How

to

feel

Good

as

you

age

JOHN BARNETT

How

to

feel

Good

as

you

age

A Voice of Experience

VanderWyk & Burnham
Acton, Massachusetts

Published by VanderWyk & Burnham
A Division of Publicom, Inc.
P.O. Box 2789, Acton, Massachusetts 01720

This publication is sold with the understanding that the publisher is not engaged in rendering legal, medical, psychiatric, or other professional services. If expert assistance is required, the services of a competent professional person should be sought.

This book is available for quantity purchases. For information on bulk discounts, call (800) 789-7916 or write to Special Sales at the above address.

Library of Congress Cataloging-in-Publication Data

Barnett, John, 1930–
    How to feel good as you age : a voice of experience / John Barnett.
    p.   cm.
    Includes bibliographical references and index.
    ISBN 1–889242–07–1 (hc.). —ISBN 1–889242–08–X (pbk.)
    1. Aged—Psychology. 2. Aged—Health and hygiene. 3. Aged—Conduct of life. 4. Aging.
5. Quality of life. I. Title.
HQ1061.B365   1999
305.26—dc 21   99–35903
                                                                                    CIP

Interior book design by John Reinhardt Book Design
Cover design by Rob Johnson
Cover photograph by Al Francekevich

FIRST PRINTING
Manufactured in the United States of America

10 9 8 7 6 5 4 3 2 1

To Claude V. DeShazo, MD,
mentor and friend,
who advised:
"If you have something to contribute,
don't wait for anyone, just start doing it,"
and
to members of Renewal,
a health support group
that he founded.

Contents

Preface: When the Student Is Ready, the Teacher Appears

"Mr. Barnett, I am sorry to say you have cancer." Cancer would be my teacher for the next chapter in my life.

This diagnosis of a life-threatening illness propelled me into a self-examination. Where had I gone wrong? Was it too much fat in the diet, a sedentary working life with no aerobic exercise, a love of cigars? Maybe it was an inability to handle stress or bottled-up emotions. The truth must lie somewhere in that mess. My task now was to learn from the past and apply those lessons. I wanted a future.

On reflection, I saw that my schooling had not prepared me well for life. I had not learned to respect myself and others, or to value proper food, exercise, mental health, and the joy of contributing to society. Medical doctors had removed my tonsils, fashioned leg casts, and written prescriptions for medicines. From them I had learned nothing about nutrition, good habits of living, physical activity, mental well-being, and spiritual soundness, nor about the evils of tobacco, alcohol, or drugs. In church I saw no spirit-mind-body connection. What about our government, which is charged with the public's physical and mental health? I could think of no wisdom from it that might have protected me from cancer.

No, it was chiefly from my own family that I had learned as a child what might help me to get through life. In retrospect, that was a trifle compared to what I learned on my own after my cancer diagnosis. This hard-won recent learning is what I pass along in the following pages to you.

On my bookshelf is an autographed copy of *Peace, Love & Healing* by Dr. Bernie Siegel, the famous facilitator of healing and of health. I was inspired by the few words I exchanged with that great man. Four weeks after we spoke, to my shock, I received the cancer diagnosis. You can be sure that I read avidly every word of advice in Dr. Siegel's book about assisting in my own recovery. I was ready when the teacher appeared.

The American Cancer Society led me to a wonderful local support group called Renewal, founded in 1982 by Dr. Claude DeShazo. Those survivors challenged me to read, listen to tapes, visualize positively, change my diet, relax, meditate, exercise, take vitamins and supplements, keep a journal, laugh, verbalize my fears, and question everything my doctor told me. Being a "good" patient in the sense of accepting without question whatever therapy is prescribed, I learned, can be accepting a death sentence. Instead, as my own physician, I must do my homework and fight every inch of the way for the treatment my knowledge and intuition tell me is right for me.

As I researched available literature while planning my new future, I found plenty of books on midlife and retirement. There was, also, an abundance of books on death and dying. Little guidance exists, however, for the long and wonderful times in between, which can last for 20, 30, or even 40 years. These years can be the best of your life, your "prime time." The guidelines herein are intended for those at any age who, well or sick, could get more from life by putting more deliberate thought and action into it. And—instead of letting you turn your back on the end of life as if that were an option—these guidelines will help you prepare for and embrace the later years and suggest how to exit life eventually with peace of mind, body, and spirit. Equally, this book is a reference for those giving care to mates and aging parents and friends. Information is power, at every stage of life.

The future belongs to those who prepare for it. While we are healthy, we can plan anything we wish. But where I work in a hospice center, even patients with limited life expectancy can make plans. One woman decided to speak her extraordinary life into a tape recorder for the benefit of her heirs. Another planned to mail a note every day to someone she had not seen in a while and probably would not meet again. Some others in the same condition simply stared at the ceiling and waited. But why be hopeless when, with a little effort, hopefulness is still possible?

Psychologists tell us that the most satisfying times of our lives are when we are striving to overcome challenges. Especially since surviving cancer, I now ask myself, "What is the accomplishment that would bring the most satisfaction to me this year?" Then I make a plan, sometimes in small steps, to do it. Periodically I check my progress. To keep life interesting, my goals should increase in complexity; that is, they should keep me stretching.

Introduction to Book Parts

In this book, Part One explains the multitude of options all of us in America have that can help us keep healthy in body, mind, and spirit and thus ensure the foundations for happiness. I show how to make a plan, get in charge and stay in charge, and set goals and work with them. Part Two discusses the interrelationship of good nutrition and good health, thereby extending your prime time for additional years. Communicating your needs effectively to health care providers, family, and friends is the subject of Part Three. How will they know how to help you if you don't tell them what you need?

The one constant in life is that life is not constant. Change takes place all around us, sometimes at a frightening pace. In the last few years and months of life I may be forced to make greater lifestyle changes than at any other time in my adult years. Keeping up with the options available and staying independent and in control means making a friend of change. The older I get, the more challenging change becomes. But it will avail me nothing to simply stand in place and rant against the world passing me by. Part Four emphasizes staying in control of where you choose to live and how you manage your financial and legal matters by being proactive in decision-making. Independent living in your own home can be prolonged if planned ahead. And leaving your home need not be traumatic if anticipated.

Part Five glimpses the world after you are gone, asks how you want to be remembered, and offers suggestions on actions that might yet be taken to ensure that your life will have had meaning. As the birth-days go by, there is much satisfaction in knowing I have taken care of the loose ends in life. I will scale down my possessions for simplicity and peace of mind. Family heirlooms and personal treasures will go to the ones whom I want to receive them, preferably while I am still here. More importantly, all bridges with relatives and others will be mended. I will not leave an enemy in the world. My wishes will be detailed in writing now, which will save my family much sorrowful decision-making and expense after my death. Although friends may arrive with a heavy heart to pay last respects, my preplanned memorial service will ensure that they walk out with a smile, refreshed.

Working with seniors and the terminally ill is an investment for the future. In addition to becoming a better caregiver, I know I am preparing to be a better care receiver. I hope this will make it less stressful for me and for those helping me when it is my turn to be cared for at home or elsewhere. In days of old, people used to pray for an easy death. I believe I have already ensured an easier one. Part Six examines dying from three perspectives: the spiritual, the mental and emotional, and the physical. It explains the hospice program and gives reasons why it is currently superior to all other end-of-life care options, both for the dying and for their families and caregivers.

Part Seven shifts focus from the recently deceased care receiver to the surviving former caregiver. In working with recently bereaved persons, I have found that not everyone grieves in the same way. Indeed, some survivors cannot even fully complete the tasks of grieving. We do not so much recover as adjust. There are many resources to help us through this difficult period, but the best are not necessarily the ones we would expect, that is, the resources of friends and family. Finally, steps are suggested for a surviving spouse or mate to reenter the world as a new person entitled to a new start in life. After many years as part of a couple, it is strange and frightening to reenter society as a single person again. This is a time for self-assessment and definition of who we are and what we want for our future. There may be a crying need to rebuild our lives quite differently from the way we lived before our loved one's death.

Acknowledgments

I wish to acknowledge Akemi Matsumoto, whose inspiration launched me on the idea for this book. For their helpful guidance, I thank the following social workers, chaplains, specialists (on fitness training, gerontology, aging research, bereavement, and nutrition), an attorney, a nurse, and hospital and hospice staff: Leroy Anenson, MDiv, David Bucher, MSW, Sue Carlson, MAPS, Marge Danskine, RN, Roger Decker, MTb, BCC, Claude DeShazo, MD, Suzy Favaro, MSW, Don Fleming, LLM, Allison Garr, MBA, FACHE, Aloha Hart, Alexandra Hepburn, PhD, Kristin Hirano, MS, RD, Bruce Johnson, MDiv, Sandi Johnson, MSW, Warren Ladiges, DVM, Sue Matyas, MS, and Liz Taylor. Sylvia Tacker's plea to "cut out the fat" rings in my ears. Lawyer Jim Miles did a critical review that helped polish the rough spots. The reference librarians at the Bellevue Regional Library were most generous in searching and finding hard-to-get material. Helen Webber and Pat Moore, my editors, gently and wisely guided me to a higher standard of craftsmanship. My wife, Yoko, was patient during my many hours in captivity. To all of the above I repeatedly send out thoughts of gratitude and peace.

Cancer has taught me to cherish the present, to hope for the future, and to keep my foot pressed firmly on the accelerator. I hope you will find that the following guidelines will add quality to your present and to your future.

Value Your Body, Mind, and Spirit

Invitation to a Different Dance

If you do what you've always done,
  you'll get what you've always got.

If you think what you've always thought,
  you'll do what you've always done,
    and you'll get what you've always got.

If you learn as you've always learned,
  you'll think what you've always thought,
    you'll do what you've always done,
      and you'll get what you've always got.

AUTHOR UNKNOWN

CHAPTER ONE

Goals for a Quality Life

Everything of importance to you is concerned with your body, thoughts, or spirit. Part One examines these three areas and explores how you can take charge of your life, add quality to your future, and improve your prime time.

Prime Time

Just what is prime time anyway? It may be the most important time of your life. Psychologist Abraham Maslow said that this is the time of life when we can finally become all that we have the capacity to be—in his word, "self-actualized." Picture this: Your children are grown and gone. You are occupying the nest alone or with your mate. If you are not already retired or cutting back, you are considering it. Financial pressures are not as great as they once were, and you have some disposable income to use as you please. You have a home that is comfortable for you; the surroundings please you. There are plenty of interesting things to occupy your time, and you do have enough time to follow your main interests.

Your health is still pretty good; you can get around all right and even take some long trips. Your mind works okay; forgetfulness is not an ever-present concern. (Even young people forget where they put the car keys, or stare into an open refrigerator, probably with about the same frequency as you.) Occasionally there are contacts with family members. You are happy to baby-sit the grandchildren sometimes, and happy also when they are picked up to go home. Friends call and come by; you do not have too many, nor too few. In a word, you are content with your present lot. You wish it could continue this way forever. This is your prime time!

Life Is About Change

It is too easy for us to accept the idea that life is fixed and unchangeable. Leon Martel, author of *Mastering Change: The Key to Business Success*, said, "We live in a world of change, yet we act on the basis of continuity." Change finishes old ways of action but creates new opportunities. A Pew Charitable Trusts poll asked working and retired Americans about expectations and actual life. Almost half of those working said they see retirement as "a chance for a new beginning." However, among those actually retired, only one-third reported their nonworking years have been a new start in life. More, 39 percent, said that retirement has just been "a continuation of life before," and 20 percent said it was "a step down" from before.

How to Feel GOOD As You Age looks into your future. What will happen after your prime time has peaked? Those open to change will stand the best chance to extend their prime time. Those unprepared could face many years of later life with diminished quality. It is said that at age 65, 38 percent of our remaining years can be characterized by a severely restricted dependency, often accompanied by resentment and anger. You already possess all of the ability you need to beat that statistic and succeed. And it is never too early to start preparing.

Time, Your Most Precious Resource

Whether it is 30 years or three months, time is the thing in your favor. It is the commodity that no amount of riches can buy. Yet it is the very thing we sometimes fritter away as if it were totally without value.

WHAT INSURANCE COMPANIES SAY ABOUT YOUR LIFE EXPECTANCY

AGE	YEARS REMAINING MALE	YEARS REMAINING FEMALE	AGE	YEARS REMAINING MALE	YEARS REMAINING FEMALE	AGE	YEARS REMAINING MALE	YEARS REMAINING FEMALE
50	33.37	36.26	67	17.54	20.35	84	6.97	8.36
51	32.34	35.26	68	16.76	19.53	85	6.55	7.84
52	31.33	34.27	69	16.00	18.72	86	6.15	7.34
53	30.32	33.28	70	15.26	17.92	87	5.77	6.87
54	29.32	32.29	71	14.53	17.13	88	5.40	6.43
55	28.32	31.31	72	13.82	16.34	89	5.06	6.01
56	27.34	30.34	73	13.12	15.57	90	4.74	5.62
57	26.37	29.37	74	12.45	14.82	91	4.45	5.26
58	25.41	28.41	75	11.79	14.08	92	4.17	4.92
59	24.47	27.46	76	11.15	13.36	93	3.92	4.61
60	23.54	26.53	77	10.53	12.65	94	3.69	4.32
61	22.62	25.60	78	9.94	11.98	95	3.48	4.06
62	21.73	24.69	79	9.37	11.32	96	3.29	3.81
63	20.85	23.79	80	8.84	10.68	97	3.13	3.57
64	19.99	22.91	81	8.33	10.07	98	2.97	3.36
65	19.15	22.04	82	7.85	9.47	99	2.84	3.16
66	18.33	21.19	83	7.40	8.91	100	2.71	2.98

Transactions of the Society of Actuaries, vol. XLVII (1995), page 865, projected to the year 2000

What do the actuarial tables tell us? Remember, insurance is a business. Companies are there for a profit. They invest millions of dollars in research to predict the future. They want to know how long you will live. That information tells them how much they should charge you for premiums. And insurance companies are notoriously conservative. They do not want to make errors that will cut into their profit.

You can add months or even years to the above if you do not smoke and if you wear your automobile seat belt all the time while riding in a car. Remember, everyone runs a 50 percent "risk" of outliving his or her life expectancy.

You may be surprised by your expected longevity! (The fastest-growing age group is the 85-plus category.) You may have some doubts. But, believe me, the insurance industry has no doubts about how long, on average, you will live. They are banking on it.

Live to 100!

Dr. Walter Bortz throws us a challenge in his book *Dare to Be 100!* Have you ever wondered, "How long do I really want to live?" Then perhaps your thoughts turned apprehensively to issues of physical health and quality of life. But who would not want to reach 100 if life were still fun? Look at the former Olympic athlete, born in 1898, who bounded to the stage at the opening ceremony of the 1996 Atlanta Olympics. He moved like a man 25 years his junior. It cannot be all genetics and genes. Surely, attitude and action count for much.

What changes would you have to make in your life if you decided today to beat the actuarial statistics and also have a quality life? Changes, to be exciting, must be thought of in a big context. Sometimes our ideas might be so big that they frighten us. It is a good kind of excitement. But ideas, to have value, cannot merely be considered but must be put into action. Nothing gets started until it is begun.

Taking Charge

Are you in charge of your life? Really in the driver's seat? Or is your life directed by a mate, caregiver, or child? Or, by not planning, have you simply opted out? How are the decisions made that ultimately affect your independence and even happiness? If you have an external focus of control, then you believe in yourself only if you are validated by others. Life is happening to you while you remain passive. Someone else is controlling your choices. That could be a miserable, hopeless, and frustrating feeling. But you can change to an internal focus of control; you can validate your own personal experiences and trust your own choices. You are the one responsible for your life. And you can do it! You got this far, didn't you? No one knows you as well as you know yourself.

At every age we need worthwhile goals and a reason to jump out of bed in the morning. Get in charge and stay in charge! Make the decisions for your own happiness and enrichment today. Decide that you want to live each day with excitement and passion. And, while you are at it, make the decisions today for that time in the future when your physical or mental condition may prevent you from adequately expressing your wishes. Nothing can improve your quality of life more immediately than the knowledge that you are firmly at the helm of your own ship.

Inspiration

In an interview in Holistic Health News, June 1997, Dr. Bernie Siegel said that information doesn't change people. They have to have inspiration. Often, that inspiration is learning that they are not immortal. He remembers his son who said, "Yeah, batteries not included," and that, to Bernie, is the essence. "You have to bring your energy, your inspiration, your batteries. We can give you the instruction, the survival behavior, the list, but you have to have a reason and the energy to do it," he says.

At the same time, if you keep doing the same things you have always done, you will keep getting the same things you have always gotten. For me, cancer was inspiration enough. I learned that I wanted to lengthen my living years, shorten my dying years, and make every day really full of rewarding experiences. Also, I am still bent on accomplishing some difficult project, perhaps just to prove to myself and others that my life yet has value. Is there anything in this world about which you can still feel passion? When he devised a master plan for Chicago in 1909, Daniel H. Burnham said, "Make no little plans. They have no magic to stir men's blood." Yes sir! No spectator sports for me. I want to be a star player.

Making a Plan

All right. Suppose from the figures on page 5 that you are forecast to have 20 years left on this planet. (You may have more, but you have to start planning somewhere.) What will you do with them? Will it be "business as usual"—perhaps a lot of television and nothing else in particular? Ashleigh Brilliant, author of epigrams collected in books such as *Appreciate Me Now and Avoid the Rush*, said, "The greatest obstacle to achieving my goals is that I don't know what my goals are." Many people stop planning when they consider themselves old, be that at 60 or 100. Not planning for the future is to deny that it is coming, and that deprives you of control over it.

Eventually, will someone you have never met take you by the hand and lead you to someplace you do not know? That is the scenario for those who hold time to have no value, who do not exercise their control, and who have no plan for the future. Or are you going to beg off, saying, "I have a chronic illness." Does that prevent your making a plan? Read what Meredith Titus, PhD, recommended for people with chronic illness in the June 1995 issue of the *Menninger Letter: Your National Resource for Mental Health*: "Set priorities. Despite the limitations caused by chronic illness, it is possible to set personal and family goals based on what is really important." Or are you missing your chance to influence the big issues because you get totally consumed by the small ones?

Think about it. What is it that you want to do? What do you really want to accomplish in the remaining time? Remember, this is your precious life, your one time around in your present form. Realize that the future does not have to be like the past. Eighty percent of the future we want, it is said, requires some form of giving up the past. In life there are still options to be exercised. When you put your goals into writing, a flood of resources immediately begins to pour in from all directions. Magic happens! Uncover your inner resources. When your mind knows that your body will follow, confidence will increase.

Goals: Short-term, Mid-term, Long-term, and Lifetime

Vince Lombardi, the son of the professional football coach, understands vision. In his book *Coaching for Teamwork*, he wrote: "Some people don't set goals, and justify it as a matter of principle—'I don't believe in this goal setting stuff.' If that sounds like you, understand one thing. Without goals, dreams, a vision—today will look the same as yesterday and tomorrow will look the same as today." Remember that commitment drives goals. What do you really care about?

Ambitious goals may take time. In the meantime, we can also be working on short-term goals. Or perhaps a monthly goal will contribute to attaining a bigger one. For example, if a 12-month goal for a nonwalker is to walk a mile in 15 minutes, a 1-month goal might be to walk daily as far as possible within 15 to 30 minutes.

In setting goals, think in terms of four time periods: 1 month, 6 months, 12 months, and lifetime. You can set one or two goals in the body, mind, and spirit categories for each time period. In that way, you can be stirring several different pots at the same time. I have heard it said, "Perseverance is not a long race; it is many short races one after another."

Physical Health Goals

Take stock of your previous major health problems and your current condition. Will you decide that you will not age according to an ordinary time line? What would you have to do to accomplish that goal? Think about getting proper nutrition, looking and feeling good, maintaining your ability to walk a fair distance, and taking measures to prevent disease. Consider also any medicines you are taking as well as any supplemental vitamins and herbal remedies. Are you satisfied with your doctors and other health care providers and the medicines and advice they have given you? Review your use of tobacco, alcohol, and the like.

A friend's story is inspirational. She injured her back and found it extremely difficult to turn over or to get out of bed by herself. Her commitment was never to be that vulnerable again. This led her to start doing pushups to develop upper-body strength. She now does 20 pushups every morning without fail and is a picture of confidence. Perhaps you believe that you should work out physically three times per week. Success increases motivation; therefore, commit initially to two times a week and benefit from realizing your goal.

What would it cost you in time, effort, and money to achieve your health goal? Is it worth it to you? Now make a list setting forth one or more of your physical health goals for your lifetime, 12 months, 6 months, and 1 month. Examples are provided.

My Physical Health Goals

LIFETIME

Exercise.
Strengthen muscles.
Stretch.
Keep functional and healthy to enable living without assistance
until age 85 or longer.

12 MONTHS

Make my home safer and more convenient by installing grab bars
and air conditioning.
Lose 12 pounds.
Walk one mile in 15 minutes.

6 MONTHS

Thoroughly study my body's major weakness.
Investigate alternative treatments.

1 MONTH

Find a new doctor.
Join a health club.
Walk one mile per day; increase speed gradually.
Lose one pound of weight through change in diet.

Mental and Emotional Health and Well-Being Goals

This category concerns your attitudes toward the people and events in
your life. It includes your thoughts when you are alone, your interactions with others, depression, mental stress affecting your health, and
dealing with old anger, sadness, and regrets, as well as your current
activities, work, and hobbies. This is where you will set goals such as
traveling to see new places, staying connected to old friends and family, joining a support group, improving your mind, learning to play
bridge, volunteering in worthwhile activities, having more contact

with people of the opposite or the same sex, teaching, and mixing with younger people.

Or perhaps you will spend more time smelling the roses. In other words, what use of your mental inner resources and time will contribute best to your future life satisfaction and happiness? Think for a while and then write down your goals for mental and emotional health and well-being. List one or more for each of the four time periods.

My Mental and Emotional Health and Well-Being Goals

LIFETIME

Live each day as if it were my last one.

12 MONTHS

Travel to my ancestors' birthplaces.
Take a course in creative writing and get a poem or story published.
Reestablish relations with relatives and friends.

6 MONTHS

Bond with grandchildren or neighbor's child.
Learn to play bridge.
Study alternative living arrangements for my future.

1 MONTH

Write letters to three relatives or old friends.
Complete a will and a living will.
Forgive an injury.

Spiritual Health Goals

When you think about God or a supreme being or an afterlife, are you comforted, or confused and afraid? Have you wanted to talk about this with a sympathetic listener, a sounding board who would not criticize your beliefs no matter how outlandish they may seem? Would you like to feel more sure and comfortable in your beliefs and also receive additional spiritual information to expand your understanding?

What could you do to feel good about your spiritual health? You could read a spiritual or religious book, attend worship services, meditate, schedule an appointment with a minister, priest, or rabbi, take a course of instruction, or join a discussion group with people of similar spiritual interests. Often, hearing yourself talk to others will help you to bring forth and confirm what it is you really do, and do not, believe about the spirit. Think about your spirit and what it would take to make you feel right and comfortable during the remainder of your life. Set goals in the four time periods.

My Spiritual Health Goals

LIFETIME

Daily be aware of my spirit.
Keep my spirit at peace.

12 MONTHS

Study an Eastern religion.
Observe my intuition and trust it.
Reevaluate my spiritual beliefs.

6 MONTHS

Write a statement of what I believe.
Find a spiritual director.
Take scriptural study classes.
Go to a place of worship.

1 MONTH

Keep a daily journal of my thoughts and prayers.
Often sit in a quiet place and sense my oneness with all living
things.

Focus and Feedback

Take four recipe-size index cards. Label them: "Lifetime Goals," "12-month Goals," "6-month Goals," "1-month Goals." Combine your physical, mental, and spiritual goals on each card. Now your Lifetime Goals card will show your lifetime goals for physical, mental, and spiritual health. Complete all four cards, date them, and keep them handy, perhaps on the refrigerator or mirror. Review them at least weekly. Draw a line through the goals you attain and note the date completed. Add or replace goals at any time as needed. Before retiring for the night, ask yourself, "What have I done today to reach my goals?"

After reading Chapters Two, Three, and Four, you may want to review this chapter and rethink your goals. Then, to help ensure success, make a declaration of your goals to one or more close relatives or trusted friends. Hearing yourself state your commitments in front of others imprints them deeply in your mind, empowers you, and asks your friends to witness your resolve. Turn your goals into reality!

> There is something in every one of you that waits and listens for the sound of the genuine in yourself. It is the only true guide you will ever have. And if you cannot hear it, you will all of your life spend your days on the ends of strings that somebody else pulls.
>
> —HOWARD THURMAN, THEOLOGIAN

Each day I put forth the effort to take care of myself, work out, eat healthy food, deal with my feelings and not bury them in a giant bag of Doritos. This has changed my life-I have been freed from my own personal prison.

OPRAH WINFREY

FROM MAKING THE CONNECTION

CHAPTER TWO

Are All Your Moving Parts Still Moving?

THIS CHAPTER EXPLAINS self-care options available to you for staying physically healthy, slowing the aging process, living a quality life, and looking and feeling good. Chapters Five and Six will cover nutrition and self-care.

Your Most Important Health Provider

Believe it or not, this is you. There is no one in the world who knows your body and your mind as well as you do. It is not possible for any doctor to know you that well. You know the source of your genes and the illnesses of your parents, which could eventually become problems for you, too. But read the words of Dr. Walter Bortz: "Heredity has about 15–20 percent to do with how long and well you will live. It's not the cards you are dealt but how you play the hand."

You know your childhood and adult illnesses, your allergies, and certain foods that seem to affect you unfavorably. Your upbringing resulted in particular attitudes toward pain, illness, and healing— ideas about what, and what not, to take to a doctor. Upbringing may also produce some hypochondriacs and some who postpone seeing a doctor until it is almost too late.

You know better than anyone else what causes you to worry and what produces stress, causing mind-body illnesses. You know your sleep pattern, your energy level, what you eat, and whether or not you sometimes abuse alcohol or other drugs. You know your past sexual partners. (It is said that when you have unprotected sex you are exposing yourself to the sexual diseases of everyone before you who ever had sex with that person.) You know how much planned exercise you get. But do you also tell the doctor how many miles you walk when shopping, golfing, or fishing?

For the above and other reasons, you must take responsibility for your own health. It is no longer acceptable simply to get an annual physical checkup and then forget about health for another year or until you become ill. What follows are guidelines for your active involvement.

What Is Aging?

Dr. Warren Ladiges is a pathologist on aging with emphasis on the immune system. His definition of aging is "a gradual failure of self-repair." The visible signs are such things as graying hair, less muscle mass (especially in men), menopause, wrinkling of the skin, lessened tolerance to foods, increased frequency of illnesses, and weakening of eyesight and hearing.

There are also invisible indications, Dr. Ladiges says. The stomach produces less acid, causing a failure to utilize protein. The colon loses its friendly bacteria for digestion and requires more fiber to keep moving. Hormone levels change, and calcium is drained from the bones, causing osteoporosis in both women and men. The pancreas is overworked with high intakes of sugar and refined carbohydrates, causing adult onset diabetes. The blood's lipoprotein balance may produce high cholesterol. Antioxidants in the cells decrease, weakening the immune system and making the body susceptible to disease. Aging is the major risk factor for cancer, heart disease, stroke, diabetes, arthritis, Alzheimer's disease, and osteoporosis.

Slowing the Aging Process

You have no control over the genes you inherited. But you have complete control over all three areas that can speed or slow the aging process. They are (1) your dietary habits, (2) how you handle emotional stress, and (3) your exercise or activities. Let's talk about exercise first. After eating, sleeping, and breathing, the most important thing you can do for yourself is to *keep moving your body*. It is true that we are all unique in the makeup of our genes, in how we accept stress, and in the functioning of our metabolic systems. But the biochemical response to exercise is the *same for everyone*. Exercise can go a long way to make up for deficiencies in other areas.

At least 50 percent of physical decline associated with aging can be prevented by increasing physical activity. The Centers for Disease Control and Prevention (CDC) estimates that lack of regular exercise is responsible for the deaths of up to 250,000 Americans each year—about 12 percent of total deaths. But if you start exercising, (1) you will reduce your chances of dying prematurely, (2) you will cut the risk of developing heart disease, colon cancer, diabetes, high blood pressure, or osteoporosis, and (3) you will be better able to control your weight and resist depression and anxiety. In addition, by living a longer and healthier life you increase the opportunity to achieve important goals that you might once have thought impossible. Isn't life worth the effort?

In "Can We Grow Young?" (*Parade Magazine* April 20, 1997), Dr. Ronald Klatz and Carol Kahn cited a study of 17,000 Harvard male graduates showing that those who burned between 500 and 1000 calories a week (e.g., walking 5 to 10 miles) had a 22 percent lower risk of death. And burning 2500 calories a week added one to two years to their longevity. But, even if a longer life were not assured, with regular exercise you will look and feel better over the rest of your lifetime.

If the average person burned at least 150 calories per day through exercise, America would see significant reductions in heart disease, high blood pressure, diabetes, colon cancer, anxiety, and depression. What must you do to burn 150 calories? Walk two miles in 30 minutes. Garden for 30–45 minutes. Wash and/or wax your car in 45–60 minutes. Cycle five miles in 30 minutes. Dance fast for 30 minutes.

Excuses, Excuses

Some people grew up with hard work, such as our farmers, miners, and those who experienced the Great Depression. The idea of exercise as medicine is strange to them. This is revealed by their post-retirement sedentary lifestyle, obesity, and poor health. A public health nurse told me that many people avoid exercise in the mistaken fear that it will make their health problems worse. The truth is the opposite. Inactivity is extremely destructive to the human body. That is why hospital patients are up and moving soon after surgery. Others may believe they are too old to benefit from exercise. Yet people well into their nineties get the same benefits as younger people.

I have heard the cop-out that people avoid exercise because they are afraid of increased appetite and pounds. According to an article in *Medicine and Science in Sports and Exercise*, most people who exercise eat about the same as they would if they did not work out—or only slightly more. However, by exercising regularly you are likely to become trimmer and fitter even if your weight stays the same, since you will be building muscle and using up body fat. You don't have the time? As an inducement, tape your favorite TV show and allow yourself to watch it only when you are exercising.

Many men, according to a physician friend, take better care of their cars than they do of their bodies. Their hearing is tuned in to the purr of their car's engine, and they notice even small changes in sound. They perform regular oil changes and cleanings for their autos but do not heed the body's need for regular exercise or a physical checkup. Do women put a higher priority on the appearance of their hair than on their health? As a motivator, write down your excuses for not exercising. A study at Appalachian State University in Boone, North Carolina, showed that people who wrote down their barriers to regular exercise and devised ways of dealing with those barriers when starting a program did twice as well in exercise frequency and intensity as those who did not write down anything.

Aerobic Exercise

About three fourths of Americans are either totally or mostly sedentary—they get little or no exercise. Until the 1930s and 1940s people used to mow the lawn, shovel snow, hang laundry, walk to the store, and rake leaves as a normal part of daily life. The most important health findings in recent years, and they keep getting reaffirmed from every quarter of the earth, are that (1) regular exercise is necessary and (2) the good that results affects our mind and spirit as well as our body. Aerobic exercise moves your body, gets your lungs working and your heart pumping for a sustained period. As you make exercise a habit, your blood cells begin to use oxygen more efficiently—you can do more with less.

The number one cause of death in the USA is cardiovascular disease. Over 60 million Americans have hypertension. Only 50 percent of those people know they have it. For the best general health, we should exercise aerobically on a daily basis. For some people, this means running seven days, for others, walking seven days. My compromise is to do vigorous aerobic exercise Mondays, Wednesdays, and Fridays, and to walk with my wife on the other four days. Yes, staying fit is challenging. But what do you think of the alternative to fitness?

You can walk, jog, cycle, swim, use a cross-country machine, treadmill, stair climber, etc. In its February 1999 issue, Consumer Reports published the results of a survey of readers who had bought over 8000 home exercising machines in the past five years. Users were most satisfied with motorized treadmills for managing weight and reducing stress. The survey did not include the new elliptical equipment, which is low-impact and thus protects the joints, and which can involve more muscle groups than the treadmill. Cycling bikes used to be either touring or mountain styles. The new "comfort" bikes enable the rider to sit comfortably erect and depend on automatic shifting of gears. Find an exercise that suits you and to which you will be faithful, day in and day out. It is a mistake to try to fit exercise in and around other activities in your life. Start with the resolution that you will exercise daily. Carve out a time when your mind and body are most agreeable to movement. Then, fit the rest of the day's schedule around exercise, not the other way around. Put in the center what is important to life.

Walking Is Basic

It does not take much exercise to protect people against a premature death. The February 11, 1998, issue of the *Journal of the American Medical Association* reported a study by Dr. Urho Kujala of the University of Helsinki. Sixteen thousand healthy men and women in a national registry of twins were tracked for an average of 19 years. This is the first large-scale study to separate out mortality due to genetics from mortality due to lack of fitness. Those who took brisk, half-hour walks just six times a month cut the risk of premature death by 44 percent. Even those who walked less often but still walked were 30 percent less likely to die prematurely than their sedentary twins.

The National Sporting Goods Association reported that of 56 sports and fitness activities, walking is number one in popularity. Seventy-three million Americans walk every day, up 4.3 percent from the previous year. Try to walk 30 minutes per day at a brisk rate. Even if you use a walker or cane, you can move once every day up to the limits of your physical endurance. While you are young, you can live without programmed exercise. However, after middle age your functional abilities will be impaired without it. On the plus side, even in people who begin at an older age, the positive effects of exercise are realized very quickly. Not only is walking good for the heart, but as a weight-bearing exercise, it also helps to retard bone density loss and prevent fractures.

Treat yourself to a new pair of good walking shoes designed to protect against shock. An exercise shoe loses half its shock-absorbing ability after about 300 miles of running or 300 hours of aerobics classes. Not only that, because of their chemical composition, new shoes deteriorate simply sitting in the store. Be sure the ones you buy are fresh. Serious walkers and joggers should replace their shoes every six months. You will feel the difference. Your knees and feet will thank you.

Progress should be gradual. If you are not walking now, start with 15 minutes twice a week and increase by 10 percent a week until you are walking 30 minutes daily. This will ensure a safe, effective workout and decrease the chance of injury. In the winter you do not have to go south to enjoy good walking. Nationwide there are more than 40,000 shopping malls. At least 2400 of those malls have specific provisions to let walkers in before shopping hours. Many have walking clubs. Walking clubs can also be found in some zoos.

Find a friend who wants to exercise with you. Agree to motivate each other by telephone calls to confirm your workout appointment. The time will pass more quickly with a friend beside you. Listen to music while you exercise. Music helps people stick with a workout program, lessens the feelings of fatigue and stress, and makes exercise more enjoyable. It promotes better breathing and muscle coordination. Swing your arms and lengthen your stride. Short steps inhibit your balance.

Exercise and Illness

Individuals who have exercised regularly prior to cancer treatment have a higher tolerance to cancer therapy and recover more quickly. The motivation to continue exercise throughout cancer treatment shifts from prevention to survival. Also, diabetics who exercise regularly heal more quickly.

Did you know that exercise stimulates the brain to produce endorphins? Endorphins are a natural chemical and pain killer. That explains why our arthritis may not be so noticeable after we exercise. Exercise even if you have to take pain medicine to do so. (Take medication one-half hour before exercise.) Otherwise you will get into a Catch-22 situation. That is, you will not exercise because it hurts, but without exercise you gain none of the pain-killing benefits of exercise. It is a downward spiral.

Arthritis and Exercise

Exercise for arthritis sufferers means a program of movements prescribed by a doctor, physical therapist, or occupational therapist specifically related to the affected joints and surrounding muscles. *Range-of-motion exercises* help maintain normal joint movement, relieve stiffness, or restore flexibility and movement if it has been lost. Each joint should be moved through its complete range of motion daily to minimize stiffness and to prevent loss of motion, which can result in deformity.

21

Strengthening exercises help maintain or increase muscle strength since weak muscles add to joint problems. *Isotonic resistance exercises* move the joint against a weight or other form of resistance. Rubber tubing or resistance bands are safe and easy to use for this kind of exercise. *Isometric exercises* tighten a muscle but do not move the joint. For example, you can increase arm strength by using your hands while seated to push up against the underside of a table or desk.

Vigorous exercise that aggravates inflammation in the joints is harmful. If you have exercise-induced inflammation lasting two hours or more, you have done too much. Join an arthritis exercise class with a proper instructor. PACE (People with Arthritis Can Exercise) is a group recreational program devised by the Arthritis Foundation. Or consider exercising in a swimming pool, which absorbs the impact of your movements and also makes you more buoyant. If you are afraid of slipping, wear water shoes to give you confidence and lessen the impact of each step.

Challenging Your Body

Periodically, challenge the body-conditioning goals you have set for yourself. Here is my own learning experience. For my primary aerobic activity I use a cross-country machine. While it produces an elevated heartbeat, there is no impact, so it is easy on my arthritic knees. After 30 minutes of moderate exercise, I used to stop and press the machine's "distance" button to find that I had moved the equivalent of about 2 miles. One day the exercise machines in the health club were fitted with new devices showing simultaneous readings for time, speed, distance, and caloric consumption. I began to focus on speed rather than time and found ways to increase speed with just a little more effort. One month later I set a new personal distance record of 3.74 miles in 30 minutes! It was both a physical and psychological lift. Since then I have bested that mark and might aim even higher someday. Satisfaction in life comes from reaching our goals and then challenging them. Keep your goals within reason for your condition.

Deep Breathing

Could it be that my dad was right after all? Dad had always encouraged me as a youth to throw out my chest and breathe deeply. Naturally, I did not pay much attention. However, Dr. Andrew Weil's book *Spontaneous Healing* lists deep breathing from the diaphragm as promoting health and healing. He wrote, "Breathing may be the master function of the body, affecting all others." It's free. Make it a part of your daily routine. And remember that lung function is an indicator for survival in older age. For varieties of breathing techniques and for general interest, see Dr. Weil's book.

Stretching and Flexibility

When backing a car, some drivers turn their heads to get full views of what lies behind. Other drivers depend solely on their mirrors, a less-safe alternative. Don't let neck inflexibility put you at risk for a fender-bender.

In the mornings we wake up stiff and uncomfortable. Then is the best time to do some simple stretches before undertaking anything else. Bob Anderson's classic book *Stretching* provides examples of morning, eye-opening stretches as well as daily stretches. He provides a special set of exercises for people over 50. I often start my day with his back-relaxing stretches. Hold each stretch for 10 to 30 seconds.

Why stretch? Among the reasons offered by Mr. Anderson are these: feeling more relaxed, improving coordination, maintaining range of motion, and just plain feeling good. Also, as we age we tend to have a poorer sense of balance and are more subject to falls. This is especially true in unfamiliar circumstances. We all know of cases in which bad falls have put people in wheelchairs for the rest of their lives. Staying flexible will help to prevent falls, and learning to fall more naturally will lessen the disastrous effects if you do fall. Besides that, flexibility looks good and feels good. Isn't it worth 10 minutes a day? Talk your mate into joining you.

Strength Training

Michael Segell, in the April 1997 issue of *Sports Afield*, wrote that the average male's muscle strength declines by approximately 20 percent between ages 20 and 50. During the next 20 years it drops by 30 percent and then falls sharply after that. There is no reason the same findings would not generally apply also to women. But a frail elderly person can double or triple his or her muscle strength in just a few months. Yes, even those in their eighties and nineties show improvement after supervised strength training. This means that muscle mass is increased, thereby making it easier to climb stairs, unscrew jar lids, lift grocery bags, and so on. We reduce body fat, increase muscle, and even look better. A test group of aged seniors found that strength training benefited their walking speed and balance. Two of them were able to throw away their canes. A recently discovered additional benefit is that strength training slows the loss of bone density. That means less osteoporosis and greater protection from breaking bones as a result of falls.

Other tests show that women dieting without exercise will, in addition to losing fat, also lose muscle, bone, and lean tissue. When women do strength training along with their dieting, they gain lean tissue and muscle and lose only fat. In one test both groups lost about the same amount of weight, but the exercising group lost more fat and obtained a better, longer-lasting result.

When can we predict a person's ability to be able to live independently in older age? The Department of Geriatrics of the University of Washington found that chronological age is not the best predictor. The more reliable measurement is strength and aerobic fitness. In particular, you should work on your upper body muscles including triceps and shoulder muscles. These muscles are used when you get up out of a chair. Women, typically, need to build upper body strength.

Older women are recently embracing strength training using weights because they know it will reduce the risk of osteoporosis. Women need not fear developing unwelcome big muscles since they lack the testosterone to become bulky. The standard practice is to begin with 12 slow repetitions, using a comfortable weight, and gradually build up to three sets of 12 to 15 repetitions before increasing the weight. However, even one set of only 8 repetitions will produce results. You can take pride in knowing that you have reversed one aspect of the aging process. That is, your muscles are being restored to a younger condition. You will experience an increase of self-esteem and self-confidence.

To avoid stressing your heart, always expel the air from your lungs as you are lifting a heavy weight. (Likewise, when sitting on the toilet and somewhat constipated, exhale before bringing any pressure on your intestines. This will protect your heart.)

Remember, physical decline leads to frailty, which leads to loss of independence and control. Stay strong and in control. Think of your fitness program as a tripod consisting of aerobics, flexibility and balance, and strength training. Only three legs of approximately equal length will provide a sound foundation. Are you short-changing a part of your foundation?

Health/Fitness Club

As much as being a condition, fitness is an attitude. Aging, also, is both a condition and an attitude. Consider joining a health/fitness club. It was not until I faced retirement that I decided, definitely, to develop for myself a program for fitness. Until then my exercise had consisted of tennis and of walking partway to the office each day. Most people I know, myself included, are not necessarily open to nonsport exercising. Of course, we feel very good after completing a workout, and we know we have done ourselves a favor. Repetitious training by itself, however, is not very exciting. I decided the only way I could keep up the discipline was to join a club, and I did it. It is somewhat embarrassing to admit my first reason for doing so, but it was frugality. It bothers me greatly to waste money. Therefore, paying a fee every month was the sure way for me to make regular use of the facilities. No way would I pay for something and not use it. Also, I could easily rationalize that the money spent was actually an investment in my future good health. That was ten years ago.

My second reason for joining was the presence of other people. It energizes and encourages me to keep going when I can see other people who are also working on their health goals. Working out regularly at home alone would absolutely not work for me. It's like the difference between watching a football game at the stadium or reading about it in the newspaper.

Some people naturally experience a feeling of self-consciousness or even fear when they contemplate entering a modern workout room. The array and variety of aerobic and strength machines is intimidating. How do they work? What is the trick for adjusting them to my height and strength? Am I the only one who does not know what to do? I may not look very good in gym shorts. Will others stare? How do I gain confidence and comfort? Believe me, these feelings disappear quickly after you jump in. A session with a personal trainer can be a helpful introduction.

What I had not anticipated was the camaraderie that developed with others whom I regularly see on my Monday-Wednesday-Friday workouts. I found that people quite naturally became nodding acquaintances. Eventually, I looked forward to encountering certain delightful people and even had lunch with some. Now, I feel as if entering the exercise room is just as comfortable as coming home. Sharing information and socializing occur regularly among exercisers who do not reject fellowship

Nor do I begrudge the time I spend in promoting my fitness. It stands to reason that as I age, I will be investing an increasingly large proportion of my day in keeping fit, making sure that all moving parts are moving to the optimum. To do the opposite is too easy, and too deadly. Spending time in this way is vastly preferable to using time (and money) waiting in a doctor's reception room or lying in a hospital bed.

Personal Trainers

Here, again, I initially had some trouble spending money on myself. However, now I consider personal trainers worth their weight in gold. For about $40 you can have a personalized fitness program prepared for you at your health club. (This service might be cheaper or free at community centers. Or, share the cost of a trainer with several of your friends.) You will learn the proper way to do stretches and to use weights and machines. This gives you the confidence that you are doing the exercises best suited for your body and in a safe manner. You will receive a card showing each exercise, how much weight to use, and how many repetitions to perform. If in doubt, check with your doctor first. Believe me, it is really satisfying to find that your strength has increased and that you can move up to the next heavier weight. In my sixties I had to donate some sport coats and shirts to the local clothing bank because the chest (no, not the waist!) size no longer fit. That had never happened before.

To promote motivation and to keep my routine interesting, I now use a trainer every six months to set out a new program. My trainer has recently introduced to me the concept of "function" exercises. This is a combination of the strength, flexibility, balance, and motor responses that keep us "functional" even as we age, which is more important than strength by itself. Having your own personal trainer is not very expensive and lends professionalism and confidence to your exercise program.

For additional information, contact the American Medical Association at **http://www.ama-assn.org/consumer/interact.htm** and choose the Personal Trainer option for a questionnaire, text with exercises, and a guide for designing a fitness program.

Vanity, a Powerful Motivator

Charles Garfield, the author of *Peak Performance*, wrote: "The most powerful human motivator of all is the desire to be proud of ourselves in the pursuit of something we care about deeply."

I admit to being a bit vain about my appearance. I believe vanity is a powerful asset that will contribute to my long-term health. Early on I decided that the appearance of a roll of belly fat hanging forward over my belt buckle did not suit the image I have of myself. Nor do I wish to present such an appearance to others. Contrary to what weight loss programs usually recommend, I do weigh myself every morning upon arising. If the scale shows that I have gained a pound or two from the previous day, I alter my food intake to drink more liquids, eat a smaller quantity of food, and be sure to have more vegetables and fewer starchy carbohydrates. I know my proper body mass index, and I know that exceeding it means I am shortening my life. Be timely. Remember the old maxim: "A stitch in time saves nine."

Develop a realistic picture of a self-image that would please you. Learn what you will have to do to attain it. Although I prefer to age without the benefit of cosmetic surgery, I know people who have raised their self-esteem by undergoing it. It is proven that individuals with low self-esteem are sick more often, become depressed, and seem to age more rapidly. An improved appearance can motivate us to take additional steps to improve our self-care and increase our enjoyment of life.

Personal Hygiene

It is important to keep your body clean. Older men living alone, it seems, sometimes fall out of the habit of regular bathing. You might be tempted after retirement to bathe less often, thinking that you may go out less and come in contact with fewer people. As we age, even small routine chores like bathing, which formerly were easy, now become harder to do. It is best to bathe regularly by whatever means you can. You will feel clean and fresh and have the confidence that your presence will be acceptable anywhere. Even your spirit rises on stepping out of a bath.

People who cannot bathe every day, and those with hemorrhoids or arthritis, will appreciate the convenience of a "washlet" toilet, which can be mounted in place of the regular toilet seat. It washes the anal area with a stream of warmed water, thus ensuring cleanliness without agitation.

One of the best days for many women is when they have just come from the hairdresser. They look good. They feel good. And they know it. Older men, again, are less careful of their appearance and sometimes let their hair grow beyond what is neat and presentable. If cost is a concern, inexpensive and even free haircuts are available. Shampoo your hair every time you bathe or, at least, three times weekly. (A dermatologist recommends rotating each month among three different brands of antidandruff shampoo to keep your scalp clean. Because the body increases its resistance to chemicals, always using the same brand will eventually prove ineffective.) For the homebound, someone can be called in for hair care. Or ask your partner or close friend to do it, perhaps in exchange for a good neck massage by you.

Dress

Earlier in my life, when I was crazy about tennis, I had an instructor who told this story. "When I played tennis at the University of Wisconsin, I didn't care what I wore; just cutoff jeans and a T-shirt were fine. One day I invested in regular tennis shorts and shirt," he said. "It improved my game." I'll always remember how he said it. "You look good! You feel good! And you play good!" It's true!

It is important what image we hold of ourselves and what image we convey to others. We should keep clothing clean and neat. When I pull a previously worn garment from the closet, I inspect the front and back for stains while it is still on the hanger. Stains are easier to see in that way, and you might avoid embarrassment later. Over the years our body measurements change, and some clothes might require alteration for a good fit. The fact that "it just feels comfortable" is not sufficient justification for continuing to wear a garment that ought to be in the ragbag.

It is okay to buy used clothing. Your clothes will be cheaper, and you will help our world by recycling. Do not stay at home simply because you "have nothing to wear." Likewise, if there are clothes in your closet that you have not worn in a year, it is unlikely that you ever will wear them. Donate and make someone else happy.

Looking Pleasant

I am convinced that our unconscious facial mannerisms act as a deterrent to socialization. Grandchildren cannot understand why Grandpa is always frowning. What happens is that we do not see well, our eyeglasses don't fit, we cock our heads to use bifocals, we strain to hear conversation, our hearing aids are uncomfortable, or we have other physical problems. In addition, we may be worried that our car will soon need a new transmission. When others address us, we greet them with deep, wrinkled frowns, squinty eyes, and upturned chins. If you don't believe it, watch the reactions of older people at the supermarket checkout counter. Then give some thought to correcting any physical problems or bad habits that prevent you from presenting a pleasant appearance to others.

"But you look so lovely when you smile." The trouble is, we have forgotten how to smile and now do it less often. Practice in front of a mirror. Would you like to be greeted by you today? You will be surprised what a difference a warm smile makes to shop clerks, friends, and, especially, to relatives. (What makes us think we can get by giving our own relatives a less pleasant face than we give to outsiders? It's a bad investment.) Make a smile your customary appearance. You will feel better knowing that you put your best face forward.

Touching and Sexual Activity

Swedish physiologist Kerstin Uvnas-Moberg said, "There are deep, deep, physiological connections between touching and love." Gentle stroking and massage stimulate the body to produce the chemicals it needs. One chemical produced is oxytocin, sometimes called the love hormone. It serves to dampen pain and make us feel less anxious and stressed. Be a hugger! It pays.

Psychologist Tiffany Field, director of the Touch Research Institute at the University of Miami, found that after office workers received a 15-minute massage, their brain waves showed a higher alertness level, and they could complete a math test in half the previous time and with only half the errors.

The Starr-Weiner Report on Sex and Sexuality in the Mature Years questioned over 800 people aged 60 to 91. Seventy-five percent considered their sex lives at least as enjoyable, or more so, as when they were younger. Among other good effects, sexual activity can decrease the severity of headaches and can relieve arthritis and back pain. Researchers at the University of California, San Diego, found that after a nine-month test, those men who participated in strenuous aerobics reported a 30 percent increase in intercourse and more satisfaction in it.

Viagra was developed as a heart medication but became popular among men as an anti-impotence treatment, and it has changed the sex lives of millions. But the story is not finished. Now Viagra is being tested on women and has been shown to enable an easier orgasm. Be careful, men! We do not know where the story will end. Simply stated, sexual activity does not have to end until you want it to end.

Sleep

Sophia Loren said in 1996 that sleep is one of her "secrets." She said, "I sleep a lot, soundly and without nightmares, avoiding TV temptations." If you have seen recent photos you would say, "Obviously, it works for her."

In 1910 Americans averaged nine hours of sleep each night. That, of course, was before TV. Today we average just seven hours. One out of three Americans say that they have sleep problems. Either they can't get to sleep or they can't stay asleep. Only 5 percent of adults function well on less than six-and-a-half hours of sleep according to the American Sleep Disorders Association. The National Sleep Foundation reported that most healthy adults need between seven and nine hours of quality sleep every 24 hours. Older people who exercise moderately on a regular basis take less time getting to sleep at night and generally sleep longer and more soundly. This is a finding of sleep researchers at the Emory University Sleep Disorders Program in Atlanta and at the Stanford Center for Research. A leisurely walk after dinner also helps people sleep.

Daytime naps are good if they do not prevent evening sleep. There is a dip in alertness about eight hours after we arise. That is why more accidents occur between 2:00 P.M. and 4:00 P.M. Some companies know this and have been encouraging employees to nap from 15 to 20 minutes in the afternoon. The result is higher efficiency and greater output. Yarde Metals built a nap room in its corporate headquarters in Bristol, Connecticut. Having allowed time for naps, 42 IS, a computer consulting firm in Berkeley, California, saw expenditures on soda and coffee for its employees drop by 30 percent.

Suggestions on how to improve sleep appear almost weekly in the press, radio, and TV. For example, try to get exposure to sunlight early in the day to help set the body's clock. Bad sleep tends to move in a downward spiral. If you believe your sleep is lacking and you cannot correct it yourself, see a doctor or ask to be referred to one of the 300 sleep centers throughout the country for a thorough sleep study. One woman who did so found that, as she slept, her periodic leg movements were awakening her. A medication helped to improve her sleep.

Lengthen Living; Shorten Dying

Using National Center for Health Statistics data, Dr. Eileen Crimmins of the University of Southern California found that on average, American men spend 13 years of their lives with a disability, and women spend 14.9 years. The July 1997 issue of the *University of California at Berkeley Wellness Letter*, in an article on caregivers, cited almost 13 million Americans (7 million over 65) as needing assistance to carry out such simple activities as eating, dressing, and bathing. Granted, this life is worth clinging to even with a disability. But invalidism does not have to be the penalty of old age. Why not do everything in our power to postpone the start of a disability and reduce the severity of it?

The trick is to lengthen the quality time when we can enjoy our independence, maintain the ability to accomplish our cherished goals, and experience satisfying relationships. Then shorten the downward spiral and avoid dying in one-hour installments in our doctors' waiting rooms. Statistics show that medical expenses in the last two years of life are about three times greater for people who die at age 70 than for those living past 100. There may be a crucial window of self-care opportunity extending from your fifties to your seventies that could make all the difference in the world in the length and quality of your prime time. By following the guidelines outlined so far, you will almost certainly increase your disability-free time and decrease your dying time.

The Most Important Gift

You may think that your children will be pleased to find in your will that you have left them money, a house, jewelry, and so on. Don't kid yourself. Taking care of *yourself* is the most important gift you can leave to your adult children. (Think about it.)

> If you doubt you can accomplish something, then you can't accomplish it. You have to have confidence in your ability, and then be tough enough to follow through.
>
> —ROSALYNN CARTER

You have just read about the options for maintaining the healthy state of your body, and only you have control over that happening. The next chapter explores the options for promoting your mental and emotional health and well-being.

Don't do things in order not to die. It never works.

BERNIE SIEGEL, MD

CHAPTER THREE

Strive for Mental and Emotional Well-Being

THIS CHAPTER OFFERS guidelines on how to extend prime time by influencing what occurs in our minds and emotions. These options may also be considered for use in your Chapter One goals for the rest of your life.

Your Amazing Brain

Your brain weighs only about three pounds. Yet, over a 70-year life span, it will store perhaps 100 trillion bits of information. That is the equivalent of 500,000 sets of the Encyclopaedia Britannica. Even the most advanced supercomputer has a less complex wiring system than the human brain. Each brain neuron is connected to more than 1000 others. Scientists previously thought that the brain's structure was unchanging from birth. Now we know that neurons grow smaller or larger and make new weblike connections as the brain constantly learns and remembers. Steven Hyman, Director of the National Institute of Mental Health, said, "It's as if there were little gremlins running around rewiring the circuits all the time." This information is a challenge to all of us, but especially to those of us aiming to extend our prime time.

Mind-Body Connection

Some people do not love their bodies. Granted that we might not have been given the face of Venus. And our knees may be a little weak. But we should thank our bodies for working hard and for carrying us this far in life. To fail to be grateful or, even worse, to dislike something about our body is to have the mind and body working against each other.

The mind-body connection is very real. Numerous experiments demonstrate the power of the mind over the body. Consider the effect of the placebo on patients who think they are getting real medicine. In study after study, at least 30 percent of patients benefit from treatment with a placebo—a pill, injection, drink, or patch that contains no medically active ingredient. Hypnosis, too, has been the source of much evidence for the mind-body connection. Hypnotized patients, through the power of suggestion, can exhibit symptoms for which there is no physical basis, such as the rash of poison ivy.

When we think of medicine generally, most of us realize that there is a Western school and an Eastern (Asian) school. There are actually many more varieties than just these two. Of all the medicine types practiced throughout the world, did you know that Western medicine is the only one that has separated the treatment of the body from the treatment of the mind? Prior to the seventeenth century this division did not occur, even in Western medicine. If you go to less traditional doctors in the USA, such as doctors of naturopathy, the condition of your mind will be given equal consideration with the condition of your body. Many doctors formerly trained in Western medicine, too, are working to end the mind-body split in Western medicine.

In an Associated Press article dated December 31, 1996, Dr. Michael L. Freedman wrote: "Another idea that has gained general acceptance is one that suggests the way older people think can affect their physical well-being. The new medical field, called psychoneuroimmunology, is based on the premise that positive thinking can have positive effects on the immune system, bolstering the body's response to infectious diseases and certain other maladies." Some doctors say that as many as 75 percent of the patients they see have problems that are more mental than physical. Wouldn't you like to have your mind working for you to maintain your health?

The Value of Work

In her mid-sixties Lauren Bacall, the movie actress, said, "What is the point of being here if you're not involved? To me, you must keep working. When I still have curiosity and energy and want to do things, that tells me I'm alive."

Currently, just one in eight Americans over age 65 works. We are accustomed to a fixed age of retirement and to the use of "early retirement" in corporate restructuring. This policy is not good for everyone and presents problems for our country's fiscal policy, labor markets, and productivity. In the future we can expect to see the opportunity to work later in life expand due to a gradual extension of the retirement age and flexible part-time work. If you enjoy your work, keep working as long as you are able. There is nothing like it to keep your mind and body active.

Of those over age 65 today, 88 percent do not work, leaving only 12 percent who do work. This is almost the reverse of the expectations of today's baby boomers, 80 percent of whom expect to work after age 65 and only 16 percent intend not to work. The 50-year trend toward earlier retirement has been halted and turned around. The typical retirement age is 62 but increasing.

Many of the 3.8 million Americans age 65 and older who have jobs want to remain in the work force. Some older workers have high-interest jobs about which they are passionate, and they believe they are making a difference in the world. Others are escaping boredom and asserting their self-esteem. Some people not yet eligible for Medicare continue to work to enjoy health care coverage. No matter what the reason, the additional income can be well used, especially by older men and women left alone by the death of working spouses. On average, Social Security will cover just two thirds of an older middle-class person's needs. AARP research claims that as of the year 2000, the fastest growing part of America's work force will be in the 55–64 age group.

For fast, efficient, and inexpensive job searches put your résumé on the Internet or answer an Internet ad. The U.S. Department of Labor and state agencies have set up America's Job Bank, advertising approximately 600,000 openings at any given time. One man who failed to find a job through traditional print classified ads tried the Internet and received calls from 70 companies.

One acquaintance, Fred, was in his seventies. He had nursed his wife through a three-year fatal illness. The doctor bills left him living in a small apartment without much interaction with others. His pension income fell short of enabling him to have a carefree retirement. Fred had a good driving record and was hired by a large car-rental company to move its rental cars from one location in the state to another. He worked only about four days per week. Driving was easy, and he enjoyed the good fellowship with other employees. The extra income let him enjoy his chief hobby, playing blackjack once a week at a nearby casino. No solitary, stay-at-home TV-watching for Fred. If his style does not actually add years to his life, it will surely add quality.

We have been raised to believe in the nobility of work. It confirms our sense of self-worth, provides income, and can be the most enjoyable activity in the world. Look at artists, craftspeople, writers, and others who go on working in later years. As long as you enjoy work, why not continue? One doctor's advice for healthy aging is: Never retire.

Modify Work to Suit You

A new term coined in the late 1990s is the "boundaryless" work force, where an individual is paid to accomplish a specific job without regard to where or what hours the employee works. The Bureau of Labor Statistics claims that in 1997, 21 million people regularly did some work at home and another 25 million had flexible work schedules, nearly double the numbers recorded in 1991. It is okay to reduce hours from full-time to part-time, according to your needs. If you chose an occupation that permits you to taper off rather than quit, you made a smart move. It is also okay to take a cut in pay. (However, working for money gives some people a sense that the value of their work is recognized.) Keeping your hand in your life-time occupation enables you to keep abreast of developments. There may also be health insurance and other benefits.

Many cannot bear to think that they will completely sever an interest in what had been so close to them for so very long. Others cannot wait to retire from boring work and are just counting the days. But are they also planning how to use their leisure time usefully, which is said to be a test of our intelligence? Is there other work you have dreamed of doing, possibly at home and with the help of a little schooling at a local college or vocational training school? Being a teacher's aide can be very rewarding and could involve as little as 90 minutes a day. What about opening a small business that you would enjoy? Consult the Small Business Resource Center at **http://webcom.com/seaquest/sbrc.** Mark Twain said: "Work and play are words used to describe the same thing under differing conditions."

Independent Living

No lifestyle requires you to keep using your brain more than continuing to live in your own home. You must remember everything that needs to be done to keep your home running in good order. And living at home requires you to keep your body moving to perform the many tasks of just staying alive. You may sometimes dream of moving into a different style of living to simplify your life. However, it is complexity that keeps life interesting, full, and rewarding. When you no longer have to make decisions, when everything is done for you, when you lose your options and control, life becomes uninteresting and boring. And when that happens, your mind becomes less active and your body ages more quickly. Your lifestyle should allow you to exercise the maximum amount of independence of which you are capable.

Study

Census figures show that there were 468,000 college students ages 50 and older in 1996, an increase of 43 percent since 1990. We are blessed with an abundance of opportunities for continuing to improve our minds, often at little or no cost. Many colleges offer older adults special tuition rates of only a few dollars per credit hour on a space-available basis. Senior centers have study programs that are appropriate to seniors' needs and are taught by experts. In many communities a public monthly service brings books, books on tape, compact disks, magazines, and videos to the homebound. One older recipient reported: "I've visited many lands and places [through books]. They've done a lot to bring me back to life."

Distance learning is the term for what used to be called correspondence courses. Lectures may be delivered on videotape or on the World Wide Web or as telecourses. Students often talk with their professors by e-mail or voice mail. Here are some recommended Web sites:

http://www.geteducated.com	This is the Adult Education and Distance Learner's Resource Center.
http://www.gradschools.com	Gradschools.com is a comprehensive on-line source for graduate school information with over 40,000 program listings.
http://www.petersons.com	Petersons.com is an education and career center for distance learning and executive education.
http://www.nucea.edu	University Continuing Education Association offers higher education opportunities for part-time and nontraditional students.

Taking courses was never so easy, nor so much fun. No grade point average has to be maintained if you do not need credit.

Many cities offer specialized training in law and other subjects in return for a commitment to volunteer your service for a year. What a wonderful way to learn and to make a contribution to society! Programs offered by Elderhostel and other organizations provide opportunities to travel domestically and internationally while learning at a local college or other institution. They also offer service- and research-oriented vacations worldwide. These are good ways to meet and socialize with others, both elders and youth.

Now is the time to pursue your educational dream. Just think of the satisfaction and heightened self-esteem that result from learning a foreign language. A doctor I know has reduced his practice so that he can spend time in a Mexican village and study Spanish and Mexican culture. He loves it! Keep your brain active and mix with others of similar interests. This is a sure prescription for happiness.

The Computer Challenge

Many people find the world is passing them by because they lack motivation to meet the challenge of computers. But consider the many benefits. As an advanced form of communication, the Internet offers contacts with millions of interesting persons at a very low cost compared with the cost of long-distance telephone calls. Many people stay in close contact with their children through the Internet. Thus, using the Internet is both entertaining and useful.

In most public libraries the catalog is computerized. Library staff offer free classes or one-on-one instruction on how to locate books, magazine articles, and more. Also, you may use computers at the library and access the Internet without cost. About 40 percent of American households have computers. Prices have dropped below $500 for a computer, with the monitor costing an additional $150. A computer teacher advises: Keep a small notebook beside your computer and make notes for future reference on how you accomplished certain operations. It beats searching through an operations manual each time you get stuck. Here are some ways to enjoy tomorrow with a computer:

- Write your family history.
- Do a home inventory.
- Balance your bank account.
- Follow your investments.
- Create your personal address book.
- Play solitaire or bridge.
- Write a novel.
- Compose poetry.
- Keep a greeting card list up-to-date.
- Make greeting cards.
- E-mail relatives and friends.
- Keep the church records or print a bulletin.
- Make labels for greeting cards or storage boxes.
- Start a family newsletter.
- Get on the Internet and find: health information, late-breaking discounts on airlines and hotels, jobs, humor pages, and people with interests like yours.
- Visit these Internet sites:
    http://www.50plus.org
    http://www.seniorsearch.com
    http://www.thirdage.com
    http://www.retiredlifefun.com
    http://www.seniorsite.com

Those with chronic illnesses report gaining much useful new information and support through the Internet. The average person can learn about any aspect of medical science, including the latest research, powerful new drugs, and alternative therapies, and can better prepare for visits with doctors. Until now, this knowledge was solely in the domain of health care professionals. Some medical Web resources are the American Medical Association, Mayo's Health Oasis, the Food and Drug Administration, the National Library of Medicine, and the U.S. Department of Health and Human Services.

In one instance, doctors had been unable to determine the cause of a boy's mysterious health problems. However, through the Web, the boy's father gathered information about a rare disease with symptoms similar to his son's. With this information doctors were able to accurately diagnose the boy's illness and treat it successfully. Some widows have been motivated to start learning how to use a computer in order to access financial information left on the home computer by their late husbands.

If you fear being embarrassed in a teacher-student relationship, find a child to teach you. A friend had a wonderful experience with his grandson who visited for two weeks at vacation time. The child convinced the grandfather that he ought to have a computer. They shopped for one together and the grandfather learned to use it from his own grandson. What a wonderful bonding experience and what a treasure of memories for both sides! Also, they now have the means to continue communicating with each other via e-mail.

Memory

"First you forget names, then you forget faces, then you forget to pull your zipper up, then you forget to pull your zipper down," says Leo Rosenburg. However, in truth, the ability of a healthy older person to retain information and recall it is not much different from that of a young person. One real difference is that we get annoyed and blame ourselves when we forget where we put our eyeglasses; the teenager just laughs it off. A traumatic event such as a job loss or a death in the family does certainly affect our memory for a time, but it should come back again. If it does not, see a doctor. Many physical causes of memory loss can be treated. In addition, there may be courses in your community on ways to assist your memory.

I have found a simple way to avoid memory overload and frustration and, at the same time, increase my productivity. Every Sunday I lay out a weekly activity plan. You might want to try this system. Take a recipe-size index card and divide it into eight columns by drawing three vertical lines on each side. At the top of each column write the day and date. Title the eighth column "memo," and use it for extra items and information. Fill in your appointments, errands, and the things you wish to accomplish each day. Check them off when done. Add more when you have time. Jot down ideas whenever they pop into mind. I simply carry my card in my shirt pocket for easy reference; I like it better than an appointment book. Throw away or file the card when completed. Practicing this kind of time management is a good stress reducer.

Create

Artistic and craft activities can not only occupy our minds and bodies, they can also eliminate stress as our minds are intently focused on our creative activity. The hours simply whiz by, and we are without a care in the world. And we can decorate our homes or give as gifts those precious items made with our own hands. Our offspring will continue to treasure them long after we are gone. Creativity is not a monopoly of the young. Many famous artists first began their work late in life. Your life experience may contribute positively to your creativity. Look for course offerings at colleges and technical schools and senior centers.

Travel

What is the destination you have always dreamed of? Mine is Borneo, to see the Dayak people who live in houses on stilts over inland waterways. There is nowhere on earth you cannot go; an enterprising travel agent can make arrangements. Most places can be visited by group tours. Even wheelchair-accessible destinations abound. There is no reason to forgo your trip of a lifetime.

Youth Hostels are very economical and are not limited to the young. Older people make up 10 percent of the membership. Elderhostels are for age 55+ and have both American and international programs of study tours, foreign home stays, and service experiences. Participants love them.

Seniors can get special fares from air carriers. Most airlines award seniors a 10 percent discount on any ticket simply for the asking. All major airlines sell senior airfare coupon books. Continental offers the Freedom fare; Delta, the Skywise program. (If you are traveling to a funeral, ask the airline for a 50 percent discount for bereavement travel.) Watch the newspapers for special seasonal fares, which are even cheaper. Or shop by computer at Priceline.com and bid on a fare. Fares are usually cheaper if you do not depart on Sunday, Monday, or Friday, and if you can start at midday rather than earlier or later.

Start calling travel agents and national tourist associations of foreign countries. Free of charge they will send stacks of brochures, guides, and maps. Ask your travel agent or the travel desk of your club or senior center to set up a group tour to the destination of your choice. Then talk it up with your friends to fill the vacancies. Or take a memorable vacation with your grandchild.

Volunteer

When you give yourself to others, you are twice repaid. The productive capacity of America's older population is generally underutilized. About one half of all Americans do volunteer work, averaging more than four hours weekly. (That means millions never volunteer.) Yet many, many more volunteers are needed. We could not function without them. With more volunteers, we would have an even better America. An added plus is revealed in a Michigan study of 2700 people over a 10-year span, which showed that doing regular voluntary work dramatically increased life expectancy.

Volunteer possibilities exist in every imaginable field, many in work that would surprise you. Some are as simple as answering the phone. Others require months of study and training. The training, often by notable professionals in the field, is an education and experience in itself. The Peace Corps combines opportunities for volunteering with foreign travel. There are nearly 500 volunteers older than 50, and the number is growing.

I have known several volunteers who were such a good fit in their place of volunteering that they were offered and took paying jobs, which made both sides happy. Though volunteer work is nonpaying, it need not be expensive for the volunteer; when filing your IRS tax return, remember to deduct 12 cents per mile on Schedule A for the use of your automobile while volunteering.

My own life has been enhanced in so many ways by the volunteer training and volunteering I have done. I have met wonderfully devoted and intelligent people and have created warm friendships. In retrospect, I can say that my volunteer work has been even more satisfying and eye-opening than my career work for remuneration. Working as a volunteer gets you outside yourself. The focus is no longer how the other person can benefit my work goals and pocketbook; I aspire to benefit him or her, without any thought of material return.

Please note that volunteering is particularly recommended to those experiencing difficult problems in their own lives, such as a serious illness or depression. Giving to others will definitely enhance your own life. It diminishes your self-centered cares and increases your self-esteem. Look up some volunteer opportunities today. Check the newspaper. Call any facility that provides care to people. Contact a library, museum, senior center, or school.

Care-Sharing

A health maintenance organization (HMO) called Elderplan has found "care-sharing" to be an innovative way to help its members, to save them money, and to recognize volunteer time. For each hour a member volunteers to help another member—for example, to go grocery shopping or to fix a broken towel bar—that credit is banked and can be drawn on by the volunteer to receive help in the future. Some people volunteer from their own homes simply by telephoning other members. Their work helps keep members out of hospitals and nursing homes and translates into savings for the HMO. It would be a worthwhile project to start this system in your HMO, church, club, or other organization.

Quiet Times

Blaise Pascal wrote: "Our achievements of today are but the sum total of the thoughts of yesterday. We are today where the thoughts of yesterday have brought us—and we will be tomorrow where the thoughts of today take us."

If you find yourself daydreaming, you are participating in a healthy and natural mental activity. Scientists say that, just as dreaming occurs every 90 minutes while we are asleep, daydreaming occurs every 90 minutes. From noon to 2:00 P.M., when body temperature is highest, daydreaming occurs more often. Purposefully schedule quiet times in your week. Watch the ocean waves, visit a museum, or sit in a park. There is nothing wrong with just observing the world go by. Many of us are so caught up with doing "important" things that we do not spend time with ourselves. It is the quiet times when we really get to know who we are and what we need.

Socializing: Meeting Emotional Needs

Just because you have lived a long time does not mean that you have less desire to satisfy the same emotional needs you had as a younger person. In her book On Our Own, Dr. Ursula A. Falk says, "[O]lder adults crave emotional satisfaction, positive reinforcement, and pleasurable experiences as much as anyone else." If you are lonely, get to know caregivers and other people who come into your life. Seniors receiving Meals-on-Wheels deliveries sometimes look forward to social interactions with the delivery people as much as the food being brought.

Give priority to close relationships, the people and things that are important to you. Remember that you tend to become like the people with whom you associate. Therefore, it is very important to spend most of your socializing time with people who make you feel vibrant, happy, and optimistic.

Say "no" to unreasonable requests. And graciously decline without an excuse invitations that do not interest you. If you make excuses, a similar invitation may come again in the future. It is a measure of your self-esteem to be able to tell the truth quickly. It shows that you can deal with the consequences. You will be respected for your forthright reply. If you encounter someone acting toward you in a way that is not helpful to you, let them know in a courteous manner and request a change.

Mix occasionally with younger people. Volunteer at an elementary school. Or get to know students through college class participation. This will increase your understanding, tolerance, and happiness.

We benefit from examining our attitudes from time to time as we consider reaching out to socialize with others. Following is a checklist adapted from Daniel Goleman's bestseller, *Emotional Intelligence*:

1. Know your emotions: recognize your true feelings as they happen.
2. Manage your emotions: have them but keep them under control.
3. Motivate yourself: use emotions to accomplish a goal.
4. Empathy: sense how it is to be in someone else's shoes.
5. Social skills: manage your response to others' emotions, and utilize the ability to persuade, negotiate, and cooperate.

Listening is an art. We should listen more than we talk. How much can we learn when our mouths are moving? You have seen people who interrupt or try to top a story with an even better one of their own. You will be a popular friend if you can listen more than talk. It is all right to let others teach you something you already know. Richard Moss, MD, said, "Our unobstructed attention is the greatest gift that we can share with anyone." It is the heart of a good relationship.

When people tell you that they need some advice, often what they really need is a chance to speak and to hear themselves speaking. When they have had a chance to talk, they will usually figure out for themselves the solution to their problem. As enjoyable as it might be to give advice, resist the temptation; just listen, paraphrase back, and affirm.

Family and Friends

It is a lovely sight to see a couple walking hand-in-hand. Occasionally, you will find a couple who claim to do everything together. However, people report the most positive moods when they are with friends. Retirees, also, are often happier with their friends than with their spouses. Friendship involves common goals and common activities. Couples should not feel guilty if they regularly spend some time apart from each other and with friends.

Men and women experience different emotional changes as they grow older. The psychologist Carl Jung talked about this midlife transition. Women are said to become stronger, more assertive, and more self-directing, whereas men tend to become softer, more intuitive, and often more dependent.

Don't assume that life with your mate and your other family members will flow along effortlessly without much care on your part. This is far from the truth. In reality, a family needs constant investments of time, energy, and compassion in order to function well. If we could treat our family as well as we treat our friends, there would be bliss on both sides. As the anonymous verse says,

> We flatter those we scarcely know, we please the fleeting guest;
> But deal many a thoughtless blow to those who love us best.

Consider that you and your mate could be together for 30 additional years or more. Therefore, if you would like to spend more quality time with your mate and enhance your relationship, you will have to work at it. Begin by thinking about what it would take to make your life together really great, and then go for it. Plan fun time with your partner. Find ways to create more energy and keep life full and interesting. Listen to the way you talk to your mate. Do you sound excited and interested? You cannot control your mate, but you can put more energy into controlling yourself and giving this most important relationship your best shot.

News Is Negative

Cut down on TV and radio news. News programs are largely negative. That is what sells. If you do not believe it, test it for a while. How many times have you seen repeats of the same tragic news scenes? How did it make you feel? The effect is to darken your mood and outlook and to generate distrust of people. Some stories awaken memories of past tragic experiences. This "media grief" can affect your appetite, sleep, and energy level. It is true that, for better or for worse, TV and whatever else you put into your mind become part of the person you are. (On average, Americans spend more than 4 hours per day watching TV and less than 20 minutes reading a book.)

Suppose that, while you were reading your daily newspaper, someone bent over your shoulder and ordered, "Read this news article but omit that one. Spend 2 minutes on this column and only 30 seconds on the other one." When you watch TV news, that is exactly what is happening. You are giving control of your mind and emotions to total strangers. But by making newspapers and news magazines your primary news sources, you retain subject choice and your emotions are less taxed. Select and ration news intake yourself rather than indiscriminately absorbing everything beamed at you. Don't expose yourself to information overload.

News is not normally your own reality. It is extreme and violent. Instead, spend time with activities that make your spirits soar. Change your major exposure from pessimism to optimism. You will be surprised at your improved outlook after you have ignored the news for a while.

Women and Health

Women live longer than men. At the age of 105, this difference between the sexes disappears and death rates are the same. However, who wants to wait that long? Some factors in the disparity appear to be the smoking and drinking habits of the two sexes and the larger number of male deaths from homicide, suicide, and accidents. Here is an interesting sidelight that appeared in a 1998 issue of the *Proceedings of the National Academy of Sciences*. John Allman and his colleagues at the California Institute of Technology reported that two species of monkey have been found in which the males do most of the child-rearing and live 20 percent longer than the females. It seems that active involvement with raising their young lengthens rather than shortens the monkeys' lives. Does this apply also to humans?

Women seem to incur more illness and depression earlier in life, which may help them to build inner strength as well as support systems they can fall back on later. Women have a greater responsibility for caregiving to members of their families and to others. In fact, about 75 percent of the money spent annually on health in recent years has been accounted for by health care decisions made by women. Perhaps because of this nurturing role, women develop four key factors in living long and well, according to research done by Dr. Royda Crose, author of *Why Women Live Longer Than Men . . . and What Men Can Learn from Them* and coordinator of the Center for Gerontology at Ball State University.

1. **Resilience** Women are better at wellness and adaptation.
2. **Flexibility** Women seem to be more flexible emotionally.
3. **Connectedness** Men want to accomplish tasks without being shown. Women get help from a network of friends when they cannot manage alone.
4. **Engagement with life** Women are more focused on activities outside themselves, which might be why they live longer.

Listen up, men!

The Male Problem

The dangerous time for men is between the ages of 45 and 65. They may feel that they have done it all and ask, "What is left and where do I fit in?" There can be a letdown. This is the time when they are confronted with making a satisfactory passage to their later years. Whereas women have built supportive networks of friends from whom they may receive and to whom they may give help, men often face aging and loss of strength and control alone and afraid. They cannot allow themselves to appear vulnerable but, on the other hand, are advised to be more sensitive and to cultivate their feminine side. Unable to confront the challenge of change, many men continue unhealthy lifestyles such as stress-filled work, smoking, and overeating. Or they retire to the couch to watch TV.

This crisis period is an important time for introspection, for developing the belief in one's ability to handle whatever the future brings, and for input and help from a loving mate or mentor. Married men, more than married women, are likely to rely exclusively on their spouses for nonprofessional consultation about worrisome health symptoms. Married women, on the other hand, consult about their own symptoms with other women and with health care professionals, as well as assuming responsibility for monitoring their husbands' health.

Positive Affirmation

Who am I? Until recently I entered the word *Retired* in the occupation blank of my Internal Revenue Service Form 1040. Now I enter *Writer*. There is a huge difference in how it makes me feel. People say, "I'm just a housewife" or "I'm only a volunteer." Both of those are responsible, important jobs. Be careful what you call yourself. Even the term *cancer survivor* may not be the most important designation that tells who you really are.

A simple exercise such as writing your own résumé can bring a big mental lift. Recently I updated my work résumé for the first time in years. Upon completion I reviewed my formal education, work, accomplishments, and activities. True, I have gotten much from the world, but I have also contributed to it. Even if you are not applying for a job, update your résumé and notice how it makes you feel.

A friend tells himself five times daily: "I am feeling well." He claims that this positive affirmation works. Or you could substitute: "I am feeling at peace." Write down affirming thoughts and post them in prominent places in your home. Clip uplifting and encouraging messages from newspapers and magazines and carry them in your wallet or handbag. For 30 years, until retirement, I carried a pocket appointment book. Each new year I would remove my collection of wonderful sayings from the old book and tape it in the new one. I read one or more sayings every day. Who would not feel protected and at peace after reading the 23rd Psalm? It is impossible to be reminded too often of inspiring and calming thoughts.

Music

Music is good therapy. Those who enjoy it are blessed. One day I was feeling down for no reason that I could discern. I flipped the radio on to jazz, the music that makes my body move. Soon I was feeling good! It was that simple. Music as therapy is coming into its own. Many hospitals use it. About 70 American colleges and universities offer undergraduate or graduate degrees in music therapy. Music reduces anxiety, lowers a fast heartbeat, and is relaxing. Sometimes patients who cannot be accessed in conversation will react to familiar tunes. Keep a supply of your favorite mood-lifting CDs or tapes handy and use them liberally.

Laughter

Recently I had an experience that caused me to question whether I am keeping up with the world or falling behind. When I exercise at my health club, I drink a lot of water. One day I went to the men's room and was standing before the urinal. I was the only person visible, but I noticed that the door to one of the stalls was closed and it was, apparently, occupied. Almost immediately a man's voice came from that direction: "How ya doin'?" I wondered, *Does he know me? How could he tell? Maybe he can identify me by the design of my athletic shoes.* "Okay," I replied. "How are you?" His reply was unintelligible to me so, not wishing to appear rude, I simply said, "Yuh, yuh." I felt a little uneasy, having never before carried on a conversation with a stranger in a men's room stall. There were some more remarks from within the stall I could not follow. Presently, the door opened and out stepped a total stranger, *talking on a cell phone.* He did not know me at all and had not said one word meant for me. I washed my hands and got out of there quickly. Boy! Did I feel stupid. However, the story got laughs later when I shared it at home.

The experience taught me that in this digital age, cell phones can be found *everywhere*. And it also gave me a refresher lesson in the healing power of laughter. Laughing lowers blood pressure and strengthens the immune system. Drs. Lee Berk and Stanley Tan of Loma Linda University found that laughter causes the brain to produce a natural euphoria through the release of endorphins. During laughter the flow of stress hormones is blocked and the sense of self-esteem and well-being increases. Laughter provides a good abdominal workout. Children laugh about 400 times a day; adults, about 15 times.

Have you heard any good jokes lately? If humor does not come naturally to you, then share with your friends a funny experience about one of your grandchildren or your dog. Or research humor on the Internet or humor books in the library, or rent a comedy video.

Tears and Whining Time

Tears may help to remove from the body a residue of unwanted chemicals resulting from stress. This may be why anger and sadness subside after crying. William Frey, a biochemist and author of Crying: The Mystery of Tears, found that 85 percent of women and 73 percent of men report feeling better after they have shed tears in stressful situations. This useful, free therapy is available to humans but not to other animals. Permit yourself to benefit from it.

A busy clergyman says that at times throughout the day he used to find himself dwelling on negative thoughts. For example, he wished he had handled a situation differently or had used different language or did not have to tackle a certain project. Now he finds it more helpful to postpone entertaining those thoughts individually. Then, in a fifteen-minute period once a day, alone, he allows himself to feel the negative emotions of those things over which he no longer has any control. In the long run, this is more efficient and satisfactory. He calls it his "whining time."

New Experiences

If you are healthy and your level of activity does not require you to keep a weekly written schedule of appointments, then either you are too uninvolved with life or you have a memory like an elephant. No matter what your age, there is no limit to your capacity for growth. You can predict who is going to do well in the aging process; it is the person reaching out for new experiences, reading new books, and following current trends. Push yourself sometimes to get out of the same comfortable routine. For example, perhaps your reduced requirements have not recently taken you into a giant hardware or sporting goods store or the housewares section of a department store. Visit one. Walk up and down the aisles. Observe what new products are available. You might happen to find the item to solve a problem you have been experiencing. Or register for a course or join a group that is somewhat "out-of-character" but interesting. Boredom means you are avoiding risk-taking. It is a sign that your lifestyle is too safe and predictable. Taking a risk may cause anxiety, but it will be an exciting anxiety.

Long-term brain power is promoted by staying physically, socially, and intellectually active. Your educational level is less important than the activity of learning. Brain function impairment is a result of disease, not age. The more we ask of the brain, the better it ages.

> The greatest trouble with most of us is that our demands upon ourselves are so feeble, the call upon the great within us so weak and intermittent, that it makes no impression upon the creative energies.
>
> —ORISON SWETT MARDEN

A spiritual life of some kind is absolutely necessary for psychological "health."

THOMAS MOORE, CARE OF THE SOUL

CHAPTER FOUR

Assess Your Spiritual Health

THIS CHAPTER EXPLORES our spiritual options, which will complement and reinforce our physical, mental, and emotional options.

Spirituality, Religion, and Humanity

Everyone is spiritual. Not everyone is religious. Our spirits inherently seek a relationship to a source of power beyond human limitations, that is, a divinity. Some people say that the spirit is the same as the soul and that both are a kind of energy or light. A few humans claim to be able to see this energy as a person's aura. This is the derivation of the halo we see around the heads of holy people in painting and sculpture. Some massage therapists report feeling their patients' energy fields.

Religion is usually a group experience. Most of us are too frightened or unready to seek a personal connection with the divine other than through an established religious group. There is safety and comfort in worshipping with others like us who are on a similar spiritual journey. On the other hand, some pursue individual spiritual journeys.

In his bestselling book, *Care of the Soul*, Thomas Moore wrote: "In a very real sense, we do not cure diseases, they cure us, by restoring our religious participation in life." If you have ever been near someone who had a fatal illness, you must have thought about your own mortality and realized that you, too, must die someday. These thoughts tend naturally to occur more often as we enter the later decades of our lives. Perhaps that is why belief in God seems to strengthen as people get older. About 50 percent of older adults say they attend church at least weekly. Some with disabilities avoid or lessen depression with religious coping, that is, by prayer, faith in God, and Scripture reading.

You may question human's purpose on earth and the meaning of your own life. This is a good time for stocktaking. "Am I comfortable with what I believe? If a doctor told me today that I have an incurable illness, how would that affect my spiritual and religious beliefs and practices?" You have been holding your beliefs for a long time. Would you be comfortable continuing as you have been doing? Or would you make a change? What change, if any, would help you face the end of life with more acceptance? You can choose the course that will bring the greatest satisfaction and peace.

Values

Society could not function well without values. Over thousands of years, and with the help of the world's great religions, we have established orderly guidelines for human interaction. Most people in the USA have been influenced by the Ten Commandments. These begin by dictating the rules of relationship between God and human beings. But most of the commandments set out rules for proper relationships among humans.

Theologians tell us that humans have free will. Therefore, just as there are rules of conduct, there are also reasons why in some instances humans find it expedient not to follow those rules. America was founded on the ideal of individual liberty. Personal independence is valued; the individual is as, or more, important than the group. In contrast, some other societies such as Japan, for example, expect citizens to sublimate individual wishes for the greater good of the group. Americans find this concept difficult. Individualism is our preference.

It is fashionable to proclaim our independent attitudes in such slo-gans as "do your own thing," "let it all hang out," and "Numero Uno." These are used to justify individual actions that are not neces-sarily in the best interests of the entire community, or that even go against the community's interests. Some of our children and grand-children have been raised without a religion-based set of rules and without any substitute code of values to which they can refer. They quite properly look to adults as role models. There they observe actions that are ambivalent or contradictory. Even theologians con-found us with their "situation theology." A certain action is wrong, but if the conditions are a little changed, what was wrong is now accept-able. Is this God speaking, or people?

As I grow older, I find that it is the tried and true religion-based values that give comfort and serve me well in telling right from wrong in my everyday life. This is not to say that the church organiza-tion itself is always right. One must separate dogma and doctrine from values. I suffered a painful experience as a young adult as a result of blindly following the advice of a clergyman who, naturally, wished me to follow church doctrine. Wisdom in aging may mean rejecting some of the trappings of religion and holding in our hearts that spiritual guidance we know to be right and true, the guidance that comes straight to our hearts from God.

A famous potter told me his story. Wishing as a young man to learn proper ceramic making, he spent four years in the country's most renowned technical college. After graduation he settled on his life's specialty, producing pottery in the traditional folk-craft style. He said that it took him twenty years to unlearn his college training and reach the simplicity and purity of true artistic creation. I suppose that his hands were then guided by the spirit or God within him. Similarly, a time comes when we must examine our own hearts. Which values are eternal, good, and true? Which are false, superficial, passing, and unworthy of our commitment? To the thinking person this self-exam-ination becomes a daily practice.

Accountability

Accountability is answering for your conduct. How is it possible that one can be accountable to God, but not to other people? When is the last time someone told you: "It was my fault. I am sorry. Henceforth I will be more careful"? When did you last say such a thing? Answering for our mistakes seems to be out of fashion. We are encouraged to make excuses and avoid responsibility: "It just happened. A computer error. Someone else's fault." Insurance companies advise us not to admit being at fault in an auto accident even if we know the fault was ours. A former U.S. President, Harry Truman, was said to have had a sign on his desk in the White House. It read: "The buck stops here." Putting personal convenience before accountability poisons your spirit. Stand up and be counted, whether in your relationship to the divine or to humans. It is never too early to make the decision: I am accountable for my actions to God, to my neighbor, and to my own individual, sacred spirit.

To your children and grandchildren you are a role model. Your efforts to avoid unhealthy habits, to take care of yourself physically and mentally, and to reach composure in your spiritual beliefs form the image they see of an aging adult, one whom they respect. It would be a first if some aspects of your life were not imitated by them. Are you living the life you would want them to live?

The Spiritual Person

The spiritual man or woman, regardless of religious affiliation, recognizes everyone in the world as a brother or sister. Speeding up when the traffic light is about to turn red is unacceptable to spiritual people, as it's not only discourteous, it risks an accident with another person on the road. At the public campground they will leave their campsite in better condition than they found it; their brother or sister will be the next camper. Spiritual people will not catch more fish or take more game than is legal or they need to feed their families. They will recycle goods and keep the ecosystem as pristine as possible. They will not waste the precious resources of the earth. They know they have benefited from those who came before and will leave enough for the billions who will come after. "Voluntary Simplicity" and "Simple Abundance" will be their themes.

Spiritual people will decline an additional drink of alcohol, knowing it could harm others and will most certainly harm themselves. They will follow their hearts in electing honest lawmakers who will work to satisfy the long-term needs of their entire country and even of their brothers and sisters in foreign countries. The spiritual person will voluntarily help people in need and will send prayers or strengthening thoughts their way.

The spiritual spouse will do everything possible to uplift and support his or her mate and care for and teach their children. To degrade or put down any living thing lowers our own humanity and spirituality. Whether or not they accept the idea that we are made in the image and likeness of God, spiritual people know that if they truly act as if they love their neighbors as themselves, and if they honor their own God-given spirit, they will be satisfying God's law.

The Spiritual Person Without Church, Synagogue, Mosque, or Temple

Spirituality ought to be maintained and deepened through spiritual exercises and quietness, either in community or by oneself. The name of the denomination or religion is less important than whether or not the faithful live good lives by any objective measure. Many people eventually drop out of regular attendance at church, synagogue, mosque, or temple. Perhaps they do not wish to put in the effort necessary to grow. Or they have outgrown what that particular faith community has to offer. Alone, it is a challenge to cultivate spirituality. The Reverend Dale Turner said, "People seldom improve when they have no other model but themselves." To continue growing, some regular spiritual practices must be incorporated into your daily routine. Suggestions follow.

Upon arising in the morning, a spiritual person might step outside to be closer to nature and make some sign of obeisance, a bow or an uplifting of the arms, in recognition of a spiritual authority. (A Native American teacher told me that he cannot begin his morning by offering his prayer indoors.) Such a person might inwardly say, "Thank you for permitting me to witness another day. Thank you for my night's rest, for my health, for bread on the table and a house in which to eat it, for my family, my livelihood, and for this place to which you have guided me. You have showered on me many blessings for which I am grateful. In the course of today I will encounter many fellow creatures, some whom I have never met before. Help me in our meetings to enrich their lives and make us all better for our encounters. Teach me how to be at one with all living things, for there is a commonality of life in all of us. As I turn to go inside my house, show me how to be especially compassionate to the family you have given me. Teach me how I can best conduct myself in all ways this day."

For the unaffiliated spiritual person, a period of meditation or quiet thought will be a part of each day. Since spiritual growth should never end, there will be study of books or tapes to deepen spirituality. The day should be a constant outpouring of positive thoughts and actions, directed both inward and outward, toward the goals of spiritual support, growth, and peace. Before retiring, a brief reflection on the course of the completed day is appropriate, noting especially areas for improvement. It will be important to have a guru or spiritual advisor with whom one can talk once a month or once a year. This kind of spiritual life, of course, is open to everyone, churchgoer or not.

The Spiritual Person and Communal Worship

When you worship together with other believers, you are benefiting in several ways. There is a community of like-minded brothers and sisters who affirm and support each other in their faith. A pastor, rabbi, or other spiritual leader ministers to the spiritual needs of the congregation, presides at ritual ceremonies, and provides ongoing education in the form of readings, sermons, lessons, classes, and counseling. Worshipers can leave the service with the hope that the spiritual nourishment received will help sustain them through the week. Spiritual reinforcement opportunities are varied and abundant. Human needs for interaction are met by social functions. Millions of

Americans look forward to weekend service as a highlight in their lives, and they hope to emerge better for it.

Through the course of long habit, it sometimes happens that although we apparently are quite religious, in fact we have become rather without spirit. We attend church regularly but do not follow the command to love our neighbor. We are "Sunday faithful" but leave our professed values in the church when we depart. Some "faithful" doggedly continue church attendance long after it has become only a routine. Their hearts and spirits are not in it. They may hold to the hope that, in spite of themselves, someday something they see or hear will inspire them to begin living the life their religion holds as the ideal. Or they may attend out of fear of God's wrath or to get other people's approval. Perhaps they just like to experience a familiar religious feeling for one hour each week. If you professed to be a believer in your particular religious faith, would there be enough evidence available from your daily life to prove it?

For most of us, having community in our faith life is extremely helpful. If you do not attend a regular worship service, you can at least choose to associate with spiritual support groups or individuals who uplift your spirit. You may decide to join others in some church-sponsored study and discussion groups even without being members of the congregation. Together you will talk, explore, challenge, encourage, reinforce, and pray. It is important for our own development to be able to hear ourselves speak what we believe and to receive the stimulation of others' witnessing and responding to our witness.

Am I Missing Out?

Faith communities provide a support, a sense of life's meaning, and a reason to focus beyond the self. Many of us have spent years as members of an organized religion. If you are not doing so now, are you missing out on something that would improve your quality of life, right here on earth? If your heart tells you that you might like to attend church, mosque, temple, or synagogue again, look for ways in which you might do it.

Ask a friend to accompany you to a house of worship. This will give you some support, and you can discuss your experiences afterward. Or go straight to a member of the clergy and have a talk about whatever is on your mind. There are no dumb questions about religion. If your previous contacts with your place of worship were unsatisfactory, ask a friend whom you admire to take you to his or her place of worship. Try several different worship experiences to find a place where God seems to be speaking to your heart.

Do you think God cares under what denomination you worship? I say, No way! Yet many intelligent adults feel guilty if they do not follow the religious traditions of their childhood. They would prefer abstaining altogether from attendance rather than go somewhere new. Such is the sustaining power of our early experiences, for good or for bad. However, it is better to do *something* for ourselves than to do nothing.

Homebound

Friends are usually happy to give you a ride to a place of worship. However, if you cannot make it, ask the clergy to visit you or to send someone, even if you have never attended. In addition to clergy, congregations have lay persons who volunteer to visit the homebound to discuss spiritual matters, to read, to take communion, to console, and to listen. Or ask a friend who seems spiritually well-grounded to visit and talk with you, whether or not he or she is a member of a congregation. Radio and TV religious services can be very stimulating and uplifting right in the convenience of your own home. If you have a computer, the Web has more than a dozen religious sites for education and stimulation.

Prayer in the USA

A *Newsweek* poll published March 31, 1997, revealed statistics on prayer in the USA. How do you stack up?

- 54% of adults pray daily; 29% pray even more frequently.
- 82% pray for health or success for members of the family.
- 75% pray for overcoming personal weaknesses.
- 87% say that they believe prayers are answered.
- 82% continue faith in God even when prayers are not answered.
- 54% say it was not God's will when prayers are not answered.
- 79% believe that God hears and answers prayers for those with incurable diseases.
- 82% believe that in answering prayers God does not have favorites.
- 51% think that prayers about sporting events are not answered.
- 36% say that financial or career success is never the object of their prayers.

Prayer Is Effective

If, while thinking of a power or strength beyond yourself, you say, "I hope my daughter makes it home without an accident," that is a prayer! Many of us were trained to believe that we had to repeat memorized prayers or else they were not effective. It is not necessarily so. C. Norman Shealy, MD, PhD, author of *Miracles Do Happen*, warns: "Watch your thinking because every thought is a prayer." Caregiving, if done with a good heart, can be a prayer. Receiving care can also be a prayer.

Visualize outcomes when you pray. Do not merely pray that some illness be removed; see in your mind a tumor shrinking in size and disappearing. This has actually happened!

Pray for those who are sick. Several double-blind scientific studies have indicated that those who are prayed for recover more rapidly. In 1988 cardiologist Randolph Byrd, MD, published his study of 393 heart patients at the hospital of the University of California at San Francisco. Half had received standard medical care only. The other half also received prayers daily from born-again Christians, although neither the patients nor the hospital staff, including Dr. Byrd, knew who was receiving prayers. The startling outcome was that, compared with the control group, the patients receiving prayers required fewer antibiotics, had less congestive heart failure, and were less likely to suffer from pneumonia. Rather than finding that the question of prayer fuels the old quarrel between science and religion, we find that science may actually verify the effectiveness of prayer.

One view says that healing comes from interaction with a community offering its prayers for you. That belief casts doubt on our ability to heal ourselves effectively without community. Anne Harrington, PhD, a professor of the history of science and a participant in a Harvard Medical School symposium on "Spirituality and Healing in Medicine," cites studies that show a 50 percent increase in survival time for cancer patients who use group support. Invite others to pray for your healing. It may be more effective than relying only on your prayers for yourself. At the same symposium, Rabbi Rachel B. Cowers made the point that a person cannot heal him- or herself alone but needs the support of a community.

Traditionally, medicine has been associated with religion. Many of our hospitals are church-connected. Interestingly, however, studies show that today's physicians and psychologists are less religious than the average public. In addition to prescribing medicine, can we expect our doctors to pray for our recovery? You had better ask. I know one neurosurgeon who prays for his patients. Miraculous cures have occurred.

If you do not want to pray, simply send strengthening thoughts to your friends and loved ones. The result for them will be helpful and you, also, will feel better.

Is the Kingdom of Heaven Within You?

Many Christian churches say that at the Last Judgment our mortal bodies will be raised up to heaven for all eternity, or damned to hell for the same duration. That should be enough incentive for walking the straight and narrow. But not everyone believes in a life after death. Some people believe that death is the end of the body and the spirit. Jennifer James, PhD, author of *Twenty Steps to Wisdom*, wrote in her newspaper column: "You may find 'ashes to ashes, dust to dust' depressing, but I find it comforting. If I desire immortality, I must raise children to carry on my genetic code and my character. I must plant gardens, write for the future and leave my memory in the minds of those younger than I am. If I am not going to be reunited with family and friends in an afterlife, then I must love them now. For me, every day is life just as it is for all the other species, not a preparation for an afterlife."

Spiritual Maturity

Childhood Scripture study is like a suit of clothes. It served us very well when we were children. But do you think adults can be well served by the same clothing they wore as children? When is the last time you studied something of a spiritual nature? Was it in Sunday school? Give yourself the chance to take a fresh look at adult-level spiritual nourishment, preferably in a group. Be in a dialogue with reality. You may stimulate your thinking in a way you did not expect.

An Indian proverb says, Everyone is a house with four rooms: a physical, a mental, an emotional, and a spiritual room. When you think about it, most of us tend to live in one room most of the time, but unless we go into every room every day, we are not complete people. Do you believe that you are here to accomplish a special purpose? You will be a happier individual and will help to create a better world when you decide what you came here to do.

Intuition

The famous psychologist Carl Jung said that humans function in four ways: feeling, thinking, sensing, and intuiting. Nowadays we are being encouraged to trust our intuition. "Intuition is clear knowing without knowing how you know. It is the deepest wisdom of the human soul," according to psychologist Marcia Emery, author of Intuition Workbook.

You have had the experience of the mind producing certain effects on the body. Fear makes us rigid; love is relaxing; and pride in accomplishment increases our feelings of positive power. These reactions are explained chemically by the flow of neuropeptides. It is not unreasonable to believe that a reaction can also move in the opposite direction, that is, that your body can send messages that are not registered in the brain as actual thoughts. These intuitions or "gut feelings" tell us, for example, that we have an illness even when the doctor cannot find anything wrong. I believe that intuition is linked to the spirit. Try learning to trust your intuition.

Meditation

I knew that I needed a calming practice in my life. None of the meditation books I studied did the trick. Finally, what did work for me was to take a meditation course with an instructor. Now, whenever my brain tells me that I need refreshment, I take a 20-minute meditation break. I feel as if I have received the good effects of an hour's nap, without any bad effects. Meditating twice a day is ideal.

Meditation calms and energizes the body and the spirit. During meditation our rates of metabolism, heartbeat, and breathing decrease. Brain waves slow down. Meditation also strengthens the immune system and promotes wellness. There is ample evidence for its good effects against hypertension.

Although meditating is a spiritual and mental exercise, it can be consciously religious or not religious at all, as you choose. For example, as a mantra or chant, some may repeat the pilgrim's prayer over and over. Others will repeatedly say or mentally visualize a Sanskrit word that has no meaning for them. You may choose as your focus any word you wish, such as "peace." Meditation is versatile and effective. If you decide to try it, do not give up without studying with a teacher.

Keeping a Journal

Journaling has been described as a way to rediscover the spiritual, as a path to mental self-care, and as a means of reaching our inner depths. Try keeping a daily journal of your actions, thoughts, and feelings. As you reread your entries, try to identify patterns of thought and feeling that might deserve further investigation and study.

It is believed that journaling strengthens the immune system. The *Journal of the American Medical Association* for April 13, 1999, reported a study of 112 patients with asthma and arthritis who were asked to keep a journal. The control group wrote only about their daily schedule. The other group wrote their thoughts about and reaction to the trauma of their disease. Afterward an independent physician found 24 percent of the control group to be clinically improved as compared with 47 percent who wrote about the trauma of their chronic disease. For more information on journaling, see *Journaling for Joy* by Joyce Chapman.

Dreams

You may well benefit from taking time to record and interpret your dreams. Most people ignore their dreams, and many claim that they do not dream at all. Doctors have proven that everyone dreams during sleeping periods of rapid eye movement (REM). Not everyone remembers dreams upon awakening, however. Dream specialists claim a direct correlation between everyday life and dreams. They say that disregarding the meaning of a dream is like receiving a letter and leaving it unopened, and that dreams are messages from our subconscious to our conscious selves. The Bible and other sacred books contain references to humans receiving messages in dreams. Experts say that if we disregard our emotions and intuitions, they often emerge anyway in our dreams. Some doctors believe that dreams can provide a warning of an illness.

There are ways to work with our dreams. For example, write about your day's thoughts, feelings, and actions just before retiring at night. Finish with a question or problem for incubation during sleep. Keep a pen and paper on your nightstand. Force yourself to awaken and record your dream when you realize you have had one. Then go back to sleep without further thought. Failing that, record your dream immediately upon arising for the day. Try to pick out any relationship between your dream and the question or problem you wrote down. For more information consult your library or attend a lecture on dreams.

Body, Mind, and Spirit

Dr. Rachel Naomi Remen in the March 1996 issue of *Personal Excellence* states: "Denying the spiritual is bad for your health. Much illness may have its roots in unrecognized spiritual distress—issues of isolation, of anger, the feelings people have that they don't matter or that nobody matters to them."

Many new reports and books link the spirit and the body. A healthy body is a good foundation for a good spiritual life. Conversely, religious or spiritual conviction seems to motivate us to take better care of our bodies. *The American Journal of Public Health* in 1997 reported a 28-year study of more than 5000 residents of Alameda County, California. Those who did not attend church regularly had an annual death rate 36 percent higher than those who did attend regularly. The latter group's longer life expectancy was explained by improved health practices, increased social contacts, and more stable marriages. Look at the many new books linking spirituality and religion with fitness, diet, and the like. The body is the temple of the spirit.

If, after reading this, you find that you are content with your spiritual beliefs and practices, you may decide to make no changes. However, you can test your thinking as follows. Spend some time visiting or taking care of a terminally ill relative or friend. Or volunteer in a hospice program. See if your thinking supports you in the harsh reality of life. You will have done yourself and your friend a great service. Also, you will have prepared for your own future.

We are not human beings having a spiritual experience.
We are spiritual beings having a human experience.

—PIERRE TEILHARD DE CHARDIN

You have completed Part One. Reexamine the goals you set for yourself in Chapter One. Make changes where appropriate and then move on.

Part Two

Think Nutrition
and
Avoid Disease

It's a very odd thing
As odd as can be
That whatever Miss T. eats
Turns into Miss T.

WALTER DE LA MARE

CHAPTER FIVE

You Are What You Eat

JUST BECAUSE YOU have been eating all of your life does not mean that the foods going into your mouth are the ones best chosen for your health, longevity, and quality of life. If you are eating in the way your parents ate, you are probably way behind the times. Ideas on proper nutrition have changed, and there is yet much to be learned. This chapter will introduce you to some of the latest findings.

Weight

I lived and worked outside the USA for a period of my life. When I returned to live again in America, I could not believe my eyes. What had Americans been doing to develop extra inches and bulges over their bodies? As the expression goes, "Americans were digging their graves with their forks."

Since then, it has not gotten any better. The National Center for Health Statistics has told us that more than 50 percent of us are overweight! One third are obese! That is up from one quarter in 1980. And worse, this trend is *accelerating*. We are taking fatness as the new norm. The number of people who agreed with the statement, "People who are not overweight look a lot more attractive" declined from 55 percent in 1985 to 28 percent in 1996. This excess baggage is putting too much strain on frames not designed for it. After all, we are not pack horses. Excess weight causes mobility problems; the joints just will not handle it. (In 1992 the *Annals of Internal Medicine* reported that women who lost 11 pounds decreased the odds for developing osteoarthritis of the knees by over 50 percent.) Excess weight also forces our hearts to work in excess of their intended capacity, thus causing overload and subsequent shortening of lives. In addition, obesity is a contributing factor in the development of adult-onset diabetes. Almost 10 percent of all health spending, or $60 to $80 billion annually, goes to treat health problems associated with obesity.

Some blame obesity on genes: "But my whole family is overweight. It's just our metabolism." It is true that some of us are genetically programmed to burn calories at a slower pace than others. However, let's not kid ourselves. Michael Fumento, author of *The Fat of the Land: The Obesity Epidemic and How Overweight Americans Can Help Themselves*, stated in the May–June 1998 issue of *Modern Maturity* that this difference in metabolic rates amounts "at most to the equivalent of burning the calories in two pieces of hard candy a day." Sadly, the fatter you are, the sicker you will be and the shorter will be your life. You can find more information about weight and weight loss at the Weight Loss Control Center: Tip of the Day Web site at http://www.arbon.com/wgttip/home.htm.

Caloric Restriction

Scientists have known since 1935 that rats can live up to 50 percent longer when put on caloric restrictions. The National Institute on Aging announced that a similar study on monkeys, started in 1987, shows the same trend. Reducing calories by 30 percent makes the monkeys' bodies work much more efficiently. Monkeys that eat less have lower metabolism, lower blood pressure, and lower levels of triglycerides (fats). They have fewer cancers and less heart disease than monkeys on a higher-calorie diet. A compound called pentosidine, associated with the onset of age-related diseases, is produced in smaller amounts with caloric restriction. Dr. George Roth of that institute said, "I don't see any reason why what applies to these monkeys wouldn't also apply to humans."

Brain-Mouth Connection

"You don't have to be hungry to eat."—Sign displayed at a doughnut shop

Fully half the women and one quarter of the men in America have tried to lose weight. For the life of me I cannot figure out our national compulsion to gratify ourselves by stuffing our mouths. For want of a definitive answer I have concluded that there must be a substantial number of us who are stressed, frustrated, and unhappy. Without knowledge of how to address our underlying problems we turn to food, the most available desirable substance.

Why is it so difficult to lose those unwanted pounds? Nature wants the body to maintain the weight it presently has. This survival mechanism is not helpful in these modern times of plentiful high-calorie foods. Fat cells produce a chemical called leptin, which is supposed to signal the brain that you should stop eating because you have sufficient energy reserves. When fat people reduce caloric intake and lose weight, they reduce the amount of fat in their cells, and leptin levels decline. The brain then gets the message that energy reserves are falling, which causes the body to conserve energy and increase the appetite. This is why dieters experience the yo-yo effect and put those hard-to-lose pounds back on again.

Perception of the nutritional value of what we eat affects the volume of food we consume. When subjects in a food study were told that the lunch they were eating was low-fat, they consumed *more* calories than usual the rest of the day. But when told that they were eating a normal meal, they ate less later. In fact, the nutritional content of the lunches was identical.

A Harvard study published in the September 1996 issue of the *New England Journal of Medicine* showed that people who live longest have body mass indexes between 19 and 22. In 1998, a University of North Carolina study involving almost a third of a million subjects reported the same numbers. Are you overweight? Here is the formula to calculate your body mass index. Multiply your weight in pounds by 705. Divide by your height in inches. Divide again by your height. If the result is 25 or more, you need to lose weight. That's all there is to it.

Food Pyramid

The U.S. Department of Agriculture has substantially revised its guidelines on recommended percentages of foods from the basic food groups—the so-called Food Guide Pyramid. (Only about two thirds of Americans say that they are familiar with the Food Guide Pyramid.) The USDA's Food Guide Pyramid is recognized as a political compromise among scientists, the government, and lobbyists representing beef ranchers, dairy farmers, and other interests. One objection is that it puts too much emphasis on animal protein and does not distinguish among sources of protein. It lumps foods like red meat, poultry, fish, dry beans, eggs, and nuts into one group and recommends that people eat two to three servings per day. However, most of us eat too much animal fat. The USDA has admitted that its approach to the public has not worked. Its advice was posted on the Internet: "Enjoy your steak twice as much. Eat half of it in the restaurant and take the rest home to enjoy the next day. Enjoy a rich dessert more. Share it with a friend."

In fact, the human body does not need animal fat at all. Vegetable oils can adequately provide whatever fat is needed. (Meat does have other desirable nutrients, which, however, may also be found in non-meat products.) For the contents of healthy, traditional diet pyramids for the Mediterranean, Asian, and Latin American areas, as well as for a vegetarian diet pyramid, contact Oldways Preservation & Exchange Trust in Cambridge, Massachusetts, at (617) 621-3000.

In 1991 the National Institutes of Health launched a "Five a Day for Better Health" program. The intent was to persuade Americans to eat a minimum of five servings of fruits or vegetables a day to ward off cancer. Why was five servings selected? Actually, some members of the committee that promulgated the recommendation wanted to advocate nine servings per day. That number was rejected because public health officials feared that many Americans would regard the number as unachievable and would tune out the message. In fact, only about half of the population consumes enough vegetables and fruits to improve their chances of warding off colon cancer. The message to me is that I will not look to my government for clear and accurate guidance on keeping my health. That responsibility is mine, and requires consulting a variety of available sources.

Here are some interesting findings. Research psychiatrist Dr. Joseph Hibbeln at the National Institute on Alcohol Abuse and Alcoholism did research that showed that a diet high in consumption of fish, especially cold-water fish, is linked to lower rates of depression and hostility. Epidemiologist James McDonald Robertson of the University of Western Ontario found that foods rich in vitamins E and C (or supplements of those vitamins) may reduce the risk of eye cataracts by as much as 50 percent. A diet rich in fruits and vegetables and low-fat dairy products reduces high blood pressure in those with mild hypertension just as effectively as the most commonly used hypertension drugs. This was a finding in a National Institutes of Health study reported in the *New England Journal of Medicine* on April 17, 1997. With about 60 million Americans suffering from hypertension, many of them having only mild hypertension, much money could be saved simply by changing diet and eliminating drugs.

Fats

Fat is as important in our diet as protein and carbohydrate. Fats are saturated or unsaturated. Saturated fats are found in meats, dairy products, and coconut and palm oils. These fats ought to be severely restricted in our diets. Monounsaturated fats include olive oil, canola oil (made from rapeseed), and peanut oil. Polyunsaturated fats include corn, safflower, and sunflower oils. This last group, according to Dr. Andrew Weil in his book *Spontaneous Healing*, can damage cell membranes. He recommends eliminating them altogether. This leaves us with olive oil, most recommended, and canola and peanut oils, very distant runners up.

Another fat category is trans fat. It is the result of a manufacturing process that produces "hydrogenated oils." Food manufacturers use this process to turn liquid oil to oil that is solid at room temperature. Examples are margarine and vegetable shortenings. When you read food labels, you will find hydrogenated or partially hydrogenated oils in many foods, especially snack foods. Trans fat makes up about 10 percent of the calories in a typical diet.

Pay attention, now, because trans fat is a big killer. The Harvard School of Public Health charted the eating habits of 80,082 apparently healthy nurses. Fourteen years later, 939 of them had died of heart disease or had suffered heart attacks. The study found that those who consumed the most trans fat were 53 percent more likely to suffer a heart attack than those who consumed the least. Dr. Walter Willett, chairman of the nutrition department at the school said, "[I]ntroducing trans fat into the American diet is the single most harmful thing the food industry has done in the last 100 years." Where is trans fat chiefly found? In margarine, pastries, crackers, "buttered" popcorn, chips, cookies, and deep-fried foods. They advised eating much less of these foods and switching to unsaturated fats such as olive oil.

Fat is one of the most concentrated sources of calories. Fat has twice the calories per ounce of either carbohydrates or proteins. The bottom line on fat consumption is: (1) limit it to 20–27 percent of your total caloric intake (for most Americans it is about 33 percent); (2) use olive oil and, occasionally, canola oil; (3) eat only lean meat or poultry and only in small quantities a few times a month or, at most, two or three times weekly; (4) cut down on butter, cheese, and whole milk products; (5) eliminate altogether the trans fat found in hydrogenated oils and also cut out all deep-fried foods; and (6) eat more salmon, sardines, herring, mackerel, and bluefish, which are high in good omega 3 fatty acid.

Fat-free does not mean calorie-free. For example, if you consumed 100 extra calories a day—as in a glass of wine or a tablespoon of mayonnaise—you would be adding 700 additional calories a week, putting on about 10 pounds of extra weight in a year. Plant-based foods do not contain cholesterol, which comes from animal foods (meat and dairy products). However, cholesterol-free foods may not reduce your cholesterol level if those foods are high in saturated fat, for example, coconut or palm oil. Robert Pritikin, whose father started the famous Pritikin Diet, pointed out that an often-unsuspected source of fat for women is in salads. After adding the dressing, the salad becomes 60–70 percent fat. It is not the kind of fat that creates cholesterol, but it does create extra calories and, therefore, pounds. An appropriate serving of meat is three ounces, about the size of a deck of cards. One helping of potatoes is one cup, about the size of your fist. For healthy nutrition we must consider calories, portions, and variety, as well as fat.

Nutrition As We Age

The need for calories decreases with aging, but the need for specific nutrients increases. We need more proteins because we are not absorbing them as efficiently. Eat more whole grains and beans, especially soybean. Fruits and vegetables are full of nutrients; consume nine servings daily. Beginning as early as age 50, the production of antibodies falls as the immune system starts to decline. But the rate of decline may be slowed by an adequate dietary intake of nutrients such as vitamin B-6, beta carotene, and zinc, and the use of vitamin and mineral supplements.

Between 25 and 50 percent of people over 65 are short on key vitamins and minerals. Don't take a chance. Take an all-purpose vitamin plus the minerals magnesium, calcium, selenium, and chromium. You may need to take extra pills daily to get sufficient vitamin E (200–800 IU), vitamin C (250–500 mg), and calcium (1300–1500 mg). These supplements do not replace a balanced, healthful diet. But be aware that our daily caloric requirement decreases 5 percent from ages 55 to 65 and another 5 percent from 65 to 75. Try using smaller plates. Put away leftovers before sitting down to eat.

A special word on calcium. For years we have known of its importance in strengthening bones and preventing osteoporosis. Although the daily recommendation for calcium intake is 1300–1500 mg, on average Americans consume about 30 percent less than the recommendation. Most older adults may be well-advised to consider taking calcium supplements. To be most effective, calcium supplements should be taken with vitamin D, magnesium, and/or potassium. If you take more than 500 mg of calcium supplements a day, spread the intake over two or three dosages during the day. Make use of this inexpensive, wonderful mineral.

Taste and smell provide enjoyment and are important to good nutrition. Some older people complain that they cannot taste their food. They may be in danger of malnutrition. Declines in these senses may be caused by illnesses such as Parkinson's and Alzheimer's, by medications, and by surgical procedures. Salt and sugar added to food may reach dangerous levels for those who suffer from high blood pressure or diabetes. Look for safer seasonings that produce no known bad health effects. Dental problems can cause some people to avoid foods hard to chew, which, nevertheless, may provide valuable nutrients. If you have a sore mouth or a medical condition that drains your energy, use a pressure cooker to do your entire meal. The nutrients are not lost, and the food will be soft and easy to eat. If swallowing is difficult, juicing is an alternative, but it does not provide significant fiber or protein if the pulp is removed.

Don't assume that just because you feel well your food intake is right for you. (High blood pressure, for example, has no obvious symptoms until it is very high.) The Department of Agriculture reported that of the people surveyed, 81 percent underestimated their food consumption. Record your food and drink intake in a typical week. Show your record to a nutritionist or dietitian. (Doctors are rarely good sources of nutritional information.) For your own knowledge, you could take your food diary one step further and include where you ate your meal, your emotional state, how hungry you were, how long it took (never spend less than 20 minutes at a meal), and whether other people were present or not. Then analyze the results for trouble spots and habits you can change.

Food co-ops and health-food stores are good sources of nutrition information and often sponsor specialty cooking classes in, for example, low-fat and vegetarian cooking. The world's number one database for learning food content is the USDA's Nutrient Database for Standard Reference at **http://www.nal.usda.gov/fnic/foodcomp**. It includes over 6000 foods, is kept up to date, and is free.

Processed Foods

Eat whole foods insofar as possible. Processed foods, while convenient, lose much of their nutrition, are high in calories, and have too
much sodium and preservative added in order to maintain shelf life
in the supermarket. I have eliminated or severely restricted processed,
starchy carbohydrates from my diet. I do not want added weight,
marginal nutrition, and added workload on my pancreas. Therefore, I
rarely eat pasta, pizza, pancakes, or bread. I frequently eat brown rice
and beans cooked together but restrict my intake of white rice.

Processed foods are lacking in fiber, which is necessary for digestion. Whereas we are supposed to consume 25–35 grams of fiber per
day, Americans typically eat only 11 grams. Soluble fiber may lower
cholesterol and regulate blood-sugar levels in people with diabetes. It
is found in dried beans, vegetables, oat bran, and whole-grain foods
made from oats and barley. Insoluble fiber does not dissolve in water;
it provides bulk, which aids in the transit of wastes. It is found in
fruits, vegetables, wheat bran, and whole-grain foods made from
wheat, corn, and rice. You will get more fiber from fruit than from a
serving of most breakfast cereals. For example, you would have to eat
two cups of a popular processed oat cereal to get the same 4 grams of
dietary fiber found in one pear. What is it worth to have an easy
bowel movement and improved health? The best way to avoid
processed foods is to plan your whole day's wholesome menu on the
previous day—and don't deviate from it.

What's on Your Plate?

As a kid, I formed a set image of an appealing dinner. Whether in a
magazine ad or at our own table, a big piece of meat or fried chicken
occupied the center of the plate. On either side of the meat would be
string beans or corn and potatoes. There was white bread, a green
salad, a glass of milk, and, for dessert, apple pie, sometimes with ice
cream on top. If I was still hungry before dessert was served, I could
fill up on extra helpings of potatoes or, perhaps, another slice of
bread.

The current appearance of the ideal dinner plate, appropriate for all of us, has changed considerably. The centerpiece of the plate, replacing the meat, is a large mound of cooked vegetables of all kinds. To one side, as an accessory, is a small piece of broiled fish or white meat. Additional protein can be provided by beans and whole grains such as brown rice. A green salad is served with a low-fat dressing or just lemon juice. If the beverage is milk, it will be nonfat. Dessert is fresh fruit—no baked desserts at all. Second helpings are available and tend toward more vegetables and salad rather than additional fish or meat.

No starchy, processed carbohydrates are present on the ideal dinner plate—no bread, white rice, pizza, or pasta. Potatoes are nutritious when eaten in moderation and without gobs of butter, cheese, sour cream, or gravy. Try them with nonfat yogurt and/or chopped green onions. If you cannot manage to get sufficient protein from other sources, you may have to depend on bread, which should be whole grain—no white flour at all. You may initially lose a few pounds on this diet until calories burned are in balance with calories ingested. Some people concerned about their health are already eating like this.

Precisely because we do not yet know everything about nutrition, we should remain open to new, scientifically proven information. However, it is obvious that the old maxim of simply relying on moderation and balance in selecting foods is too unclear to be useful. Moderation for some might mean eating red meat only once per day, while balance could be interpreted as having a leaf of lettuce in a luncheon sandwich and a vegetable with the main meal. Moderation in alcohol consumption is a term even more loaded with varieties of interpretation.

The fact is that much of what we stick in our mouths is really not food for the body. Pastries, chips, and crackers contain comparatively little nutrition but much that is unnecessary for our bodies. (These foods do temporarily gratify us emotionally.) You wouldn't pour maple syrup rather than gasoline into the fuel tank of your automobile. All human bodies have certain nutritional needs. Educate yourself on what they are and shop accordingly.

Dining Style

Style is also important. Make meals appealing. Use good china and glassware. Add fresh flowers to the table. Whether you eat at home or at your workplace, eat in one set place—no open grazing from fridge to living room and all stops in-between. Sit at the table and slow down the speed of consumption. Lay down your fork between bites. Give your body time to release the hormones that tell your brain when you have had enough. Reward yourself with a treat occasionally, but in small quantities.

Unless you are as skinny as a bean pole and terribly short on time, do not eat *anything* while walking or driving a car. You will not appreciate the fact that you have eaten, and the foods typically eaten "on the run" tend to be the worst kinds for your health. Did you know that 25 percent of adults skip breakfast altogether? This figure is up from 14 percent in 1961. Don't skip meals. Instead, budget a few extra minutes at home and eat with "mindfulness." If you are trying to lose weight, it is necessary (but not sufficient) first to make dietary adjustments, and second, to increase your activity output, that is, burn more calories. The third leg of the weight reduction tripod is this: Change your behavior patterns. When you can do all three, you will succeed.

"Chew Each Bite 28 Times, Johnny"

As a child I heard the above instruction from my mother countless times. Now I am telling her the same thing. Since stomach acid in the older person is greatly diluted, proteins such as meat may not be properly digested. Older adults are quite commonly protein deficient. The smaller the mass of the protein we swallow, the better the chance that stomach acids can prepare it for maximum digestion. Unfortunately, older people may have mouth or teeth problems that prevent thorough mastication. Some doctors recommend that older adults stimulate the production of digestive juices with cayenne pepper or even take hydrochloric acid capsules. "Chew your food, Mother."

Individual Diets

For more years than I care to remember I had been plagued with canker sores in my mouth. They were extremely painful and lasted about two weeks. As the frequency increased I began experimenting and found that they could be almost totally eliminated if I did not eat navel or mandarin oranges. For two years I denied myself the pleasure of oranges, which are also a good source of vitamin C. Then I discovered that grapefruit, also a good source of vitamin C, did not cause a mouth problem for me. Now I buy grapefruit by the case and enjoy them immensely.

Some diets have been helpful with particular illnesses. I had a friend who was able to keep his cancer under control and extend his life by following the macrobiotic diet of George Ohsawa, whose approach is both physical and spiritual. Some people believe that since no two human beings in the world are exactly the same, it follows that ideal diets, also, will have some variation from person to person. If you are not satisfied with your health, it pays to experiment with what you eat.

Why Be a Vegetarian?

There are many kinds of vegetarian diets. Some avoid all foods of animal origin. Others include one or more of the following food groups: dairy, eggs, fish, and poultry. If diets are well planned, vegetarians are no more susceptible to deficiencies than meat-eaters. This is especially true if dairy products and even a little fish or chicken are included. (If you use milk and yogurt, buy the nonfat kind containing bifidus and acidophilus.) Of course, vegetarians may eat fruit. For cancer prevention, however, vegetables are preferable. They provide greater cancer protection than fruit and do not add to the load of simple sugars that can upset people with a high glycemic index. The vegetable-fruit consumption ratio should be 2 or 3 to 1.

The *University of California at Berkeley Wellness Letter*, vol. 14, April 1998, observed that vegetarians are usually thinner and have less cholesterol and coronary artery disease than meat-eaters. They have easier bowel movements and a reduced risk of diabetes, gallstones, and several types of cancer. Most good restaurants now have one or more vegetarian entrées to cater to the growing number of vegetarians.

At the Market

Everyone knows the disastrous effects of grocery shopping before a meal rather than on a full stomach. Everything in the store cries: "Eat me! Eat me!" It is particularly tempting if there is a bakery on the premises. Some people tear into the bakery sack while still in the store's parking lot. Most people link a particular aroma to a childhood memory. For example, the smell of freshly baked bread can produce an emotionally intense reaction, more intense than the reaction produced through other senses such as sight. To eat wisely, stay away from all baked goods except for 100 percent whole-grain bread.

Take a course in reading labels. Did you know that ingredients are listed in order of their amounts by weight? Therefore, a whole-grain cereal or bread will list whole grain as the first ingredient. If sugar or corn syrup or trans fat (hydrogenated oil) appears among the first three or four ingredients listed, put that item back on the shelf. It's not for you if you are trying to lose weight, or even hold your own. Average Americans get about 20 percent of their calories from sugar and about 33 percent from fat. (The Center for Science in the Public Interest says that Americans consume 152 pounds of refined sweeteners per year, up 24 pounds since 1970.) Packaged, processed foods generally occupy prominent places on the grocery shelves at eye level. The foods you want, the nutritious foods, tend to be on the higher and lower shelves—and they are cheaper, too.

The biggest beef-eaters are lower-middle-class households with children. They average 14 servings per week. (The *American Medical News*, vol. 39, no. 6, states that lower-income families eat far more expensive [packaged and canned] foods than middle- and upper-income families but get less nutrition.) Overall we Americans average eight servings of beef per week, but around 10 percent of households eat no beef at all. A 3.5-ounce beef patty may be labeled "lean" (or "extra lean") and either "10 percent fat" or "90 percent lean." These labels refer to the percentage of fat by weight, not the percentage of calories from fat. Half of the calories in a "lean" patty come from fat. According to dietitians we should limit beef to two to three servings per week (at most) and limit each serving to three ounces. In my opinion, once a week is plenty if you are getting sufficient protein from other foods.

If I order seafood stew for dinner at a restaurant, the next morning I can feel that my fingers are swollen from water retention due to the high salt content. Instead of ingesting 800 milligrams of salt, which is typical of canned soup, look for the word "healthy" on the label, which means it contains less than 480 milligrams. This is still 20 percent of the Recommended Daily Allowance (RDA). Actually, the RDA is not a good indicator of nutrition requirements for everyone because it is intended for those 51 years and older in normal health. More age categories should be added to RDA listings since nutritional requirements change. Also, the government should add a range for minimal need, for toxicity levels, and for conditions of illness.

There are various lists of "superfoods" that seem, more than any others, to provide the optimum ingredients for longevity and disease prevention. Most lists include the following vegetables: broccoli, cabbage, avocados (good fat), spinach, kale, tomatoes, garlic, and onions. Good fruits include berries, citrus fruit, grapes, and raisins. Soybeans are extremely blessed in nutritious and anticancer properties. If tofu, soy milk, or roasted soy nut butter do not appeal, try frozen green soy beans ("edamame" on some labels) in the pod. Boil for three minutes, cool, and pop them in your mouth directly from the pod. Great fun to eat as a snack, and they are about 12 percent protein! Or, if you have good teeth, munch on unsalted, dried soybeans as you would peanuts. Good nuts include almonds, peanuts, cashews, and Brazil nuts. Buy them dried but not roasted; roasting usually adds unneeded fat, sugar, corn syrup, salt, and chemical preservatives.

Snacking

For many people, sticking to three meals per day is not a very realistic plan. A "pick-me-up" at midmorning and midafternoon can regulate blood glucose levels and metabolic rate, reduce stress, pacify our appetites, and increase our productivity. One working woman carries a bag of nuts and peeled carrots everywhere so that when the need hits she will be adequately prepared with proteins and good carbohydrates. She does not have to resort to candy bars or pastries. Even in hospitals, I have seen vending machines that dispense potato chips and other fried chips. These contain too much unhealthful fat. Substitute plain, unsalted (or low-salt) popcorn as a between-meal snack. It is nutritious, filling, inexpensive, and available. In people constantly under stress, the adrenal glands continually pump out hormones, which can make them ravenously hungry. If this sounds like you, find ways other than snacking to control the effects of stress. Maybe you need to change jobs for your health.

My weakest time is from about two hours after supper until I go to bed. We don't even keep cookies (my favorite snack) in the house anymore. Aside from not having snacks around, there are some things you can do when the urge to snack hits you at night. Promise yourself that you will hold off for five minutes. Then, get up, walk around, have a glass of water, take the dog for a walk, let the cat out, and see if the urge is still there after that. Sometimes a delay will help you to overcome the snacking impulse. Or allow yourself to have just one modest treat, such as a dish of low-fat frozen yogurt. I have found that brushing my teeth right after dinner leaves the sweet taste of toothpaste in my mouth, which acts as a short-term pacifier. If the urge hits you again, and if the five-minute rule does not work, limit the rest of the evening's snacks to fresh fruit only.

Earlier Americans kept bowls of nuts around as an after-dinner treat. Taking this cue, I always lay in a good supply of mixed nuts in the shell at year's end for the holidays and the next year. Cracking them with a nutcracker is fun and is a natural limit on the speed of consumption. (Eating shelled peanuts by the handful from a jar is a no-no.) Also, this is a good hand exercise to strengthen your grip and counteract arthritis. Try cracking nuts sometimes with your nondominant hand. You *can* control your snacking habit. But, by all means, whatever your snacking game plan is, have it firmly in place (and the pared fruit waiting in the refrigerator or the nut bowl within reach) before your vulnerable time approaches.

Alcohol

Martini drinkers have a saying: "One is just right. Two are too many. And three are not enough." The *New England Journal of Medicine* on December 10, 1997, published the results of a study of alcohol use among 490,000 men and women. At the end of a nine-year period, 46,000 had died. The researchers found that, for people aged 35 to 69, an alcoholic drink a day can cut the risk of death by 20 percent. Those who benefited the most from drinking were people with bad hearts. (Other studies have found that alcohol increases the risk of breast cancer and other diseases.) Participants averaged one drink a day for men and less than one full drink for women, less than half of average alcohol consumption in the USA. Most Americans, it seems, cannot be so moderate.

The more we drink, the more our judgment about quantity ingested is impaired. Nondrinkers should not become drinkers only for the possible benefits, since there are other ways to protect against heart disease. Drinkers are advised to limit intake to one per day. Large amounts of alcohol taken irregularly work against both quality and quantity of life and also contribute to poor interpersonal relations with family and friends.

Water

How many times have you heard it? We need eight 8-ounce glasses (two quarts) of water a day to maintain good health. As we age, our sense of thirst decreases. Did you know that most older people drink only three glasses? It is no wonder they suffer constipation problems. Some people count coffee, tea, cola, or alcohol. Far from being a substitute for water, these beverages actually increase our water output by serving as diuretics. If you consume any one of them, you must then *increase* your water consumption to make up for it. (Fruit juice counts as water.) The surest way to meet your quota is to draw off your eight cups of water in a pitcher in the morning and empty it by night. Start off each meal with a big glass of water. You will attain that full stomach feeling a little sooner.

Food and Our Environment

Some people believe that, insofar as possible, we should eat lower on the food chain in order to provide enough food resources for our increasing world population. Michael Schut, former Associate Director of Earth Ministry, wrote in *Food, Faith and Sustainability*: "What we eat, where our food comes from, and how we eat are all expressions of our embeddedness in the fabric of creation, and therefore, an expression of our vision and our faith." Many people support the idea that we should practice the *enjoyment* of eating and also consider that eating has spiritual aspects. Eating connects us to the land and to each other. Our daily food choices impact our economic, environmental, and cultural lives. If we believe this, it becomes less likely that we will abuse our bodies with the wrong selection of foods and frequent overeating.

Be aware that our food sources are increasingly contaminated from the overuse of antibiotics and hormones in the meat, dairy, and poultry industries and the importation from poor, tropical countries of produce that can make us sick. The U.S. Centers for Disease Control and Prevention estimated that as many as 9000 Americans die annually from food-borne diseases, and many thousands of others are sickened.

Be Realistic

Let's be realistic. Even well-intentioned, intelligent people may be put off at the thought of weighing food portions, calculating dietary fat percentages, and in other ways making such an enjoyable activity as eating into a chemistry lesson. The bottom line advice is to educate yourself. Then, using whatever motivations work for you, slowly reduce portions of unhealthful and junk foods, and gradually replace them with vegetables, fruits, and other good things. The process is surprisingly painless. Don't stop replacing until your wisdom tells you that your nutrition target has been reached. It's that simple!

Daily you can read newspaper and magazine articles on nutrition and health. There is hardly a more popular subject in the press. And scientists are still learning and informing us about this complex subject. The Internet offers information at such Web sites as the following:

CyberDiet at **http://www.cyberdiet.com**
Prevention magazine's Healthy Ideas at **http://www.healthyideas.com**
American Dietetic Association at **http://www.eatright.org**.

More and more it seems that the author Victor Lindlahr was correct when he wrote a long time ago, You Are What You Eat.

We tend to be crisis-oriented when it comes
to health. We only spend 1 percent of our healthcare budget on prevention.

DR. DAVID SATCHER
U.S. SURGEON GENERAL

CHAPTER SIX

Take an Active Role in Self-Care

THIS CHAPTER BRINGS the results of the latest research to bear on some of the most prevalent serious diseases and suggests how they may be treated or avoided. Better understanding of health issues means better communication with health care providers and improved treatment, subjects taken up next in Part Three.

Preventive Treatment

The most important care is the care you give yourself. The World Health Organization (WHO) defines self-care as follows:

> Self-care in health refers to the activities individuals, families and communities undertake with the intention of enhancing health, preventing disease, limiting illness, and restoring health. These activities are derived from knowledge and skills from the pool of both professional and lay experience. They are undertaken by lay people on their own behalf, either separately or in participative collaboration with professionals.

It has been said that of the total health care we Americans receive, most is actually self-administered. If, through education and self-enlightenment, we could increase our self-care by even a small percentage, the lessening of Medicare's financial burden would constitute a huge savings to all Americans. In addition to putting less pressure on the health care system, self-care helps us to get rid of symptoms more quickly. Also, it bestows feelings of control over our own health and greater independence. Self-care may earlier have been a threat to the medical community. Now the medical establishment actively promotes it. A good web site is that of You First Health Risk Assessment, which provides a free health risk appraisal at http://www.youfirst.com. MedicineNet is a good general-interest site consisting of a network of doctors producing up-to-date information. The address is http://www.medicinenet.com. Healthfinder assists you through government health agencies and institutes at http://www.healthfinder.org.

Give yourself appropriate self-examinations. How often do you strip and examine your body? In the shower room of a health club you can sometimes see older men with large, ugly, dark moles on their backs. Those spots could be precancerous, and the men might not know it. Ask your spouse or mate to examine the skin you cannot see. Ask your public health nurse what should be included in self-examinations. It is not the same for men and women.

Recently, I received a shock. A local hospital offered free skin cancer screening during national skin cancer week. I went to have a mole examined. The doctor said, "That mole is nothing, but you do have several precancerous conditions on your nose and forehead." You can be sure that I had them treated. Now I follow his advice and apply sun block every morning after my shave. I learned that skin cancer is the most common preventable and treatable form of cancer. One in five Americans will contract it. Well over 90 percent of skin cancers are curable if caught in the early stages. But 40,000 cases are malignant melanomas, which are more serious. We should avoid the sun's rays between 10:00 A.M. and 3:00 P.M. Although my warning signs had not yet progressed to actual skin cancer, the mere mention of that word scared me into action.

One Half of All Americans Die Prematurely

Two million Americans die each year. The leading causes are as follows: heart disease, cancer, stroke, injury, pulmonary disease, pneumonia, influenza, diabetes, AIDS, and suicide, in that order. Most deaths actually result from a combination of genetic and lifestyle factors.

J. Michael McGinnis, MD, MPP, and William H. Foege, MD, MPH, published a study on "Actual Causes of Death in the United States" in the November 1993 issue of the *Journal of the American Medical Association*. These two scientists analyzed 16 years of research to find out just what external factors are killing us. They found that the root causes of death over which we as individuals have 100 percent control are: tobacco (400,000+ annual deaths); diet and activity level (300,000); alcohol (100,000); infectious agents (90,000); toxic agents (60,000); firearms (35,000); sexual behavior (30,000); motor vehicles, not including alcohol- or drug-related accidents (25,000); and illicit drug use (20,000). This means that half of our annual deaths are attributable to factors we might actually control. If you do not get your full share of years, you may have only yourself to blame. Will it have been worth it?

Alcoholism

Alcohol is a factor in 40 percent of violent crimes. three fourths of the victims of spousal violence reported that their attackers used alcohol. These figures were reported by the U.S. Department of Justice in 1998. Brigid Schulte of Knight-Ridder newspapers reported in December 1997 that nearly a quarter of those hospitalized who are over age 60 are alcoholics. More older people are hospitalized for alcohol than for heart conditions. There are about three million alcoholics in America. Problems with alcohol afflict as many as 20 percent of older people, half of whom are considered to be addicted. Treatment costs our country $60 billion annually. Even so, only about 10 percent of alcoholics seek help in quitting, and 80 percent of those relapse one or more times.

Older alcoholics can be divided into two groups: those who have had a problem most of their lives, and those who begin to drink to excess only after retirement or the death of a spouse or out of depression. Alcoholics often underestimate their addiction or try to hide it. If your doctor fails to ask you about your alcohol consumption, always offer the information and be truthful. Prescription and over-the-counter medications can interact adversely with alcohol. Your doctor may possibly be the very person to turn your life around.

Alzheimer's Disease

Alois Alzheimer was a German doctor who first described this condition in 1907. He regarded it as a gradual impairment in mental functioning. People did not live very long at that time, and the disease was thought to be rare. Bill Crounse, MD, of Overlake Hospital in Bellevue, Washington, and James Mortimer of the Institute on Aging at the University of South Florida in Tampa, reported that now about 10 percent of all Americans over age 65, and about half of those over 85, have Alzheimer's disease. This is a total of more than 4 million sufferers. When you reach your mid-sixties, the chance of developing Alzheimer's disease begins to double every five years. The number of people affected is likely to grow as the aging population grows. Many do not know they have a problem because they are not aware of memory loss.

Patients usually live from four to eight years after the diagnosis. Drugs are available to help ease symptoms. Some new drugs seem to help improve mental functioning temporarily. Leon Thal, MD, of the University of California at San Diego found that 200-milligram daily supplements of vitamin E can slow, and possibly prevent, Alzheimer's disease. Lifelong exercise also seems to reduce the risk. Question your doctor to be sure he or she is keeping up with the latest research. Information and help are available on the Internet, too. Joining a support group is highly recommended.

The Alzheimer's Association has developed a list of 10 warning signs of the illness.

- Memory loss that affects job skills
- Difficulty performing familiar tasks
- Problems with language
- Disorientation with regard to time and place
- Poor or diminished judgment
- Problems with abstract thinking
- Misplacing things
- Changes in mood or behavior
- Changes in personality
- Loss of initiative

Be aware that, although no cure has been found for Alzheimer's disease, there are cures for memory loss caused by poor nutrition, inadequate liquid intake, bladder infections, vitamin deficiency, grief, depression, excess alcohol, and medications. See your doctor.

Arthritis

Ronald Klatz and Robert Goldman's book *Stopping the Clock* quotes Dr. William Castelli, director of the Framingham Heart Study, as saying that three quarters of the world's population does not get chronic degenerative diseases. Osteoarthritis affects about 37 million Americans and is caused by the breakdown of cartilage from wear and tear in the joints. Being overweight exacerbates the problem. Anti-inflammatory drugs may help the arthritis sufferer to tolerate exercise, which itself can diminish pain. (See "Arthritis and Exercise" in Chapter Two.) The nutritional supplements glucosamine and chondroitin sulfate are said to promote growth of new cartilage. A new injection treatment of hyaluronic acid claims to lubricate and protect the joints; exercise is thought to boost the body's production of this natural substance.

Rheumatoid arthritis is an autoimmune disorder and affects more than 2 million Americans. Joints in the hands, feet, and arms become stiff, painful, and deformed. Experts think that one day new treatments may make rheumatoid arthritis disappear. In 1998 the FDA approved the drug minocycline, which provides relief and slows progression of the disease. Sufferers should consult large research institutions such as medical universities or the Arthritis Foundation at http://www.arthritis.org. Arthritis is not just an old person's disease. At least half of the people who report having arthritis are under age 65.

Asthma

Asthma is a chronic inflammatory condition of the air passages in the lungs. Dr. Irwin Redlener of the Albert Einstein College of Medicine, part of Montefiore Medical Center in New York City, said about asthma: "This is the most underdiagnosed and undermanaged illness we have to deal with."

Asthma presents a public health crisis, particularly for children and the elderly. Fifty million Americans have been diagnosed, and 16 die every day. Asthma rates have doubled in the last 10 years and are still increasing. No one knows the cause for sure, but one study implicates obesity as a factor. Even a little bit of fat increases the risk, and those who are 35 percent overweight triple their susceptibility. In 1992 an expert panel issued guidelines to doctors on how to achieve long-term control using anti-inflammatory drugs. However, many doctors have either not read the guidelines or are not using them. This has led patients to rely on quick-relief medications, which do not manage the condition over the long term. Become informed before seeing your doctor, or go to a specialist.

Cancer

Cancer is a group of over 100 diseases characterized by the uncontrolled growth of abnormal cells in the body. Cancer cells often form tumors, which then spread and interfere with normal body functions. In the USA there are over 7 million cancer survivors; more than 50 percent of them will survive at least five years. Newly diagnosed cases of cancer each year total 1.4 million. Cancer kills 500,000 Americans annually and disproportionately strikes older people. Among the over-65 population, about 20 percent of deaths are due to cancer. A May 29, 1997, article in the *New England Journal of Medicine* said that cancer fatalities peaked in 1991, when 203 Americans of every 100,000 died of cancer. Since then the rate has been dropping at about 1 percent per year. A major factor in the drop, according to a 1998 report in the journal *Cancer*, has been the decline in smoking, which started 30 years ago. For reasons we do not know, female smokers are twice as likely to get lung cancer as male smokers—lung cancer deaths in women have exceeded breast cancer deaths for more than a decade.

The old theory blamed cancer on something bad hiding in our food or environment, that is, something like a virus. The new theory says that cancer comes from not getting enough of the good things, according to Dr. Walter Willett of the Harvard School of Public Health. The Cancer Research Foundation of America says that 70 percent of all cancers can be prevented through a healthy diet and lifestyle. This is extremely important to those willing to take responsibility for their own health. Exercise is very important. The Foundation claims that colon cancer rates would show a 17 percent reduction (18,000 cases) if Americans walked three hours per week. Unfortunately, 65 percent of patients do not begin to show symptoms until the disease is advanced. Colon cancer screening (covered by Medicare as of 1998) could reduce deaths, now 56,500 annually, by 50 percent, according to John H. Bond, chief of gastroenterology at the Veterans Affairs Medical Center in Minneapolis. The Centers for Disease Control and Prevention (CDC) reports that only 29 percent of those age 50 and older have had a colon exam in the past five years. The disease strikes both sexes at approximately the same rate, yet minorities and women are greatly undertested. Other cancers, also, would decrease significantly with changes in education, lifestyle, and testing.

Previously the choices in cancer therapy were surgery, radiation, and chemotherapy. Immunotherapy, or cancer vaccine therapy, was introduced for lymphoma, melanoma, and prostate cancer. Prostate cancer can also be treated by freezing and by radioactive seed implants. Light, or photodynamic therapy, has FDA approval for use on esophageal and early lung cancers and is experimental for ovarian cancer. Gene therapy will begin when a way is found to place a particular gene at a particular spot. Even if the new therapies do not wipe out cancer but simply reduce it to a chronic, manageable state, they will have benefited millions who otherwise would die. Other known tumor fighters are vitamin E and green tea.

Formerly, patients waited for doctors to tell them what therapy to start. Now information and treatment options have increased. Patients are more active in requiring information on alternative therapies and are taking a proactive stance with their doctors. If your doctor is not comfortable with this, get a new one. If you are referred to an oncologist (cancer doctor), be aware of what Dr. Sherwin B. Nuland, author of How We Die, says about them: "Oncologists are among the most determined of medical people, prepared to try almost any last-ditch effort to stave off inevitability—they can be seen on the barricades when other defenders have furled their flags." Of course, we want our doctors to be working for a cure. But if death seems inevitable, there is also value in trying to end our days peacefully and with some remaining quality of life.

Many cancer patients work concurrently with medical doctors and doctors of naturopathy. Naturopathic physicians frequently are better able to treat unwanted side effects of the chemicals prescribed by MD's and to recommend dietary changes. For example, some normally useful vitamins and supplements can work against certain chemotherapy treatments. Medical doctors, even oncologists, may not take the time to study the diet–cancer therapy relationship. Typically, a naturopath will allow more time for each visit and can also help with depression and other effects of cancer and cancer therapy. For information on the Internet, go to these Web sites:

National Cancer Institute at **http://www.nci.nih.gov**
American Institute for Cancer Research at **http://www.aicr.org**
American Cancer Society at **http://www.cancer.org**
National Alliance of Breast Cancer Organizations at
    http://www.nabco.org
OncoLink (run by the University of Pennsylvania) at
    http://www.oncolink.upenn.edu

The National Cancer Institute says that cancer costs America more than $120 billion yearly in medical-related expenses and lost productivity. When it is someday cured, we will have alleviated cancer suffering and added three years to the life expectancy of every man, woman, and child in the USA.

Depression

The Associated Press, reporting July 13, 1998, on an article in the American Medical Association's *Archives of Internal Medicine,* wrote that an estimated 9.5 percent of the nation's population suffers from clinical depression in a given year—that's 17 million people. Depression seems to hit older adults harder, affecting 25 percent of persons 65 years and older. Sometimes depression is caused by chronic illness or a toxic reaction to medications. Depressed individuals utilize more health care services, including emergency room visits, and incur higher medical costs than do nondepressed patients.

A survey of 120,000 individuals in 47,000 households showed interesting results. Women suffer depression about 50 percent more often than men do. Depression is twice as common among people with less than a high school education as among those with higher education. Black Americans are twice as likely as white Americans to report a high level of depression. People living in the country are depressed at rates equal to those of people living in the inner city; people living in the suburbs are less depressed. Perhaps this is because they have easy access to cities without the crowding and other disadvantages of city life and without the isolation of the countryside.

Matthew, a man of about 75, signed up for a seven-week course, Chronic Disease Self-Management, which I lead at a local hospital. Matthew was a widower, lived alone, had always taken care of himself, and had previously been active in his church's music ministry. When invited to introduce himself at our first meeting and state his reasons for taking the course, Matthew avoided using the word *depression.* Instead, he spoke of having inexplicably diminished interests, of not wanting to leave the house, and of an inability to get back into pleasurable activities such as church music participation. He seemed puzzled by his own condition and could not offer any reasons for it or give it a name. Later he admitted that both a doctor and a senior-center nurse had said that he was depressed. Finally, he ventured the tentative suggestion: "I guess I'm depressed." But it was less an admission than a recounting of another's opinion, the truth of which he had not necessarily accepted. Matthew missed the second meeting and told us at meeting number three that he had been unable to make himself attend the missed session. Nor could he accomplish the brief home-reading assignment or take a walk for exercise. We never saw Matthew after that.

Many older adults deny the existence of depression. Having grown up during the Depression, World War II, or the Korean War, they learned not to "waste" time on their feelings. Seniors are also more likely to have sustained losses. Most can grieve for a time and then move on. Some people get stuck in their grief. Prolonged depression triggers chemical changes in the brain that reinforce and continue the depression. Experts think that depression may suppress the immune system, making the body more prone to debilitating illness. There is a downward spiral that is difficult to see in yourself. The more depressed you are, the more your function declines. A Yale University study presented in the journal *Psychiatric Services* reported that 89 percent of people with major depression are not taking any medication for it.

Symptoms are physical aches and pains, memory loss, confusion, crying jags, weight gain or loss, fatigue, listlessness, or agitation. Other symptoms are increased or decreased sleep, lack of interest in things you normally enjoy, poor self-care, and thoughts of death or suicide. David Buch, MD, a geriatric psychiatrist at the Institute of Pennsylvania Hospital, tells us that every year 6500 older Americans commit suicide. Experts say that depression is almost always a factor. Doctors rarely detect potential suicides in the older people who commit them.

If you suspect that you might be depressed or are having a painful experience that you cannot let go of by yourself, get professional help in resolving it. Consult a physician, family service agency, community mental health center, senior center, private clinic, or place of worship. Get a recommendation from someone you can trust. Using the Yellow Pages is not necessarily a good approach, as there is no guarantee of professionalism. Some people benefit from group therapy, where they receive reinforcement and encouragement from others also fighting chronic illnesses. Consider contacting the following Web sites:

National Depressive and Manic-Depressive Association at
   http://www.ndmda.org
National Institute of Mental Health at
   http://www.nimh.nih.gov
Depression Central at
   http://www.psycom.net/depression.central.html
Online Depression Screening Test at
   http://www.med.nyu.edu/Psych/screens/depres.html.

Repressing the problem will get you nowhere. The Johns Hopkins School of Medicine confirmed in 1998 what 10 other surveys had found, that depressed people have twice the likelihood of incurring heart disease. On the other hand, working through the problem will leave you feeling lighter, and you will be a wiser person for the experience.

Diabetes

Excessive urination and constant thirst can be a sign that the pancreas is producing insufficient insulin, the hormone responsible for the absorption of glucose into the cells. About one million Americans have Type 1 diabetes, which develops in childhood and always requires insulin for control. Type 2, adult-onset diabetes, affects about 15 million people and can often be controlled by diet and drugs that stimulate the production of insulin. However, as patients age, they often begin to require insulin injections.

Diabetes is potentially dangerous, since it can result in heart disease, blindness, stroke, and other complications. Diabetes is associated with aging, obesity, diet, and physical inactivity. It is wise to stay slim and to avoid overworking the pancreas with sugar and with starchy carbohydrates that are not whole grain.

America has a rather poor record of taking care of its diabetic population. Although, in general, we spend far more per patient than any other country in the world, our preventive measures are lacking. That is why, for example, American diabetics are twice as likely to go blind or need their limbs amputated as British fellow sufferers, according to "Health Care in America," a March 7, 1998, article in The Economist. The British National Health Service works harder to make sure that insulin injections and eye tests are done regularly.

Clinical trials have begun on an insulin powder that is sucked through the mouth into the lungs. This method reduces reliance on painful and inconvenient injections. So far, it has been found to be as effective as injections, has no side effects in the lungs, and is much more popular with patients. As with other chronic conditions, diabetes patients benefit greatly from self-management classes.

The CDC reports that on average 798,000 cases of diabetes are diagnosed annually. It is a disease that often goes undiagnosed; about one third of those with it do not know they are afflicted. Doctors previously recommended that diabetes screening should start at age 45. The CDC has now lowered that age to 25 because of rising childhood obesity and sedentary lifestyle. Medical bills for the average diabetes patient are over $11,000 per year. The good news is that strict maintenance of body weight and blood sugar levels can significantly cut costs. The bad news is that primary care physicians are not providing the recommended preventive care, according to American Medical News. Deaths from diabetes have risen 30 percent since 1980 and have trebled among African Americans. If you are in doubt, a doctor or public health nurse can check you for diabetes in five minutes.

Headaches

More than 45 million Americans suffer from recurring headaches. Additionally, an estimated 16 to 18 million people have migraine headaches; 70 percent of these people are women. The National Headache Foundation tells us that approximately 90 percent of all headaches are "tension" headaches from muscle contraction. In the USA, more than $4 billion a year is spent on aspirin or over-the-counter (OTC) anti-inflammatory drugs to combat headache. Clearly, headaches are a problem that saps our quality of life as well as our pocketbooks. You should see a doctor about headaches under any of the following conditions: you are over 40 and never had recurring headaches before; the locations of your headaches change; they are getting stronger and/or more frequent; or they are accompanied by numbness, dizziness, blurred vision, or memory loss.

Examine your body for indications of clenched teeth or hunched shoulders. This may be a sign that your headache is a tension headache. If you decide to take aspirin for your headache, take it right away. Exercise sometimes helps, but it may make a severe or migraine headache worse. Another remedy that sometimes relieves headache pain is to apply pressure with your fingers to the cervical vertebrae at the back of the neck, or to squeeze the web between the forefinger and thumb until you feel pain.

Contrary to what you might think, OTC drugs are not necessarily safe for headaches. Prescription drugs are strictly regulated by the Food and Drug Administration, which requires making known both the benefits and risks. OTC drug advertising, on the other hand, is regulated by the Federal Trade Commission, which requires companies to stand behind the advertised good effects but is not concerned with emphasizing possible dangers. Doctors are now noticing a "rebound headache" effect caused by the pain reliever itself as the amount of self-prescribed medication builds up to toxic levels in the body. For that reason, keep track of OTC drug consumption and tell your doctor.

Medical doctors are inclined to treat headache symptoms with muscle relaxants and physical therapy. Naturopathic doctors, on the other hand, have found that more than half of their patients' headaches are related to food sensitivity and treat them accordingly. For example, a diet high in carbohydrates usually brings on low blood sugar. (Insulin levels increase to metabolize the carbohydrates; the insulin sends sugar into the cells too quickly, causing a drop in blood sugar; the result is fatigue, irritability, and headaches.) A remedy is to eat small, frequent meals with protein to balance the carbohydrates. Suspect foods for some people who get recurring headaches are milk, eggs, wheat, citrus fruits, corn, and tomatoes. Also suspect are the following, which constrict blood vessels: chocolate, cheese, bananas, and alcohol. Headaches are also caused by hormonal imbalance, stress, and musculoskeletal problems. If your doctor cannot find the cause, see other doctors until the cause is found. You can also contact the American Council for Headache Education through its Web site: http://www.achenet.org. Quit suffering sooner rather than later.

Heart Disease

Heart disease is America's number one enemy, killing 743,460 people in 1994, more than cancer and stroke combined, according to the *Journal of the American Medical Association*'s Health Care State Rankings for 1996. Heart disease is usually caused by a fatty diet, failure to exercise, smoking, and high blood pressure. Until 1993 the rate of this disease was falling, but the trend is now up, partly because many people who know they have high blood pressure are doing nothing about it. Would they be so complacent if they knew that one fourth to one third of patients with coronary disease experience no warning before suffering a heart attack and that sometimes the first attack is fatal? There is a misconception that after we get older it is too late to change to a healthy lifestyle. But people who stop cigarette smoking return to an average risk of heart attack after only two years. (It takes 10 years for them to return to an average risk for cancer.)

Some women have the misperception that breast cancer is their greatest threat when, in fact, ten times more women will die of cardiovascular disease. Twenty-nine percent of men in their forties have cardiovascular disease, compared with 17 percent of women. Estrogen protects women until menopause. This means they will incur cardiovascular disease about 10 years later than men. By the time people reach their seventies, about 70 percent of both sexes have the disease. And women wait longer than men to seek medical attention for it.

Over 61 million Americans suffer from hypertension, and billions of dollars are spent each year on blood pressure medications. Previous studies have shown that blood pressure can be reduced by losing weight, lowering salt consumption, and minimizing alcohol use. An April 1997 report in the *New England Journal of Medicine* is the first to show that, independently of those factors, dietary changes can reduce blood pressure. Specifically, a diet rich in vegetables and fruit and providing three servings per day of low-fat dairy products dropped systolic pressure (the higher reading) an average of 11 points and diastolic pressure (the lower reading) 5.5 points in just two weeks. This diet proved to be as effective as the most commonly used hypertension drugs.

A good blood pressure level is 120/80. One out of every two persons over age 60 has high blood pressure that is not a normal consequence of aging. Doctors had been advising hypertensive patients to maintain a ratio of not more than 140/90 to minimize health risks. A 1998 meeting of the International Society of Hypertension showed that keeping the diastolic number below 85 by medication reduces the chances of suffering stroke, heart attack, or death by 30 percent. About 20 percent of those who have elevated blood pressure in a doctor's office show normal readings when tested elsewhere. I am one of those who have "white-coat hypertension." To make sure, I asked a cardiologist to prescribe a 24-hour ambulatory blood pressure monitor, which measured my pressure every 30 minutes, awake and asleep. Another way is to measure your own blood pressure several times at home or at the local fire station and then average it.

Dr. Mickey S. Eisenberg, director of emergency service at the University of Washington Medical Center in Seattle, has published widely on the topic of sudden cardiac arrest, which, he says, strikes Americans 500,000 times per year. For reasons unknown, the electrical pulse of the heart goes out of control, causing the heart to beat abnormally and to quiver. This potentially fatal heart rhythm is known as ventricular fibrillation (VF) and kills up to 250,000 victims annually. Administering an electric shock can restore normal heartbeat in almost 100 percent of the cases if it is provided within one or two minutes. Chances of survival drop about 10 percent for every one minute in time that elapses. High-risk individuals can have a 3-ounce defibrillator implanted in their chest that automatically applies the appropriate restorative electrical shock when called for. Most people, however, must depend on emergency medical technicians who carry external defibrillators. New technology has reduced those defibrillators to the size of a hardcover book and made them almost foolproof for use even by nonmedical personnel. Increasingly they are being stocked by airlines, health clubs, amusement parks, and even Las Vegas casinos. When CPR (cardiopulmonary resuscitation) is also used, defibrillation is effective even 10 to 12 minutes after VF. (Because of the CPR training given to the general population in Seattle, the survival rate from VF in that city is 30 percent. In New York City, it is only 5 percent.) We ought to encourage our government to facilitate further development of defibrillators in order to make them affordable for every home in need and to teach people how to use them. Encourage your club, church, and senior center to provide them.

New, smaller, and quieter artificial hearts are being developed by Abiomed with the Texas Heart Institute and by 3M with Pennsylvania State University. Furthermore, Harvard scientists Dr. Anthony Atala and Dr. Dario Fauza claimed on July 23, 1997, to have grown new bladders and windpipes for a sheep and organs for other animals. It seems that spare parts for humans will be commonplace in the future. Gene therapy may be able to instruct the body to grow new blood vessels, thereby eliminating the need for coronary bypass surgery. Studies are under way. Progress is also being made in reducing the size of implantable cardiac-assist devices.

Over the past 35 years, Americans have educated themselves about the danger of cholesterol to the heart. The average adult cholesterol reading has dropped from 220 to 202 due to medications and changes in diet. The famous 50-year Framingham heart study shows that, of all people who will develop heart disease, up to 80 percent could be identified and treated years earlier if they knew their risk factors. Take tests and find out from your doctor if you are at risk for heart disease. For example, depression doubles your heart risk. Follow advice on reducing your risk. For prevention, ask your doctor about taking an enteric-coated baby aspirin daily to thin the blood, taking coenzyme Q10 and vitamins such as E and B-6, and eating more potassium, magnesium, herring, salmon, mackerel, sardines, and garlic. Heart disease is an excellent example of a disease that can be controlled by self-management. Dr. Laura Svetkey of Duke University headed a study that developed the DASH (Dietary Approaches to Stop Hypertension) diet. It proved effective in lowering blood pressure. Get a copy of the diet from the National Heart, Lung, and Blood Institute at NHLBI Information Center, P.O. Box 30105, Bethesda, MD 20824-0105. The home page address is **http://www.nhlbi.nih.gov**.

Infectious Diseases

Infectious diseases are a leading cause of death in the USA and the leading cause of death worldwide. Each year 35 to 50 million Americans contract flu. More than 20,000 die from it. A severe epidemic could result in 172,000 hospitalizations costing $12 billion in medical expenses and lost productivity. At the peak of the flu season in January, about 9 percent of all deaths in cities in the United States result from pneumonia and flu. A new flu spray vaccine can easily be taken through the nose and offers a broader immunity than injected vaccines. It is so simple to protect yourself from the common types of flu that no one should catch it in its full force.

Pneumonia causes an estimated 40,000 deaths annually, mostly among older people. One common type, especially for the elderly, is caused by the pneumococcus bacterium for which vaccination is available. About 23 million Americans over age 65 remain unvaccinated; many do not even know that a vaccine exists. Get the inoculations or boosters you should have according to your age and situation. These will include flu (annually), pneumonia (one time only), and boosters or shots for diphtheria, tetanus, and other diseases. Your doctor can give them. But unless you like to visit doctors' offices, why not use your convenient and low-cost public health service, health club, or community or senior center?

AIDS is spread by sexual contact with an infected person and by using contaminated intravenous needles. Contaminated blood transfusions are less of a problem now than previously. (But if you are going to have surgery, have your own blood drawn and stored in advance to be given back to you on the operating table.) Drugs are available to slow the progression of AIDS symptoms, but new strains are proving to be drug resistant. Probably more research money is being spent per patient to find a cure for this disease than for any other in the history of the world. Another virus transmitted by sexual contact is herpes simplex. Although not fatal like AIDS, herpes simplex causes much suffering. It is carried by about 35 million Americans, or one in five adults, 90 percent of whom do not know they have it. Protect yourself.

You are not necessarily safe in a hospital. So many people are now treated on an outpatient basis that those who are hospitalized are much sicker than their counterparts of 20 years ago. The CDC estimates that hospital-acquired infections strike 2 million patients each year and kill 90,000 of them. Infections are most commonly transmitted by stethoscopes, blood pressure cuffs, and inadequate washing of hands as health care workers go from patient to patient. If you are hospitalized, ask health care workers entering your room to wash their hands in your sight and to assign a stethoscope and blood pressure cuff exclusively to your room.

The *Journal of the American Medical Association* now associates infectious agents with a growing list of diseases, including some cancers, multiple sclerosis, and cerebral palsy. A bacterial infection that commonly causes lung inflammation may also signal a second heart attack.

Obesity

Some people say that obesity, like alcoholism, can be voluntarily reversed and is, therefore, not a disease but more of a symptom. It is, nevertheless, a stubborn condition to treat. Former Surgeon General Dr. C. Everett Koop said, "[O]besity-related conditions are the second leading cause of death in the U.S., resulting in about 300,000 lives lost each year." Some researchers doubt that the death rate is quite that high. However, the Nurses Health Study found that excess weight was at fault in about 20 percent of the untimely deaths in nonsmoking adults under 70. The number of obese Americans is forecast to double in the next three decades. A Web site to visit is Obesity.com at http://www.obesity.com.

Osteoporosis Afflicts Women and Men

It is well known that osteoporosis afflicts more women than men, due to the decrease in estrogen production that occurs during menopause in conjunction with women's generally lighter, thinner bones. However, the problem of osteoporosis for men is that it is underdiagnosed, underreported, and inadequately researched. We know from National Osteoporosis Foundation statistics that 2 million American men suffer from osteoporosis, and that an additional 3 million are at risk. One in every eight men over age 50 will have an osteoporosis-related fracture. Each year 100,000 men suffer a hip fracture and one third of these men die within a year. Tens of thousands of men also fracture bones in their spine, wrists, or ribs as a result of osteoporosis.

Bone mass reaches its peak at about age 35 and then begins thinning from the inside. By age 80, almost everyone is osteoporotic who has not taken estrogen. Now, portable machines for testing bone density can take measurements in 10 minutes in your home for about $75. Or testing can be done in your doctor's office. Take your measurements early, while there is still time to make dietary and lifestyle changes.

Low body weight is the most prominent risk factor for osteoporosis-related fractures. Both men and women need to be sure they are ingesting sufficient calcium. Ask your doctor or public health nurse to examine your diet, including any calcium supplements you may be taking. If your body is not getting sufficient calcium from food and supplements, it will leach calcium from your bones. (A thought-provoking article in Calcified Tissue International, vol. 50, pages 14–18, claims that nations with the greatest calcium and protein intake have the highest rates of osteoporosis and hip fracture, and that populations with the lowest calcium and protein intake have the lowest rates.) New medicines are being tested to give the same benefits as estrogen without the potential to increase the risk of breast cancer. Regularly walk, jog, or get some other weight-bearing exercise to reduce your risk of osteoporosis. Preventing calcium loss is much more effective than ingesting supplements.

Pain

It is a sad fact that 97 million Americans suffer chronic pain associated with various conditions and illnesses. Not only is there the physical component of pain but also the emotional component, which includes depression, anxiety, and other psychological factors intensifying the pain. It is true that science still has much to learn about controlling pain. But it is also true that pain management is undertaught in most medical schools. And doctors are afraid of the laws set up to catch those who prescribe controlled drugs to abusers and/or to themselves.

Minorities and older patients suffer more, partly because they are less likely to complain of their suffering. A study of more than 13,000 cancer patients in nursing homes showed that up to 40 percent were in pain every day. They may be reluctant to push the "call" button. But I believe you get no points in heaven by being stoic. The best pain management requires patients to be their own advocates and speak out loudly and clearly to health care staff.

Many doctors rely too heavily on over-the-counter or prescription medications, even when they seem to produce no good results. More enlightened doctors and patients will seek the help of chiropractors, massage or physical therapists, or naturopaths. Recently, medical experts convened by the National Institutes of Health found acupuncture effective in treating certain types of pain, as well as the nausea and vomiting brought on by chemotherapy and pregnancy. For many whose health insurance does not cover these treatments, they may not be options. Keep after your doctor if you are not getting the hoped-for results. Or ask for a referral to a pain center, or seek alternative solutions on your own. You will be surprised at the large number of resources available.

Caroline Myss, PhD, author of *Anatomy of the Spirit*, recognizes the body-mind-spirit connection in the matter of pain and suggests: "Pay attention to how many thoughts and attitudes you hold each day that are painful. Write them down so that you can see them clearly and can recognize the physical damage they can do to your body. You may come to realize that you dwell on painful images of yourself or on pain-filled beliefs about life." Pain is very susceptible to self-management.

Stroke

Each year about 500,000 people suffer strokes, which kill 160,000 of those people. Strokes have left more than a million people disabled. Blood clots that form in the vessels of the brain cause about 80 percent of strokes. The other 20 percent are caused by the bursting of weakened vessel walls and subsequent bleeding into the brain; these hemorrhagic strokes cause the most damage. When larger vessels are involved, larger areas of the brain are affected.

A recent survey of 1880 people in the Cincinnati area showed that only 57 percent could identify even one of the warning signs of stroke. People age 75 or older have the highest incidence of stroke but are the least knowledgeable about risk signs and factors. (But the American Heart Association tells us that those under age 65 account for almost 30 percent of strokes.) Symptoms include sudden weakness or numbness of the face, arm, or leg; sudden dimness or partial loss of vision, especially in one eye; sudden difficulty in speaking or understanding speech; sudden severe headache with no known cause; and unexplained dizziness, unsteadiness, or sudden falls.

If you experience any of these symptoms, call 911. Every minute counts. The clot-dissolving drug tPA must be given by physicians within three hours of a severe stroke to prevent disability and death. (It is not used for hemorrhagic strokes.) Fewer than 5 percent of victims reach the hospital in time to receive tPA. The drug prourokinase can be given up to six hours after symptoms start. A study found that women who suffer strokes take 46 percent longer to get to a hospital than do male stroke patients. Also, going by car is not a good idea since doctors see patients more quickly if they are brought in by ambulance. A Transient Ischemic Attack (TIA) usually lasts only minutes and is followed by a full recovery. It is a warning.

For prevention, start early to do the same good things you would do for a healthy heart. Exercise frequently, cut out unnecessary dietary animal fat, stay lean, avoid harmful stress, watch your blood pressure, take medication if prescribed, and, if over 50 years old, take a baby aspirin daily. Doctors also advise avoiding frequent hostility and anger because of their bad effect on blood vessels and the heart.

Healthy Feet

You may take about a billion steps in your lifetime and walk about 77,000 miles. With every step, the 26 bones in each foot will receive a force three times your body weight. Foot problems can prevent you from enjoying a nice walk or, worse, inhibit your mobility. For reasons unknown to me, I suddenly developed a painful right heel that shouted at every step: "You're hurting me!" I was one of the 2 million Americans who suffer each year from heel pain, the most common foot problem treated by doctors. I was told that my plantar fascia, a band of tissue connecting my heel to the ball of my foot, had become inflamed. It was 6 months before I could walk comfortably again. Some people put foam rubber "doughnuts" in their shoes under the heel to help absorb the impact of walking. What helped me were hamstring stretch exercises and standing on the edge of a stair step to slowly raise and lower the heels above and below the level of the balls of the feet, thus stretching the plantar fascia.

During the jogging boom in the 1970s, many new joggers found that their feet did not strike the ground at the proper angle, which after a time caused them to go temporarily lame. Shoe inserts, called "orthotics," were developed to correct this problem. Millions of Americans, myself included, wear them every day, in street shoes as well as in athletic shoes. Over-the-counter (OTC) orthotics sell from around $20; custom designed versions cost hundreds of dollars. A study organized by the American Orthopaedic Foot and Ankle Society showed that OTC orthotics are a good and economical first choice for many people with this problem. If they do not improve your condition, see if a doctor or podiatrist recommends a custom-made orthotic. About half of insurance companies will pay for them if recommended by a doctor. Medicare will usually pay for doctor-ordered custom-made orthotics as well. With more Americans living longer and engaging in serious walking and jogging, we will see more foot injuries and pains. Whatever your foot problem, do what is necessary to make your feet feel good and to start, or continue, walking. A healthy body is grounded on healthy legs and feet.

Dental Care

I asked my dentist, "What are the problems older people have with their teeth?" He said that we do not floss or brush sufficiently, nor do we have regular plaque removal and checkups. Our gums shrink, exposing tooth roots, which then decay faster because of less protection of the dentin area. Also, our saliva flows less, exposing teeth and gums to a stronger concentration of mouth acids.

Dry mouth (xerostomia) makes it hard to eat, swallow, taste, and speak. It is not a part of normal aging but results from various diseases or medical treatments, such as chemotherapy or radiation to the head or neck area. Dry mouth is also a side effect of more than 400 commonly used medicines, including drugs for high blood pressure, antidepressants, and antihistamines.

Periodontitis is a gum disease that destroys bone and loosens teeth. About 75 percent of adults over age 35 have some degree of it. There may be a genetic susceptibility to gum disease among about one third of the population. Improved oral hygiene can catch it early, before the bone is involved. Gum disease, plaque bacteria, and heart disease seem to be interconnected. About 60 percent of the streptococcus sanguis bacteria found in dental plaque can cause blood clots, narrowing a portion of an artery and triggering a heart attack. People with bad gums and teeth have about double the risk of dying from heart disease.

Exposed root surfaces should not be subjected to abrasive paste or powder brushings but can be protected by fluoride rinses. Many cosmetic solutions for missing or unattractive teeth can provide a younger-looking smile. Implants can take the place of uncomfortable partial dentures.

Taking care of the mouth is as important to our health as taking care of the rest of the body. I suspect that concern for the pocketbook and fear of the dentist's chair keep many away. When you don't get needed dental work, you are depriving yourself of the joys of a healthy mouth, including enjoyment of your favorite foods, a nice smile, and pleasant breath. If cost is a problem, discuss it with your dentist or the dental receptionist. Ask about paying over a year's time. Or talk to your county dental society or a public health nurse.

Eyes and Ears

Without adequate sight and hearing you will be in big trouble. Cataracts are not the most worrisome matter. Laser surgery will easily take care of that. What you must avoid is glaucoma, for it can blind you. Get your eye pressure checked yearly for glaucoma. (I know of a physician who neglected to get checked and now has permanently diminished sight.) Macular degeneration, in which the frontal vision becomes permanently blurred, might be prevented by ingesting lutein, a carotenoid found in kale, spinach, and other greens.

Have your eyes tested and get a prescription for new glasses when you have difficulty seeing. Keep your sight functioning well. If you cannot afford to pay, ask the doctor about an installment plan or about free care through VISION USA. Also, contact the Lions Club, which assists with glasses at reduced cost.

Almost one third of us aged 65 to 75 years old have hearing loss. (Cigarette smokers have nearly twice the risk.) Friends sometimes like to repeat their negative hearing aid experiences of a decade ago, which may discourage us, but remember that hearing aids have improved greatly in the past few years. I have one developed by AT&T that automatically adjusts incoming sound 20 times per second. Your doctor can recommend an audiologist who can provide individualized fitting at a reasonable price. If your hearing loss is severe, take a course in lip reading. It is effective and cheap. The ability to communicate is such a wonderful gift. Fix it; don't lose it.

Dealing with Incontinence

Incontinence affects more than 13 million Americans, of whom 85 percent are women. It robs them of their independence and spoils the quality of life. A survey by the National Association for Continence shows that people wait a long time before addressing the problem; women wait on average 3.4 years and men 1.8 years before seeing a health care professional. Incontinence is not "just what happens" as you get older; it is a condition that can be treated. Some treatments are dietary changes, bladder retraining, medications, pelvic muscle exercises, biofeedback, electrical stimulation, surgery, collagen implants, pelvic support devices, and skin care to lessen rashes.

Sweat the Big Stuff

We get scared by what the media tell us is dangerous. A Harvard study says that 40 percent of Americans are worried about getting cancer from electrical power lines or cellular phones. Yes, for some this may be a serious risk, but is it a realistic thing to worry about? By comparison, the experts are half as concerned as the general public about this risk but are more concerned about the dangers of routine X-ray tests.

Risk analysis is the science that tells us, for example, that mile for mile it is safer to fly in an airplane than to drive a car, or that an 18-year-old is at higher risk of dying in a car accident than from cancer, and vice versa for a 50-year-old. We know that eight of the top ten leading causes of death are results of our own conduct. Professor John Graham, the former president of the Professional Society for Risk Analysis, says: "By changing personal behavior, people could reduce their risk of dying early by 70 to 80 percent." The lesson: Stay focused on exercise, health knowledge, nutrition, keeping weight off, health exams, and avoiding bad health habits. Don't sweat the small stuff. Put your health efforts where the payoff is big. Make the decision today on the major changes in your life that will keep you functional and enjoying this world longer.

Health/Medical Information

The amount of medical information available is said to double every three and one half years. You can obtain it everywhere. However, if you want the regularity and convenience of keeping up with this subject in your own home, subscribe to a monthly health letter. I have learned much from the *University of California at Berkeley Wellness Letter*, which you can subscribe to by writing to P.O. Box 420108, Palm

Coast, FL 32142. Many hospitals have good health information periodicals, which they will mail to your home without cost. Just ask to be put on the mailing list. For a listing of America's best hospitals by departments, see the annual evaluation published in *U.S. News and World Report*. Here are some notable medical information Web sites:

http://www.ncbi.nlm.nih.gov/PubMed

> PubMed gives access to the National Library of Medicine's database of worldwide medical articles and citations.

http://www.healthfinder.gov   HealthFinder provides health information from and links to the U.S. Department of Health and Human Services.

http://www.ahcpr.gov   The Agency for Health Care Policy and Research gives an unbiased collection of links and resources.

http://www.rarediseases.org   The National Organization for Rare Disorders, Inc., can be searched for rare illnesses.

http://www.nih.gov/nichd   The National Institute of Child Health and Human Development is another site to check for information on rare diseases.

There is a lack of oversight on what information is put on the Web. When you search for information on the Web, you should ask yourself a few questions: (1) Is the author properly qualified? Does he or she have an MD, PhD, or ND degree? What institution does the author represent? (2) Is the study clearly identified? Does it have a sponsor with an agenda that might influence the results? (3) Is the study the result of observation or experimentation, and how many people were studied? (4) What is the date of the information? (5) Was the study reviewed by other qualified scientists? For example, studies published in the *Journal of the American Medical Association* have been peer-reviewed. Spend your time on the most reputable health information sources. Stay focused. Educate yourself thoroughly on your personal major health problems. This approach will produce better results than, say, the latest tea find that promises to melt away undesired body fat.

Senior Wellness Programs

Community and senior centers actively promote wellness and employ nurses and social workers. The researched and proven outcome-based Senior Wellness Project, which began on the Pacific coast, has been picked up in Virginia and is expanding. The goal is to create a partnership among participants, their primary-care physicians, and center staff that will improve health and functioning and reduce unnecessary medical care. Participants are self-referred or referred by health care professionals. After an assessment by a nurse, a health action plan sets goals, action steps, and monitoring.

The action plan has five components. *Health promotion* includes exercise, nutrition education, hot lunch, home safety check, weight control, and smoking cessation. *Self-management* includes a chronic conditions class, self-monitoring of blood pressure, weight, blood glucose, food and alcohol intake, and record-keeping of health activities. *Peer support* keeps the senior participant in contact with health monitors and support groups to combat depression, to quit smoking, and the like. *Nursing* provides medication review and management, health education, participant advocacy, and minor procedures including dressing changes, injections, and foot care. *Social work* provides individual and group therapy, mood management and other skill-building classes, and links with other services. Practical applications include home visits and preparing seniors for appointments with their doctors.

This program started as a controlled study with 200 chronically ill seniors aged 70 and over. Major results were these: a 38 percent reduction in hospitalizations, a 72 percent reduction in hospital days, a 36 percent reduction in medications such as Tylenol, significantly higher levels of physical activity, and better functioning in activities of daily living. A sliding cost takes income into consideration. Health insurance companies recognize the benefits and are considering the payment of premiums for their participating seniors. Wouldn't you like to spend more time out of a hospital in exchange for a greater involvement in cooperatively managing your overall health? It is too important to give away this role to someone else. Even if you are not responsible for the onset of your illness, you ought to accept responsibility for your health and participate in your recovery. Who has the most to gain?

The only wealth is health. All the rest is just poker chips.

—ANONYMOUS

Part Three

Don't Be Shy
About Your Needs

No prescription is more valuable than knowledge.

C. EVERETT KOOP
FORMER U.S. SURGEON GENERAL

CHAPTER SEVEN

Help Your Doctor Help You

COMMUNICATION WITH YOUR DOCTOR is what the doctor hears, not necessarily what you say. This chapter focuses on communicating effectively with your doctor and becoming knowledgeable about the medical system. Knowledge is empowering.

Doctor Satisfaction

An important asset in aging is your doctor. Are you satisfied with yours? Can you get an appointment quickly when there is a sudden disturbing condition? Does your doctor correctly diagnose your condition and prescribe remedies that work? From time to time, does your doctor review your medications for effectiveness and possible incompatibilities and make appropriate changes?

In the waiting room is there a friendly interaction among staff and patients? Does your doctor appear in the consultation room after only a short wait? Do you have adequate time to discuss your important concerns? Patients equate confidence in their doctors with the amount of time doctors spend listening. (A test showed that on average doctors listen to your story for 18 seconds before interrupting you and starting to talk.) Do you like your doctor's manner? Does your doctor telephone you to see how you are doing, for example, after a new medication or a long absence? Are you always able to telephone your doctor or the office staff to ask questions without scheduling a visit? Does your doctor exhibit compassion for the elderly? If you consistently answered "yes," you have a wonderful doctor. Hold onto that jewel!

A surgeon told me the following story. His family had a large, much-loved dog who was aging and suffering from a difficult heart condition. A veterinarian could offer only limited help but telephoned occasionally to check on the pet's condition. One day the surgeon had to tell the vet that the dog had died. A few days later the surgeon's family received in the mail a condolence note from the veterinarian. This was food for thought for the surgeon, who had experienced the death of many of his human patients. Would your doctor telephone to check on you, much less send a note to your survivors?

Interviewing a New Doctor

If you are dissatisfied with your doctor, get a new one. But first get recommendations. (AARP has an excellent publication for choosing a doctor. It is "Healthy Questions: How to talk to and select physicians, pharmacists, dentists, and vision care specialists.") Then meet your prospective new doctor before scheduling a medical appointment. I needed a family doctor and later was glad to have scheduled an interview appointment before getting sick. A friend suggested a doctor I'll call Dr. John Doe. Doctor Doe's nurse said that I could talk to him for fifteen minutes without charge. I brought a list of questions, some of which follow.

1. Do you believe in a holistic approach to medicine? (This means to consider the whole body, the mind, and the spirit to diagnose a problem, as opposed to looking only at the area of complaint.)
2. What do you think of the use of vitamins, minerals, herbs, acupuncture, and massage in treatment and prevention?
3. Do you ever pray for your patients? (A 1996 University of Connecticut survey of American adults found that 64 percent wanted their doctors to pray for them during their illnesses.)

4. What do you yourself do to stay fit and prevent illness? (Doctors tend not to urge their patients to practice healthful activities they don't do themselves. Doctors who practice what they preach are role models.)
5. If I have a sudden problem, how soon can I get an appointment?

There were other questions as well. To tell the truth, I felt rather impudent in talking to a doctor that way. After all, medical doctors ranked right next to God when I was growing up. We did not question them, and we usually did what they said. However, I reasoned that I am not a kid anymore. I am an adult in the last quarter of my life. It is my health and my future.

In fact, I decided never to see that doctor again. And it was not because of his answers to my questions. It was simply that I found him a "cold fish." I would not be able to enjoy my visits to him, even if he were the best doctor on earth. It was good to have discovered that fact sooner rather than later, after I had invested time and money and, perhaps, felt vulnerable because of some existing condition.

You have the option of approaching any doctor you wish. Even if your health insurance plan limits your choice, you can always state your case and ask for another doctor. Get one you like, one who is interested in you.

Allopathic and Alternative Medicine

Allopathic medicine is what your medical doctor practices on you. It is high-tech medicine, attacking diseases and microbes with drugs and surgeries. For many of us, it is all that we have ever known. The other approach is alternative or complementary medicine, which restores and promotes health through physical therapies, therapeutic nutrition, and patient-centered initiatives. Each approach makes excessive claims for its effectiveness, and each has shortcomings.

According to the World Health Organization, 65 to 80 percent of the world's health care services can be classified as alternative. We yearn for the "good old days" when doctors listened to their patients rather than sending them for complicated tests. Americans now spend

$6 billion annually on nutritional supplements, and the figure is growing by 20 percent every year. The *Journal of the American Medical Association* for November 10, 1998, tells us that in 1997 alternative medicine was used by 4 of every 10 Americans used and that $27 billion was spent on alternative remedies. This says something about where we place our trust. Perhaps in recognition of this, the U.S. government has established a Center for Complementary and Alternative Medicine within the National Institutes of Health with a first year budget of $50 million.

New Directions: The University of Arizona Program in Integrative Medicine

This program, according to Dr. Andrew Weil, trains doctors to ask and answer more questions, to offer treatments other than drugs and surgery, and to understand mind/body interactions and offer alternative therapies. Participating doctors study traditional Chinese and Indian (Ayurveda) medicine and homeopathy. They work with natural healing, nutrition, and botanical medicine. (When is the last time your doctor showed an interest in what food you ate?) They learn guided imagery, acupuncture, proper exercise, and neutralizing stress. Doctors "also study and practice the communication skills that are vital to good doctor-patient interactions." In other words, the program combines the best of old and new, East and West; the doctors examine you holistically, and with a smile. How would you like to have one of those doctors as your primary care physician? I certainly would. You, also, should aim for the best. You deserve it.

It's a Pain

No one knows your pain as well as you do. But in doctors' consultation rooms I have witnessed patients describe their pain symptoms so imprecisely that it is a wonder the physician (and the patient) benefited at all. To help your doctor choose the best treatment for your pain, you must define it as precisely as possible. Keep a record for a few days in advance of your next visit to a doctor. To help you, the Iowa

Cancer Pain Relief Initiative's *Comfort Assessment Journal* recommends a Pain Rating Scale from 0 to 5. Thus, 0 = no pain, 1 = mild pain, 2 = moderate pain, 3 = distressing pain, 4 = horrible pain, and 5 = unbearable pain. (If unbearable, call your doctor immediately.)

In addition to describing the intensity of the pain, describe how your pain feels. The *Comfort Assessment Journal* offers the following descriptions of kinds of pain: dull ache, nagging, stabbing, burning, squeezing, cutting, tingling, shooting, pressing, flickering, itching, sharp, stinging, pricking, crushing, pinching, pulsing, gnawing, boring, and cramping. Observe where the pain is, how often it occurs, how long it lasts, what gets it started, what makes it feel better, what you think causes it, and anything else you think might be helpful for your doctor to know. Have the doctor read your written record at the beginning of your visit and retain it in the file. You keep a copy.

Acute vs. Chronic Care

The current health care system is based on an acute-care model. This assumes that the patient has a single, short-term health problem that can be cured by the physician or another member of the health care team. The reality is that the majority of patients in a doctor's office or in a hospital, perhaps 75 to 80 percent, have not acute, but chronic diseases such as arthritis, diabetes, congestive heart failure, or lung problems. Here are some areas where you can take action to help yourself if you suffer a chronic condition.

1. Help improve coordination between your pharmacist and your doctor. Taking multiple medications over a long period of time often generates additional health problems, which then need more medications. Doctors are sorely challenged to manage this problem in an office visit.
2. Ask your doctor to devote some attention to your emotional and social needs. When a disease continues for a long time, patients are prone to depression because the disease is forcing some life changes and/or limiting the quality of life. Doctors are generally more comfortable managing medical problems than social or emotional problems.

3. Ask your doctor for guidance on your role in managing your disease. For example, if your doctor is thinking of prescribing a medication, ask if you have the option of changing something in your way of living that would make the medicine unnecessary, such as losing weight. Then agree on a time line for your goal. Your attitude, behavior, and lifestyle all influence how a chronic disease progresses. Also seek the help of a physical or occupational therapist, nurse, social worker, pharmacist, or dietitian. Ultimately, however, you are responsible for your own health.

Medical History

Make a record of your family medical history of serious illnesses and your personal medical history. (See "Medical Information File" in Chapter Nine.) Take a copy with you on your first visit to a doctor. This will save much time in completing forms at the doctor's office. Ask your doctor to read it in your presence. Leave a copy and ask that it be made a part of your permanent file. Discuss the illnesses of your parents and siblings with the doctor and ask whether there is anything you should do to avoid those same illnesses. Your doctor can advise you on how to assess your personal health risks, an assessment that will give you a look into your future. A friend makes a "medical calendar" for an entire year, plotting routine exams she will take, health objectives she wishes to accomplish, and types of health-promoting exercise she will do on various days. Another friend kept a "medical journal" on his son's specific illness, recording every visit or conversation with medical personnel.He found it invaluable in dealing with his health insurance company.

In 1998, the Journal of the American Medical Association reported on 145,716 adult visits to 3,254 medical doctors concerning the question of smoking. Although the Agency for Health Care Policy and Research had advised doctors two years earlier to question patients about smoking during every office visit and to provide ways to help them quit, one-third of the time doctors did not know their patients' smoking status. In only 21 percent of the office visits did doctors counsel smokers to quit smoking. Don't leave the consultation room until you are sure that your doctor understands your primary health risks.

When you are taking a number of medications, some with food and some without, sometimes two pills at a time and sometimes only one, do not try to rely entirely on your memory. A friend designed for his wife a daily chart showing each hour of the day and each of 10 different medications. In this way her complicated medication schedule could be accurately maintained and recorded. He added categories for recording such other activities as sleep, bowel movements (because some medications caused constipation), and food consumption. Doctors and nurses, then, could learn at a glance that medications were being properly taken as well as other information about the patient. This made it easier to assess effectiveness of medications and to adjust dosages. Devise something similar for yourself.

Doctors take the position that the ownership of your medical file is theirs. However, there is usually no reason you cannot have a copy. If you move, you should certainly take a copy with you, even if you have not decided on your next doctor. If you change doctors in the same city, take a copy of your former doctor's file to your new doctor. You may have to pay a copying charge, which in the case of a hospital file can be quite expensive. Ask your new doctor to make his copy from your purchased one. Then keep your copy. There may be reasons you wish to keep your home copy up-to-date. If so, tell your doctor and/or the office staff. On being readmitted, even to the same hospital, do not assume that the file listing your drug allergies will be read.

When you sign a blanket permission at your doctor's office concerning dissemination of your personal medical information, be aware that there is no federal law to protect you against abuses of that information. About 35 states have enacted some form of law to protect your privacy. Is your state one of them?

Primary Care Doctor

A doctor told me: "In this chaotic world there is a competition to get the attention you need from the medical practitioner. You would be astonished to find how a personal note of thanks, a bunch of flowers picked from your yard, or a similar gift to your physician will differentiate you in a busy schedule." Additionally, it would not hurt to spend a minute updating your doctor on your family, travels, and common hobbies or interests. Establish a bond with your primary care doctor, who should be a board-certified internist or family physician. Women sometimes prefer to select a gynecologist as a primary doctor. In that case, be sure the doctor is checking your entire body. Primary care doctors generally do a better job of keeping you healthy than a specialist does. Also, they help coordinate care and channel important information to other members of the health care team, to you, and to your family.

Ask in advance for a longer appointment if there is much on your mind. Patients who talk mainly about their pain and suffering don't give the doctor much to work with. Describe objectively your conditions. It is a mistake to drop hints about a sensitive problem and see if the doctor will be astute enough to figure out what is on your mind. Don't avoid the subject. Be proactive; show your doctor that you are interested. Present the most serious problems first. Be honest. Don't minimize complaints that really bother you. Tell your doctor everything on your mind and in your body that you think may be affecting your health.

Do not be deterred by interruptions or a hurried atmosphere in the clinic. If your doctor seems ready to conclude the visit, politely say: "I have something else important to say." Or, "Doctor, I feel that I am not being heard." Stop the doctor if he or she is being too technical. If you have difficulty understanding, take an adult child or friend with you. One woman asked permission to audiotape her visit for later referral. Her physician agreed. Do not let the consultation end until all of your important questions have been answered.

Educate yourself on your specific illness and the therapy prescribed. Ask your doctor to explain the benefits and risks of each treatment option. Bring copies of any medical articles on your condition that you do not completely understand. Request copies of articles to read at home, or get suggestions on other information sources. Your doctor will develop new respect if you show that you are serious about wanting information. Ask clarifying questions before leaving the consultation room, summarize your understanding, and ask for confirmation. Ask: "If I have further questions later, whom should I call?" If, after leaving the examination room, there is something you did not understand, ask the nurse to explain before you leave the doctor's office. After each meeting, make a written record of the diagnosis and prognosis to keep in your medical information file. If you are uncomfortable with the doctor's judgment, get another opinion. We have all heard of cases in which the doctor was wrong; the patient's intuition was right, and by dying he or she proved it.

If you maintain summer and winter homes in different cities, get a primary care doctor for each city and up-to-date health files. People without a primary care doctor sometimes depend on visits to the emergency room for nonemergency conditions. Emergency rooms are not set up to provide ongoing care, and you may get a different doctor every time. Also, after an initial check you might be asked to make an appointment later with a doctor. Costs of treatment will be higher and may not be covered by insurance, depending on the nature of the illness.

Occasionally you may be sent to specialists. Do not expect that they can be as knowledgeable about or as interested in your overall condition as your primary care doctor. The latter is like the football quarterback who may sometimes hand the ball off to other players but is crucial to the team's advance. And in instances where the specialists conclude that no cure can be found, your relationship with your primary care doctor will become extremely important.

Finally, when you believe that your doctor is doing a good job for you, look him or her in the eye and sincerely express your thanks for all the efforts in your behalf.

Are Regular Checkups Worth It?

Two-thirds of Americans do not get an annual physical checkup. This is a mistake because this outlay of only about $120 and a little time could catch a serious illness in its beginning stages and save your life. HMOs usually include an annual examination at no further cost. Fee-for-service care and Medicare do not include it. Thirty percent of people over 65 get their checkups from specialists. Generally, specialists do not do as good a job of preventive screening in checkups as do internists and family doctors.

The annual checkup for healthy patients over age 50 should include blood pressure measurement, fecal occult blood test for colorectal cancer (done at home and mailed in), sigmoidoscopy for colorectal cancer every 3 to 5 years, and a cholesterol test. Additionally, women should have a mammogram for breast cancer and a Pap smear for cervical cancer. Men should receive a PSA blood test and digital rectal exam for prostate cancer. Both sexes over 65 should receive a vision and hearing test, generally given elsewhere.

A checkup with a doctor should last 15 to 30 minutes, much of it spent in talking about diet, exercise, smoking, injury prevention, and other lifestyle issues. One problem is that doctors are not trained to do effective counseling for healthy patients. Dietary counseling, for example, is given to only one in five patients. But when doctors do offer counsel, patients listen. A study of men who drank heavily found that the men who received as little as five minutes of counseling drank 17 percent less nine months later than those who received no counseling. Arrive at your checkup with a list of questions and stay until you get answers. Ask your doctor if the test results are "good" or only "good for my age." Keep your own record of tests and immunizations. Don't depend on the doctor's staff to remind you when the next ones are due.

Health Care Decision-Making

Some older patients become passive about their health care. Perhaps an adult child or a friend is their primary caregiver. The caregiver may make frequent contacts and seem capable of doing the right thing. The older person becomes less concerned with directing his or her own care. The caregiver notices this passivity and assumes the patient is becoming incompetent. Soon the older person has turned over important decisions affecting his or her health and life. Giving away personal power to caregivers pushes you down the road to a powerless existence. The answer, of course, is to be keenly and actively involved in all decisions that affect you. Staying in control assures you of contentment and a sense of self-worth.

Changing Expectations

Baby boomers are expecting more from medicine than did the previous generation, and the pharmaceutical companies love it. Boomers expect increased longevity and want to be sure that along with it they enjoy quality. Aging has become a medical problem. In addition to medications for aches and pains, they also want remedies for baldness, impotence, bone-density loss, depression, menopausal discomfort, weight, wrinkles, sunspots, memory loss, and other symptoms of aging. And many boomers are affluent and willing to pay for the extra remedies. Already they are spending billions of dollars on self-medication with alternative drugs. For those 76 million potential customers the pharmaceutical companies are researching over 400 new drugs. The older generation also will benefit from these discoveries and the higher demands on medical science. Insurance companies are hard pressed to decide which treatments are needed for physical health and which just contribute to feeling good.

Keeping Up with New Regulations

Communication with your doctor and your doctor's bookkeeper will be improved if everyone keeps up with the changing coverage of Medicare and of your health insurance company. For example, in 1998 Medicare expanded preventive monitoring coverage for Pap smear, breast exam, colorectal screenings, mammograms, glucose monitoring for diabetics, and bone-mass measurement. These changes will enable some people to ask for and receive more frequent screenings without incurring out-of-pocket expenses. Ask your doctor what preventive tests you should be taking. When a test is recommended, ask if it will be paid for by your health insurance coverage. The Senior Law Home Page, http://www.seniorlaw.com/index.htm, provides information on changes in programs such as Medicare and Medicaid.

HMOs and Insurance Companies

The squeaky wheel gets the oil. When you encounter problems with your HMO or health insurance company, try one of the following approaches. Learn the name of the person who makes the decisions on your case. If you have made a request through channels and received no response, or if you do not like the response, write a letter, make a telephone call, or send an e-mail directly to the decision-maker. One person got attention by sending an "urgent" fax with inch-high letters.

When I see a doctor for the first time, I take a typewritten history of any symptoms about which I want advice and ask that it be put into my record. In 80 percent of all malpractice lawsuits, the determining factor is the patient's chart. (But a Harvard Law School study showed that only one in eight victims of malpractice ever sues.) Keep records of your communications. Ask for a copy of your patient chart. Enlist the help of a friend or relative whom you know to be forceful in negotiations. If you are employed, get help from your human resources director. Get your doctor or hospital medical director to write a letter to your insurance company. If your doctor will not stick up for you, find a new one. Ask patients, coworkers, friends, and nurses for names of doctors known to fight for their patients. Use the appeals system of the HMO or insurance company. Seek help from your state's insurance commissioner.

Mistakes Happen

A 1996 Michigan study found that one-third of doctors do not always notify patients of abnormal test results. The most common reason given was that the patient was expected to return to the office soon. But what if you had decided not to return soon? More than two-thirds of doctors did not always notify patients of normal test results, believing that patients would assume that all is well. Call your doctor for test results.

My own painful story began in March 1990 when I, presumably in good health, volunteered to give blood to help with a university's cancer research project. Hearing no reply, I assumed everything was normal. It was not until July of that year that I learned of the abnormal finding that eventually resulted in my cancer diagnosis. What does this tell us about picking up the telephone?

The American Medical Society polled American adults to study the frequency of medical mistakes. Forty-two percent of those polled said that they themselves, a relative, or a friend had suffered from a medical error. The top three errors were misdiagnosis/wrong treatment (mentioned by 40 percent), medication error (22 percent), and mistake made during a procedure (22 percent). Nearly one-third of respondents were involved with more than one mistake. The American Medical Society called this "disturbing." Although not every mistake is preventable, our own vigilance can minimize the harm done. If a treatment isn't helping or a medication is making matters worse, don't wait. Speak out.

Medications

In the late 1990s, pharmaceutical companies increased annual advertising costs to $1 billion. Previously, prescription drugs were advertised mainly to doctors. Now, as a result of a change in Food and Drug Administration regulations, you can find prescription drug advertisements in magazines and newspapers. They are often full-page, small print ads that contain much technical data. Doctors report that some patients always expect to have medications prescribed, even when they are useless for a particular illness, such as an antibiotic for a common cold. It has been reported that cyberspace pharmacies will introduce you to "virtual doctors" for writing electronic prescriptions. Don't do it. Every year, more than 140,000 people die after taking the wrong prescription drug or the wrong dosage. Be sure you understand the directions.

Almost half of older citizens take multiple medicines daily. List all of your medications on a piece of paper and take it with you to all doctors' appointments. Include your vitamins and herbal supplements, if any. Sixty percent of patients do not tell their doctors what herbal remedies they are taking. This is dangerous. Whenever your doctor prescribes a new medicine, show the list and ask that it be reviewed. Your doctor might not know what other doctors have prescribed for you, or might overlook his or her own previous prescriptions. Find out if you are being a guinea pig for a drug. Ask your doctor if the drug has been tested for the purpose for which it is being prescribed. A drug approved for sudden heart stoppage was also routinely prescribed for mildly irregular heart rhythms. Later test results showed that it doubled the chance of sudden heart failure and caused many deaths, according to Stephen Fried, author of *Bitter Pills: Inside the Hazardous World of Legal Drugs*. Since almost all drugs have side effects, ask your doctor if there is any non-pharmacologic therapy for your problem, such as a change in lifestyle, that you could try on a test basis.

The *Journal of the American Medical Association* on April 15, 1998, reported that drugs with similar names or appearances accounted for an estimated 25 percent of the medication errors in America. More than 1000 drugs have similar names. Doctors are being urged to write prescriptions more legibly, without abbreviations, and with precise instructions. Before leaving your doctor's office you should be able to understand the written prescription. In that way you yourself can check on the brand and generic names and the dosage.

Whenever you go to the pharmacy to fill a prescription, show the pharmacist your medication list and ask that it be checked for any incompatibilities. Ask what side effects to look for in the medications prescribed. Some HMOs provide a hot line for members to inquire about their medications. To help avoid errors at the pharmacy, avoid Monday for filling prescriptions; it is the busiest day. For refills, telephone and give your pharmacist a few days so that your prescription can be filled at a less busy time. Inquire if your refills are different in size or color.

To test your reaction to a new drug and to save money, ask your doctor for a free sample or for a one-week prescription only. If you are self-medicating with nonprescription drugs, ask for advice at the health food store or the pharmacy where you shop. Drugs and herbs produce a wide variety of physical and mental side effects. For example, cholesterol-lowering drugs are known to sometimes cause depression. People metabolize drugs differently according to age, gender, and ethnicity. A significant amount of this variability is genetic in origin. Ingesting grapefruit juice can dangerously affect the results of some heart drugs. Always give your doctor feedback on your adverse reaction to drugs. Otherwise, how will your doctor know? Finally, shop around for the best prices. They can vary greatly.

Noncompliance with Prescriptions

The Center for the Advancement of Health reported what happens when patients do not take drugs exactly as prescribed. The desired results are not attained in 30 to 50 percent of all prescriptions because they are not taken correctly. About 125,000 Americans die each year from noncompliance. Approximately 10 percent of all hospitalizations are caused by patients' improper drug use. Only about one-third of patients finish using up all of their prescription medicine. One-third stop part way, and one-third take none of it. Inability to pay is cited as one reason 20 percent of prescriptions are not filled at all. Tell your doctor frankly if you cannot afford to pay for the prescription. Help is available in some cases.

Communicating effectively with professional health care providers is up to you. It is worth repeating: "Communication is what your doctor hears, not necessarily what you say." If you have not had a physical checkup recently, isn't it in your best interests to make an appointment today? The next chapter explores staying well through communicating effectively with your family, caregivers, and other people important to you.

We could not effectively monitor Mother's health from 1000 miles away, so we brought her here. Then we found out about many health problems of which we had not been aware. She had even fallen but had not told us. I wish we had had better communication. Unfortunately, Mother did not last long after the move.

A CAREGIVER

CHAPTER EIGHT

Communicate with Caregivers and Family

THIS CHAPTER OFFERS methods for staying in touch with family, care-givers, and other people important to you, both for your sake and for their peace of mind. It includes effective techniques for more skillful-ly communicating your health care and other needs and getting others to help you. It also offers suggestions for caregivers.

Too Little Conversation

Older people tend to keep things private. They do not want to rock the boat by admitting what they really believe about their deteriorat-ing physical or mental situation. Some are afraid to discuss health issues for fear they will be put into a nursing home. As communica-tions expert Robert Bolton, author of *People Skills*, puts it, "In our soci-ety it is rare for persons to share what really matters—the tender, shy, reluctant feelings, the sensitive, fragile, intense disclosures." The prob-lem, then, is that we assume that doctors and others know what we need and will provide those things. Then we wonder, "Why didn't the doctor even look at my incision to see if it is healing well?" Or, "How come my neighbor went grocery shopping and didn't ask me if I needed anything?"

Then there is the problem of too much speaking and too little listening. "Conversation in the USA," in the words of Nathan Miller, "is a competitive exercise in which the first person to draw a breath is declared the listener." Older people can add another communications-related complaint, that is, too little caring. Malcolm Skolnick puts it this way: "Your children talk to you as if you were a child, and your grandchildren ignore you except when you have a present for them."

Still another problem is that we do not see or hear as well as before, although we may be too proud to admit it. Or we may not have the necessary money to buy new glasses or a hearing aid. Do not give yourself such a handicap. You need everything working for you in order to support your continued quality of life and your ability to communicate, to make your own decisions, and to stay in control of your life.

Self-Esteem, a New Attitude

To have a satisfactory relationship with your family and friends, your doctors and caregivers, you must be both honest and assertive. This requires self-esteem, a term that might not have been familiar to you while growing up. Some of us would prefer to refuse help rather than admit that we are not self-sufficient. Some even refuse the very services that would enable them to continue living independently. Your ability to assert yourself is a mark of your self-esteem. It requires self-confidence to be willing to take a risk on relationships.

When your doctor recommends a new treatment, ask what to expect before going ahead. Ask: How many people with my condition have you treated? What are the possible side effects? How many visits will be required? How long before I feel better? How much will it cost? Better, more honest, and more satisfactory relationships will emerge. Decide today that from now on you will be open and honest, yet kind, with everyone you meet. If the situation were reversed, you would want them to take that attitude with you, wouldn't you?

Rules of Effective Communication

The following guidelines were provided by Kathleen C. Miller, MA, a Marriage and Family Counselor. They will serve you in any relationship. They are especially effective with those with whom you find communication difficult. Practice makes perfect.

ATTITUDE

- Empathy: Be willing to stand in the other person's shoes.
- Congruence: What you feel inside must match what you are showing and saying on the outside.
- Warmth: Be the most gracious you can possibly be.

GROUND RULES

- Use "I" language. Avoid saying "you."
- Take responsibility for yourself. Do not try to read the other person's mind or expect the other person to read yours.
- Let the past be past when you speak in the present. Talk about past issues in the context of the past.
- Assume the good will of the other person.
- Throw away the words "always," "never," and "should."

TECHNIQUES

- Use feedback for listening accuracy. "What I hear you saying is . . ."
- Check out in detail; ask for clarification. "Tell me more about . . ."
- Kleenex box: Discuss one issue at a time, just the one that is sticking up. Don't bring up other issues until the first one is solved.
- Closure: Do not break off talks abruptly. Finish the issue, or set a time for continuation. Be specific. Follow through.
- Body language: When speaking, watch your tone, volume, and body language, which sometimes communicate more than words.
- Eye contact: Look directly into the other person's eyes when you are speaking and listening. To do otherwise when you

speak weakens your delivery. This is a hard skill to master and very productive of good results.

Assertive Communication

In 1995, I took a college course to learn what assertive communication is about. It was a real eye-opener. I found that I had been failing in some important areas of communication. Assertive communication was developed in the 1970s, mainly to help women talk to men. Yes, there are notable differences in the way the two sexes speak. A book explaining this is *Men Are from Mars; Women Are from Venus* by John Gray. There are also differences between the generations in the way we communicate. Assertive communication does not mean speaking aggressively. The three types of communication are these: nonassertive, aggressive, and assertive. The last one falls between the first two and is the best. When you speak assertively, you make your point honestly and clearly in a nonthreatening manner.

Robert Alberti and Michael Emmons offer the following example in their book *Your Perfect Right.* In a restaurant a diner orders a rare steak and it arrives well done. A few minutes later, the waiter asks, "How is everything?" A nonassertive diner answers, "Fine," but grumbles to his dining partner all evening. He is angry with himself, and his evening is ruined. An aggressive diner loudly summons the waiter, creates a scene, and causes friction between himself and his dinner companion. An assertive diner politely explains the problem to the waiter and asks for another steak. This time he is satisfied, generously tips the waiter, and he and his companion have a nice evening. The world would be a lot better place if all communication were like that.

Positive Speaking

Dr. J. Mitchell Perry, author of *The Road to Optimism*, says that the five basic factors you need in order to be happy are a sense of control over your life, spirituality, meaningful work, closeness, and optimism. Optimism can be learned; it results in a longer life, better health, less sickness, faster recovery after sickness, and greater productivity. A paramount factor in gaining more optimism is language.

Thoughts, feelings, and language interact with each other and produce behavior. If you change one thing, language, the resulting behavior will change. For a start you can eliminate from your speech exclusionary words such as "don't," "can't," and "won't." Talk (and think) about how you *do* feel rather than how you *don't* feel.

Dr. Perry believes that the Visa credit card is dominant over the American Express card in part because the former's slogan is inclusive and positive, "It's everywhere you want to be," whereas the latter's is exclusionary, "Don't leave home without it." If we thank someone and hear in return the expression, "No problem," it conveys a much less positive feeling than the reply, "It's a pleasure." A child returning from a trip to the amusement park will say, "It was cool!" An adult will say about the same trip, "Not as bad as I feared." Watch your language and enjoy the benefits!

Relations with Caregivers

Nowadays, parents and children spend more years in an adult relationship than in an adult-child relationship. This is different from the past. When grandchildren can observe good relations between their caregiving parents and their aging grandparents, they may be inclined to follow that caregiving role themselves. Where offspring show indifference toward aging parents, it is possible that the feeling of loving concern and helpfulness has stopped flowing from one generation to the next.

In her book *Getting Over Getting Older*, Letty Cottin Pogrebin says that older people are likely to be humored or indulged when they act crabby, boring, or hypercritical. We would not tolerate such conduct in a younger person. Older care receivers then end up being grouchy and demanding because we have permitted them to act by different rules of interpersonal communication. You should manage your emotions when you are receiving care, especially from children or relatives. If you do not, they may not feel as bound to continue helping you as you might wish. Rupturing relations with good caregivers just because you were not nice or were grouchy is not smart.

Try to create a pleasant environment. If your caregiver is not a smoker and you are one, have your home as smoke-free as possible and refrain from smoking until that person is gone. Your pets may be perfectly acceptable to you, but some people are allergic to cats and scared to death of large dogs, no matter how friendly. Put yourself in their position. Would you want to give care to a person like you? Accept help graciously. Smile. Express gratitude. Give small gifts when appropriate. All of these positive actions represent an investment in your future happiness.

To quote from Goethe: "In all situations, it is my response that decides whether a crisis will be escalated or de-escalated and a person humanized or dehumanized. If we treat people as they are, we make them worse. If we treat people as they ought to be, we help them become what they are capable of becoming."

When You Are a Caregiver

You are not doing an older person a favor if you overdo your help. Generally, it is preferable to do only what that person cannot do. Help someone to remain capable and independent, even your mate.

Telephone in advance with your expected arrival time. Try to be on time or else call to warn when you will be late. Older adults anticipate visitors and become worried and irritable when the appointed time has passed. Sometimes it may be more important to do less and, instead, enjoy each other over a pleasant conversation. Mutual sharing is usually not regarded as an element of caregiving, but it could be well received. Also, be open to the possibility of the care receiver's wish to discuss spiritual matters as a means to healing. A teacher of caregiving, before entering the patient's room, says as a reminder to herself, "From God to God." I understand this to be a reminder that she is attempting to bring a divine-centered presence to a care receiver whom she recognizes as having God within her. Frequently ask the question: "What do you need?" Do whatever you can, but avoid praising yourself for how much you have accomplished for the care receiver. It could make the receiver feel even more dependent and unworthy because she or he is incapable of doing as much.

If you are living with a seriously disabled or memory-impaired adult, you may be able to delay placing him or her in a nursing home by using an adult day center. (It is estimated that delaying admission to a nursing home by just one month could save America $3 billion yearly.) Centers provide meals and group activities in a safe environment, and the daily break will help you to last longer.

Everyone wants to give advice to elders: their children, friends, medical personnel, neighbors, and others. By now the elders usually know what they want. Well-intentioned advice is turned off, resented, or only serves to confuse. Instead, simply state an alternative possibility without actually suggesting that your advice should be taken. It might seem to be the best solution only to you.

To prevent burnout, take a really restful break after each visit. Look inward to examine what you have learned from this experience. What have you learned new about your care receiver? About yourself? If time permits, enter those discoveries in a journal. The following words help me to remember that the quantity of caregiving is less important than the quality.

Letting Go

To "let go" does not mean to stop caring; it means I can't do it for someone else.

To "let go" is not to cut myself off. It's the realization that I can't control another.

To "let go" is to admit powerlessness, which means the outcome is not in my hands.

To "let go" is not to try to change or blame another. It's to make the most of myself.

To "let go" is not to care for, but to care about.

To "let go" is not to fix, but to be supportive.

To "let go" is not to judge, but to allow another to be a human being.

To "let go" is not to be in the middle, arranging all the outcomes, but to allow others to affect their own destinies.

To "let go" is not to deny, but to accept.

To "let go" is not to nag, scold, or argue, but instead to search out my own shortcomings and correct them.

To "let go" is not to adjust everything to my desires, but to take each day as it comes and cherish myself in it.

To "let go" is not to regret the past, but to grow and live for the future.

To "let go" is to fear less and love more.

—AUTHOR UNKNOWN

Elder Abuse

In 1996 there were 293,000 reported cases of Americans 60 years or older being neglected, physically abused, or financially exploited. The National Center on Elder Abuse estimates that the real figure is over a million and that the problem will get worse as society ages. Often a relative is the abuser and/or the older person is dependent on the abuser. The older person may fear for the future if he or she is taken out of the abuser's care. One of the factors involved is unresolved tensions between children and parents that have simmered over a lifetime. Another factor is the adult child cracking under the stress of caring for aging parents. Still another factor in abuse is financial motivation. Know where to report abuse if it should happen. When it happens, get help and confront the problem. If you do not know your state's 800 number for reporting abuse, you may get it from the National Center on Elder Abuse at (202) 898-2586. Or call the Adult Protective Services office that serves your area. However, if a crime is in progress, call 911.

Keeping in Touch

Establish a regular system of communication with caregivers and neighbors so they will know whether you are okay or not. This is particularly important when you are living alone, especially if you have been ill or are in danger of falling. When my mother raises her bedroom blinds upon arising in the morning, it alerts her friend across the street. If her friend sees blinds down at 8:00 A.M., she will telephone or visit. Mother fell once. Now, before she goes down the basement stairs, she calls a neighbor and advises the neighbor to expect another call in 10 minutes when she has come back up.

Use the Telephone

Writing letters is a wonderful art. But it is insufficient by itself as a means of keeping in touch with your adult children living at a distance. Three-fourths of seniors talk on the phone with adult children at least weekly. Ask your children to telephone you at set times during the week. Make telephone time pleasant and informative. Instead of complaining about your neighbor's cat digging in your garden, assure your children that you are well and appreciate their call. Resist the temptation to talk at length about people they do not know and in whom they have no interest. But do tell them about health and living problems and successes and be open to any suggestions. They will be happy to be involved. If there are serious health problems, ask your children to get a briefing by telephone directly from your doctor. Give them the number and the best time to talk with the doctor. This applies to your main caregivers whether or not they are your children.

As older adults become increasingly homebound, a day when the telephone does not ring can cause loneliness. Call friends often to have short conversations. It will nurture the friendship, ease depression, and be a benefit for all concerned. Also, these communication routines will serve as a way of alerting others to a potential problem. When friends call and offer to help, make a note for the future if you cannot think of any immediate need. Later, call them and say, "Thank you for offering to help the other day. Now I do have a request. Tell me if you cannot do it."

Telephone Reassurance Program

Graduate students from Yale University School of Nursing worked with a regional visiting-nurse agency to follow up on patients who had been discharged from a hospital and whose visiting-nurse privileges had ended. The discharge nurse provided information regarding the patients' living situation, primary caregiver status, use of community resources, and current medications. The students recorded the results of their telephone conversations with the patients on an assessment flow sheet. Supervising nurses could then determine from the flow sheets that patients were stable and required no further follow-up. Or, patients could report physical or functional complications, ask questions, or schedule appointments. This system resulted in fewer clinic visits, fewer prescriptions, fewer hospitalizations, and greater patient satisfaction. Since calls were made by the nursing students, no additional personnel had to be hired. This is an example of a program that encouraged independent living and community-based care. Does such a program exist in your area? Could you work toward getting one started?

Telemedicine

Telemedicine is a newer technology whereby patients are monitored at home using equipment that costs about $1000. Whereas a typical home visit by a nurse costs about $90, a patient may have a televisit checkup at a cost of $15–25. This can cut hospitalization rates by one third and is especially beneficial for patients too frail to travel. The U.S. Army has a communications infrastructure in place whereby the health of soldiers may be monitored remotely in this way. American prisons, also, use technology to eliminate the security risks of transporting sick criminals to a clinic. Why, then, is telemedicine not used more widely among the civilian population? It is the fault of bureaucracy. Medicare and Medicaid have finally given approval for radiology reports to be sent over telephone wires but not to home health services. Insurance companies have followed Medicare's example.

Also, since doctors may practice only in states where they are licensed, telephone wires crossing state lines are problematical for monitoring patients. Eventually, budgetary considerations will prevail and convenient telemedicine will be practiced widely.

Children at a Distance

Seven million Americans are trying to provide long-distance care for chronically ill or failing loved ones who live far away. The number will double in the next 15 years. If your adult children live at a distance, and if a friend or church member is your local caregiver, acquaint him or her with your children. Then ask permission to let your distant children telephone your friend concerning your condition once in a while. Perhaps that person can identify a need or a problem that hadn't occurred to you or that you were reluctant to mention. Being able to talk with a third party will be reassuring to your distant children.

If your children can subscribe to your local newspaper, they can keep up with services offered to seniors in your area. If not, send them pamphlets or news clips that could be pertinent to your ability to continue living where you are. If closer contact is desirable, your children could hire a geriatric-care manager to check on you, assess needs, and make recommendations.

E-Mail

Seventy percent of seniors who have a home computer have access to the Internet. If your child or grandchild wants to teach you how to use e-mail, accept the challenge. It will greatly expand your communication capability and provide a fascinating pastime. Perhaps your grandchildren away at college keep late hours, and it is difficult to time your phone calls. They can answer your e-mail messages anytime. Failing hearing may make it difficult to communicate with family and friends by telephone but will be no problem with e-mail. If your daughter uses a computer at her office, you might be able to send e-mail while she is at work without interrupting her.

Increasingly, patients are communicating with their doctors by e-mail. Dr. Stephen Borowitz of the University of Virginia studied 1200 e-mails from patients and found that it takes only about four minutes to respond to e-mail. Some doctors have even started online consulting services for a fee. If you do not have a computer, get a TV terminal that can access the Internet. Get in step with the future.

Emergency Calls

About 9.5 million elderly people live alone. The *New England Journal of Medicine* reported a study of 367 people found "down" in their homes. Ninety were dead. Some of those could have lived if help had arrived. One woman I know suffered some crisis while taking a bath and, not being able to get out of the tub by herself, spent 48 hours in cold bath water until she was rescued. In addition to calling 911 for emergency assistance, there are several other types of alerting mechanisms. These are usually for times when you have fallen or become incapacitated.

Personal emergency response systems (PERS) enable you in an emergency to alert a monitoring center, which will respond to you and then call for help. Companies that offer these systems provide an alarm device—worn around your neck or wrist—that you can easily activate when you need help. The monthly monitoring fee is about $35, depending on the start-up cost. Radio Shack sells a similar system without the monitoring service for about $100. When you activate the device, it will dial up to four telephone numbers set by you and will play your recorded message. Also, you can speak with anyone who answers if you are not too far from your central unit. Or you can set the system to blast an emergency horn on the outside of your home. The whole neighborhood will know you are in trouble.

A retired engineer cared for his bedridden wife. He set up an elaborate system of outdoor flashing lights, which permitted his wife to summon him while he was doing yard work. Later he discovered a more effective system, a battery-powered remote doorbell. The activator button remained at his wife's bedside while he carried the bell in his pocket. The effective range was about half a block. A pager is also effective, but my friend's solution cost only $40 at the hardware store and no monthly fee. Ask your local police or fire department to advise you on ways to summon emergency help, *before* you actually require it.

Written Records

Your memory can be used for far more important things than as a storehouse of numbers and dates. Don't overburden it with details that you can put in writing. You will need three things: a handy book of personal telephone numbers, a calendar large enough to write on, and a small spiral notebook to serve as a communication log.

Telephone book Keep an alphabetized book near your phone of all the numbers you call, or even think you might call. Of course it will contain phone numbers of relatives, friends, doctors, clergy, neighbors, caregivers, and pharmacies. Make several copies of the most important numbers and give them to your adult children and other caregivers. In addition, record every new number you call for the first time. (How many times have you searched again for the same number in the telephone directory?) If you call the home delivery pizza number once, chances are you will call again. It is less frustrating and faster to find the number in your personal phone book than to look it up each time in the published book. Also, include numbers from the newspaper of new stores or services you may wish to call someday. Exchange phone numbers with new neighbors as soon as they move into the neighborhood. Be prepared to help each other.

Calendar Keep a calendar near your telephone and use it to record every forthcoming event you are considering or to which you are committed. It will contain dates and times of doctor appointments, social engagements, birthdays to be remembered, tax payments due, annual change of smoke alarm batteries, oil changes for your car, gardener's visits—in short, everything you can think of that you don't want to miss. Don't keep more than one such calendar unless you are sure to record everything in duplicate. Businesspeople keep appointment schedules; why shouldn't you? Your calendar will help you avoid frustration and also serve as a historical record of events, should you need to refer back.

Spiral notebook Keep this, also, by your telephone, but take it with you to doctor appointments. It will contain notes on every conversation to which you may wish to refer later. For example, when your doctor diagnoses a condition, write that diagnosis in the book. (Have the doctor tell you the spelling of medical words.) When the doctor's nurse telephones you to give the outcome of a test, write it in the book along with the date and the name of the person who called. Make notes also on how you felt after taking a new medication.

I know people who cannot clearly remember one week later what the doctor told them. This is usually because they did not understand it in the first place or are dependent on someone else to remember. As Dr. James Wade said, "I learned a long time ago that my patients, despite my thinking I was telling them everything they needed to know, would go home and they'd stare in the bathroom mirror and say, 'What the hell did he say to me?' " Then, too, some people like to embellish what the doctor said, or they forget things they did not want to hear. A written record will help to clarify at the time and, later, will be a correct source of information for caregivers.

> Hope is an act of collaboration. It cannot be achieved alone. We offer grains or fragments of hope to one another so that everyone's sense of possibility can grow. In this way, we can do together what might seem impossible alone.
>
> —KATHLEEN FISCHER

Part Four

Stay in
Control

We had to search in six different places in her home to find the necessary documents to process care for this patient.

A SOCIAL WORKER

CHAPTER NINE

Keep Files for Peace of Mind

THIS CHAPTER HELPS you to understand what documents you already have, what others you may need to assemble, and how to organize them all so that you or anyone can locate them when needed. This exercise puts you in control and empowers you; it contributes to your peace of mind and to that of your caregivers.

Important: Explain to your mate, children, or closest caregiver where you have stored the documents to be discussed in this chapter. Or leave in your desk a written locater directory.

Drowning in Paper

As we age, we are increasingly dealing with medical forms, doctor bills, Social Security and pension records, bank statements, investment information, and the like. Piles of unread or unfiled material are depressing. Some people with extra money would prefer to hire someone to make order out of chaos. That preference has created the need for the National Association of Professional Organizers. However, before reaching for the telephone, try by yourself to clean up one file per day or per week and observe your progress. The job may not be as onerous as you expect, since some points in this chapter may not apply to you. And other files may already be in good order.

Personal Information File

All of the following will fit nicely in a manila, letter-size folder, preferably one that ties or closes. Label the outside "Personal Information File."

- Birth certificate
- Marriage certificate
- Citizenship papers if not born a citizen of the USA
- Divorce/separation papers
- If widowed, death certificate of deceased spouse
- Full names and addresses of children, parents, and siblings
- Adoption papers
- Social Security number
- Passport
- Military records

Medical Information File

A spiral notebook measuring 8.5 by 11 inches or a three-ring binder will do the job; some may prefer using a folder with loose papers inserted in two inside pockets, or an accordion-type folder with many pockets. (Those with computers may prefer the paperless approach.) On the outside write your name and "Medical Information File." At the top of each page write the name of each section listed below.

PERSONAL MEDICAL DATA

- Your name, date of birth, and Medicare or other health insurance numbers.
- Allergies to drugs (e.g., penicillin), food, and insects. (If none, in each case write, "no known allergies.")
- Implants such as pacemaker or artificial hip.
- Chronic health problems with dates of diagnosis. These include angina (heart pain), heart attack, epilepsy, atherosclerosis (hardening of the arteries), cancer, diabetes, high blood pressure, stroke, mental illness, alcoholism, osteoporosis, and arthritis.

- Primary-care doctor, any specialization, and telephone number. Other doctors, specializations, and telephone numbers.
- Dentist and telephone number.
- Pharmacist and telephone number.
- Social worker or caseworker and telephone number.
- Emergency notification. List person to be notified in case of emergency and that person's telephone number.
- Refer to your living will and health proxy, or durable power of attorney for health care, kept in your legal file (page 163).

MEDICATIONS AND INOCULATIONS

- Inoculations such as those for tetanus, influenza, and pneumonia with dates. Also include childhood inoculations if known.
- Name of each drug currently taken, for what purpose, dosage, doctor, and date prescribed. When you stop taking it, write the date and "stopped." Do this even for over-the-counter medicine such as Tylenol or aspirin, even if not prescribed by a doctor.
- Leave a few blank pages to accommodate the recording of medicine that might be prescribed for you in the future.

ILLNESSES, INJURIES, AND PREGNANCIES

- Serious illnesses including pneumonia and bronchitis; major infections; broken bones; include dates.
- Surgical procedures including cesarean sections; hospitalizations; names of surgeons; dates.
- Pregnancies including live births and miscarriages; dates.

TRAUMAS

- Burns, loss of consciousness, other traumas; dates.

BLOOD

- Blood type. Blood transfusions dates.

HEALTH EXAMINATIONS

- X-rays, CAT scans, MRI (magnetic resonance imaging), cardiac tests, etc. Where done, prescribed by whom, and dates. Note if you are keeping these at your home.

- Routine tests including those for blood pressure, cholesterol, Pap smear, mammogram, and PSA (prostate-specific antigen); dates and results.

FAMILY HISTORY MEDICAL DATA

Some diseases run in families. Hereditary breast or colon cancer may show itself 10 to 20 years earlier than nonhereditary cancers. It will be helpful to you and your doctor for prevention purposes to know the major diseases in your family history. This record can be a gift to your children and grandchildren. Give them copies.

- List the ages your grandparents, parents, and any siblings were when they died and give the cause of each death—for example, not simply "cancer" but what kind. Also list for each relative any major illnesses and age of onset; include health problems from recurring headaches, frequent colds, and allergies. Indicate whether each relative was a smoker or nonsmoker; estimated amount of alcohol consumed; any reproductive problems such as birth defects, miscarriages, or inherited conditions.
- List any other information you think pertinent.

Financial and Legal Information File

Use a spiral notebook, three-ring binder, or folder to record financial and legal information. Write your name and "Financial and Legal Information File" on the outside.

SAVINGS AND CHECKING ACCOUNTS

- List all savings and checking accounts at banks, savings and loans, credit unions, etc., including account numbers and addresses. Indicate if held jointly with another person with right of survivorship. List the names and telephone numbers of any personal bankers.

- An easy and effective way to list your accounts is simply to tape a monthly report from your bank onto a page in your notebook. Or slip it in your folder. In that way, all the necessary information will be included and you will not have to copy by hand. At the end of each year either write in a new balance or else replace the bank's page.

BUSINESSES
- Identify any businesses that you own except for rental property listed below.

SOURCES OF INCOME
- List sources and approximate amounts of income you regularly receive. Again, fastening an actual statement into the notebook is a good way to complete this.
- Include an earnings statement if you are currently employed, Social Security income, pension and annuity income, rental properties, and major interest income.

EXPENSES
- What does it cost you to live for one year? Totaling your annual checks written and cash withdrawals made will give you this figure for a typical year. However, take into account years of unusually large expenditures such as automobile purchases or very expensive vacations, which could raise the average yearly cost of living.

DEBTS
- Indicate if you have any mortgages, major debts, or financial obligations to anyone.

CREDIT CARDS
- List your major credit cards, numbers, and expiration dates.

TAX STATEMENTS
- Attach to this page a copy of your latest Internal Revenue

Service federal and state income tax returns and the name and telephone number of your accountant if you did not complete the returns yourself.
- Include real estate and personal property tax statements.

SECURITIES

- Stock brokerage firm, address, account executive, and telephone number should be included, and whether the stock certificates are kept by you (and where) or by the brokerage.
- A listing of stocks, bonds, and mutual funds will be useful. All of this can be accomplished by fastening into your notebook a monthly or annual statement from the brokerage. It is not necessary that every transaction be recorded. But you should indicate where in your house your monthly statements are filed.

IRAS, ANNUITIES, ETC.

- Include any other pertinent financial holdings, contact persons, telephone numbers, and where records are stored.

REAL ESTATE

- List all real estate you own and whether or not the mortgages have been fully paid. Include rental and out-of-state properties and whether or not some are owned in joint tenancy.
- Attach a copy of the latest evaluation of your real estate, including your home. Include the cost basis.

PERSONAL PROPERTY

- List any autos, recreation vehicles, and boats you own, and storage place of titles.
- List valuable artworks and collections, jewelry, and computers, and where kept. Indicate where the insurance appraisals for these items are stored. Include cost bases.
- Inventory all valuables kept in your home. Put them on videotape, if possible.

INSURANCE

- Enter the name and telephone number of your insurance agent, the companies and types of insurance, e.g., home, life, health, long-term health care, auto, etc., and where the policies are kept.

LEGAL FILE

- What documents exist for indicating your wishes if you become ill and cannot make your wishes known? List where you keep a living will and power of attorney, or durable power of attorney for health care. Indicate here the names and telephones numbers of those to whom you have given power of attorney; attach copies to the page for easy access in an emergency.
- What documents exist for conveying your property after you die and for expressing your other wishes? List where you keep a will, community property agreement, or living trust. Do you have a written document pertaining to your own memorial service? Interment wishes? Indicate your lawyer's name, name of law firm, and telephone number.
- List the password to your computer files.

Other Important Contacts

PROFESSIONAL ADVISORS

- List other professional advisors not mentioned earlier, addresses, and telephone numbers. These advisors may include attorneys, financial advisors, bankers, accountants, insurance agents, stockbrokers, and clergy.

PAST EMPLOYERS

- Company names, addresses and telephone numbers, dates of retirement, contact persons, and identification numbers.

NEIGHBORS AND FRIENDS

- List the names and telephone numbers of those who have keys to your house or are important in other ways.

SERVICE PROVIDERS

- List the names and telephone numbers of those who provide you with services such as electrical or other repairs, meals, and so on.

CLUB MEMBERSHIPS

- List memberships, volunteer activities, etc., contact names, and telephone numbers.

LANDLORD

- Name and telephone number.

Safety Deposit Box

If you keep a safety deposit box, indicate the location and box number. Be sure that the names of those who should be able to gain entry have their signatures duly registered. Tell one or more of them where you store the key and/or let one hold a duplicate key. Make an inventory of the contents of the box, leaving one copy in the box and one at home in your Financial Information or Legal File notebook. Some documents will be needed immediately if you become incapacitated or die. These are, for example, a living will and a will. If you store the originals in the safety deposit box, keep copies in your Legal File.

(Some safety deposit boxes hold savings bonds that, because of their age, no longer bear interest. These are not redeemed either because the owner does not know they are fully mature or does not want to pay the added income tax on the interest income. Unless it is important to you to keep your income at a low level, it is preferable to cash the bonds and use the added income for enjoyment while you are alive.)

Hiding Valuables in Your Home

If you hide valuable documents, money, or jewels in the house (preferably in a fireproof home safe), please tell someone the location. The following is a true story of hidden treasure. As a child I often would look in wonderment at the sight of my father's wedding ring on his thick, stubby finger. The ring was unusual, a black-and-white cameo cut to depict Antony and Cleopatra, and mounted on a massive white-gold setting. Years later, Dad decided not to take it on a forthcoming trip with Mother and, instead, hid it in the house for safety. Sometime later when he went to look for it, he could not remember where it was hidden. He carefully searched all over the house—many times, in fact.

Dad has now been dead for 23 years and my mother has given up the search. Somewhere in her house is that beautiful cameo ring, which I would love to have for sentimental reasons. But where it is, I do not know. The moral: Keep valuables in a safety deposit box. But if you decide to hide something valuable at home, tell someone you trust or make a note to yourself.

Undertaking the file preparations recommended in this chapter is a big job, something that most of us do not want to do. I understand that. However, like any big challenge, if you look at it as a series of small jobs it becomes doable. I guarantee that when you complete it you will feel a sense of empowerment, contentment, accomplishment, peace, and satisfaction. You will have given yourself handy access to vital information. Your children and caregivers will thank you for your farsightedness and thoughtfulness.

> If you don't know where you're going, you might not get there.
>
> —YOGI BERRA

Be it ever so humble, there's no place like home.

CHAPTER TEN

Make Your Home Work for You

THIS CHAPTER EXPLAINS the various steps to be taken to ensure that you are able to remain in your own home, in control, happily, and as long as you wish.

This Is Where You Want to Be

Fortunately, you are still able to take care of yourself. You have considered all of the various alternative living styles. Each has its pros and cons. But you have been in your present residence long enough to know that it is the most satisfactory for you. You are near family and friends. The transportation system is good. The environment is healthy, and there are ample recreational and cultural opportunities. Besides that, there are also some nice memories connected with it. Just thinking about packing up and moving makes you tired. You definitely will stay where you are, perhaps for a long time.

That being so, now is the best time to do everything within your resources to make your home safe, comfortable, and convenient for the years ahead. Sixty percent of older persons live in homes more than 20 years old. It must have occurred to you that there are things you would like to change at home to make life a little easier and more enjoyable. Make a list of those items. Would you like a fence or storm doors? Is the electric-circuit capacity too low for the number of appliances you now have? Do you want a larger hot-water tank or an outdoor sprinkler system for watering your lawn? Would door lever handles be easier to use than door knobs? Maybe a bedroom and bath on the main floor would add to your comfort.

An Investment in Your Future

With your completed list in hand, call in a contractor experienced in working with housing modifications for older people. The contractor should be licensed and bonded. Or ask your adult child or a social worker to go over your home with you. Also, consultants with this specialty can be hired by the hour. Another alternative is to contact your local agency on aging regarding home modification and repair programs. Improvenet, **http://www.Improvenet.com**, puts you into contact with 600,000 local contractors and lets you see if they have had legal problems.

"Oh," you say, "It will cost too much and, besides, I want to leave some money eventually for my child and his or her family." Remember! The best gift you can give your adult children is to take good care of yourself. The place in which you live is of crucial importance to your well-being and to your functioning. Don't give up on any improvement meant for your comfort, safety, and enjoyment at home without first getting a written estimate. Then you can decide your priorities. Compare the cost of improvements against what it would cost to stay in a nursing home for a couple of years. You can do a lot of renovating with that much money. Also consider that some home improvements will enhance the value of your residence when it is sold in the future.

Financing Home Improvements

When you get estimates for your home improvements, calculate whether or not you can afford all of them. If you do not know, figure out your total income and expenditures in a typical year. Add any other special expenses you are planning, and any extraordinary one-time income.

If you are short financially, could you sell any real estate or personal property without detracting from the quality of your life? Could you reduce any expenses? Remember, you might qualify for decreased property taxes and utility rates, and for fuel oil assistance. Could you have a higher deductible on your auto collision insurance? (Some people continue to pay the higher premiums for $50 deductible insurance when they have not had an accident in 20 years!) Some cities provide no-interest housing-rehabilitation loans to low- and moderate-income residents to make improvements for safety and health. The loans need not be repaid until the home is sold.

If you do not have a spouse, roommate, child, or trusted friend, ask for help from your accountant or bank. The chances are that you have kept a bank account for many years. Your bank may be eager to help you without charge. In fact, when I described my mother's problems with balancing her checkbook and her inability to go out, her bank offered to send someone to her home once a month to do it for free. You never know until you ask.

Guarding Against Falls

The event that could take you out of your home faster than anything else would be if you were to fall and sustain injury. Unfortunately, it happens every day. Don't let it happen to you.

Margie Lange, RN, MSN, presents insightful information in Home Healthcare Nurse, vol. 14, no. 3. Approximately two-thirds of accidents among the elderly are falls; they are the largest single cause of death due to injury. Annually, approximately 30 percent of older adults fall, and 20 to 30 percent of those who fall incur moderate to severe injuries leading to loss of mobility and independence and to a higher risk of death. Isolated elders are at greater risk, and so are those who are sick and have reduced mobility. It gets worse as you get older. Persons aged 80 years and older are *eight* times more likely to die from falls than those 60 and younger. And those who experience one fall often experience repeated falls. Being in a nursing home is no sure protection either; 43 to 68 percent of nursing home patients fall more than once.

After the first serious fall, a downward spiral begins. The older person becomes less active, less independent, and less confident. Inactivity leads to joint stiffness, muscle weakness, and the probability of another fall. A rib fracture may put an older patient on a ventilator, resulting in pneumonia. High-risk factors are being a woman over 75 or incurring a stroke or a respiratory disorder.

What throws us off our guard is that we have done the same things without a problem all of our lives. We have climbed ladders, gone upstairs to the bedroom or down to the basement, walked across the throw rug, taken baths, and so on. These everyday events have not changed. What is the problem? It is that we are changing, slowly but surely. I do not know of anyone who is growing younger. What we must do is grow smarter. That means we must do some things more safely and relinquish doing other things altogether, or get someone else to do them for us.

Partial Checklist to Prevent Falls

LIGHTING

- An aging adult needs, on average, about three times the light that a young person needs. Make sure the lights both inside and outside your house are numerous and bright enough.
- Keep flashlights in every room.
- Put some lights on automatic timers or photoelectric cells or motion sensors.
- Keep small lamps or strong night lights working all night between your bed and the toilet, or install sound- or motion-sensor switches. What do a few cents of electricity matter when your safety and future happiness are concerned?

MEDICATIONS AND ALCOHOL

- Some medications cause drowsiness, and elders tend to become overmedicated, sometimes making mistakes in their dosage.
- Alcohol also causes drowsiness. The amount of alcohol we *actually* drink is often more than we *think* we drink.

FOOTWEAR AND WALKERS

- Are your favorite house slippers ready to be replaced? Get footwear with firm soles that will support you, and without heels that could cause a fall. They should fit without falling off when you are using stairways.
- "An Analysis of Risk Assessment Tools for Falls in the Elderly," appearing in *Home Healthcare Nurse*, vol. 16, no. 9, showed that of the patients who fell, 70 percent had been using assistance devices, mainly walkers. Do we become overconfident? Do we not use those devices correctly? Ask a physical therapist to advise you. Frequent fallers can request training on how to fall more safely.

ASSISTANCE DEVICES

- There is a whole industry selling assistance devices that make it easier for older people to walk, bathe, eat, and toilet. A specialty store clerk or a social worker at your senior center can make suggestions. Durable medical equipment for use at home can be covered by Medicare when prescribed by a medical doctor.

CORDS AND LINES

- Keep electric cords and phone lines well out of the way.

FURNITURE ARRANGEMENT

- We all accumulate lots of possessions during our lives. Don't let them throw you! Keep walkways free of clutter and much wider than you need. Could you pass comfortably through the halls and rooms of your home if you had to use a walker?
- Are chairs unstable, beds too high, or floors too slippery?

- If you have more furniture than your need, for example, pieces that have not been used in the last year, call the Salvation Army or Goodwill to pick them up. There are plenty of men and women who could use some furniture and cannot afford new purchases. It is great to recycle, and it is nice to know that someone is benefiting from your surplus. In addition, you will have simplified your life. You are not losing something; you are gaining safety and freedom.
- If carpets are wrinkling, have them stretched and nailed down. Get rid of all scatter rugs.

BATHROOM

- Nearly 90 percent of all major injuries for all age groups occur in the home, mostly in the bathroom.
- Install enough grab bars and antislip material in your shower and tub areas. Towel bars are not substitutes for grab bars. The safest way to bathe is by sitting on a plastic stool in the tub or shower and using a flexible-hose shower spray. Liquid soap or soap-on-a-rope prevents the problem of falling bars of soap.
- Grab-bar stands on either side of your toilet can be a great help in getting up and down. Also, consider getting a high-rise toilet seat. The extra height helps you to avoid knee strain and falls. (Grab bars, in general, are not covered by Medicare.)
- More than one older person avoids potentially dangerous nighttime walks to the toilet by keeping a commode or portable urinal beside the bed—not a bad idea.
- Faucet handles can be replaced with single-lever handles or foot-pedal faucets.

STAIR STEPS

- Use nonskid materials on all steps. For outside concrete or brick steps and walks, attach the nonskid material using double-sided tape that is made for laying outdoor carpets around swimming pools. It is easy to use and, later, to remove, and it works better than glue.
- Install handrails beside all steps and stairways, inside and out.

Be sure that they extend the full length of the stairs and beyond the steps.

LADDERS

- Treat ladders with the respect they deserve. Use common sense and caution. If you keep everything you need at levels that can be reached by standing on the floor, then you won't need to use a ladder very often.
- Install long-life light bulbs. When you need to change a ceiling bulb, if you are at all unsure of yourself, ask a neighbor to help you.
- You may think that you can continue to use ladders—until the last time. Make yesterday your last time.

Fire

Fire is another danger that can shorten your life. Install smoke alarms. Test them to be sure they can awaken you. Replace with fresh batteries at the same time each year, for example, every Labor Day. Keep a flashlight near your bed and a telephone programmed to call 911 at the touch of one button. Ask your local fire department for advice. It might send a firefighter to survey your home and advise you without cost.

A fire extinguisher in the kitchen is a must. Get someone to show you how to use it. Also, anytime you turn on a stove burner and leave the room, even for a minute, set a timer alarm to remind you. A woman I know has burnt up several teakettles while watching TV in the living room "just until the water boils." She would be well advised to acquire a whistling teakettle. As a security measure, consider placing fire extinguishers in areas near heating equipment such as dryers or electric motors (but not so near that a fire in such equipment would block your access to an extinguisher). Also, put an extinguisher in your bedroom that you can carry to a fire site.

Avoid extension cords. Be sure your electric cord is rated for heavy duty if used with an iron or electric space heater or frying pan. Avoid having furniture legs rest on electric cords.

Security

Here is where your local police can help. Ask them to send someone to inspect your home for security against entry. Or simply hire a carpenter knowledgeable in this field. Install or replace any locks as suggested. Install a security system if it will make you feel more at ease.

Burglars hate to be observed. Therefore, keep the shrubs trimmed near first-floor windows and doors, and keep tree limbs pruned away from second-floor windows. Plant thorny bushes near windows and/or install gravel paths that make footsteps audible. Have enough outside lights on a timer or a motion sensor, and be sure there are enough lights and located in a way to avoid creating a shadowy hiding area for a burglar. Inside, vary the time that lights go on in different rooms, and keep a radio playing and shades drawn when absent in the evening. Make an agreement with neighbors to report suspicious activity in the area. Get advice from police on building a community watch program. To make it easier for emergency vehicles to locate you, fasten reflective house numbers on the front and back of the house, and install a flashing "911 Locator" light on the front porch.

Communication Equipment

An intercom system is a handy way of calling your housemate to come take a phone call or sit down to dinner. It can be a reassuring device to check on someone who is bedridden or prone to falling. Some people use the monitors often bought for infants' rooms.

Telephone instruments are cheap. Have enough so that you do not have to run to answer one. Extra telephone jacks are easily installed. In addition to having phones in the kitchen and next to your favorite chair, put one in the bathroom and one in the basement. If you are expecting a call, take a cordless telephone outside while working in your garden. It beats running into the house and risking an accident. A mobile phone is a good investment, too, especially if you drive your own car. In an emergency you can get help.

If your adult children have expressed worry about your health or safety, install a telephone answering machine for their sakes. You, personally, may prefer not to use answering machines. But look at it from the viewpoint of your family, friends, and caregivers. It saves worry. (If you are home all of the time it may not be needed.)

When you expect to be away from home for a longer period than usual, your children would appreciate a phone call alerting them to your plans. I remember telephoning my mother, living three hours distant, countless times one evening. There was no answer. Worried, I started calling her friends, one by one, and finally learned that she was happily playing cards. (This was at 11:00 P.M. when she was 88 years old.) My mother could have called to tell me of her plans; she could, if necessary, have left her message on my answering machine.

Ask your neighbors and friends if you may give their home phone numbers to your children and caregivers. It can be a comfort—and a help. If you would benefit by a personal emergency response system (PERS), described in Chapter Eight, but cannot pay the monthly monitoring fee, ask your children to consider paying it as a continuing Mother's/Father's Day gift to you.

Maintenance and Cleaning Schedule

When my home is neat, clean, and orderly, I am more contented and at peace. I can think and work better. When my wife is on a trip, I become messy for a few days and then cannot stand it any longer. One's tolerance for a messy house is strictly an individual thing. Whenever I visit some aging adults' homes, they invariably say, "Please excuse the appearance; I just did not feel like dusting." One aging adult does not like to invite friends to lunch because they might look in her cupboards and she would be embarrassed. If the condition of your home really bothers you or prevents you from entertaining friends, do something about it.

Get rid of clothing and other items you have not used in one year. If neighbors are planning a garage sale, ask if you may add your items. Set up a housecleaning schedule. Not everything has to be done at once; spread housework throughout the year. Decide what you can do and want to do by yourself and what you should hire someone else to do. Get your carpets and upholstery cleaned when there are price specials. Isn't it worth parting with a few dollars if the return is an improved outlook and enjoyment in the place where you spend the most time?

If you are the one in the house who takes care of home maintenance, you will be doing your mate a big favor by putting the year-long schedule in writing while you are able. Instruct your mate where the water and gas shutoff valves are located, label the fuse box or circuit breakers, show how the fireplace works, and keep a list of service people such as plumbers and electricians. Both of you should learn how to live alone while still living together. A recommended how-to book is *Renovating Woman* by Allegra Bennett.

Transportation

According to some people, the greatest tragedy second to the loss of a mate is the loss of your driver's license. When you are able to drive yourself to the supermarket, to the doctor's office, and to volunteer at the school or to play bridge or mahjong, your quality of life is higher and you require fewer services. The more independence you give up, the greater is the likelihood that your quality of life will suffer and that you will spend more of your own (or others') money on your increased need for care. The ability to drive safely helps you to remain active and in a potential caregiving role for others. It postpones the time when you yourself must assume the role of a care receiver.

Contrary to what you may think, statistics show that older drivers have fewer highway crashes than younger drivers. And after about age 65 there is almost no change in the crash rate as we age. (State Farm Insurance Company offers a lower premium to drivers when they reach age 65 because the company knows older persons drive with more care.) The problem is that some older drivers give up driving too readily, having lost confidence simply because of their accumulating years, while others continue driving in a dangerous manner, unaware of their bad habits.

It would be nice if there were some way to obtain an objective driving assessment without the pressure of state driver's licensing examiners. For that reason, the National Highway Traffic Safety Administration has started a pilot project for older drivers in Florida.

Maryland and California have similar projects sponsored by other organizations. These programs consist of classroom refresher courses, computer-assisted vision assessments, and eye exercises to improve hand-eye coordination and other driving skills. Don't stop driving without such an assessment. Where functional disabilities have made it necessary to give up your license, counseling is provided on how to get around without driving. If your mate is driving dangerously, suggest an evaluation and/or a driving refresher course. Get an update on accident prevention by taking the AARP-sponsored driving course "55 Alive."

If your car is not reliable, replace it with one you can always depend on. You deserve it. (A larger car, while more expensive to operate, offers greater protection in a crash.) If you would like to know more about maintaining your car and selecting a repair shop, take a course at your community college or attend a lecture at the senior center. Finally, if you quit driving, don't stay home if you enjoy going out. Remain mobile and vital. Find out which neighbors or friends are willing to give you rides. Of course, you will compensate that person or persons generously each time, more than merely the cost of gas consumption. However, be careful of jeopardizing the driver's insurance coverage through cash payments, which put you into a commercial relationship with the driver. Instead, buy lunch or a gift, unless the driver is willing to receive cash. Keep a good thing going! By comparison, just think what a taxi would have cost. (Your area may use senior citizen taxi scrip, which is somewhat cheaper.) Be ready at the agreed time and don't load on extra destinations not mentioned in advance.

Your local community is the source of information for buses and special vans. They will come right to your door and take you to the doctor or supermarket if you have a qualifying disability. The cost is small. Also, seniors get special discounts on regular buses. Volunteer drivers will take you in their own cars to scheduled medical therapy appointments. Contact your hospital or area agency on aging office.

Mealtimes

Some older adults routinely eat just twice a day. They need less and enjoy cutting down on food preparation and cleanup time. Nutritionists advise that small, nutritious snacks between meals are a good way to go. They help maintain our energy and are easy to digest.

If you cannot cook, look into Meals on Wheels or ask if your neighbor would be willing to prepare one extra portion per day of lunch or dinner for pay. If you are alone and mobile, eat your main meal out at a restaurant or senior center for variety. Breakfast can be something simple at home, depending on your ability and interests. If you put leftovers in the refrigerator, attach a sticker giving the date. This will help you in cleaning out the refrigerator and in avoiding a possible illness from old food.

Ask a neighbor or friend to take you along to the grocery store when he or she regularly goes, that is, without making an extra trip. If you cannot get out, ask the friend to shop for you. Be sure to make a written list, give money in advance, and don't complain if a brand purchased for you is not your preferred brand. Investigate possible volunteer programs that will do your shopping for you and deliver it. Some grocery stores will take your telephone order and deliver for a fee. In my area, a company working from its own warehouse delivers grocery orders over $75 free. This is a fast-growing business nation-wide. An online offering at **http://peapod.com** also provides shopping and delivery. Some personal services companies, in addition to delivering groceries, will pick up dry cleaning, take your cat to the vet, move you to a new address, or house-sit.

Elders sometimes lose their senses of taste and smell and, therefore, their interest in food. Also, being lonely and eating alone is no fun. A good custom, enjoyed by all, is to invite a friend to eat lunch or dinner with you in a restaurant. Restaurants often offer "early bird" dinners at considerably reduced prices. Your friend will gladly drive if you do not drive. Dining out in this way accomplishes several purposes. You can repay favors. It is fun to experience new restaurants and new menus. You will have a nutritious meal. It is a social time and gets you both out into the world. "Why should I pay for my friend's lunch?" you may ask. You can work out the financial arrangement appropriate to the situation. The point to be made here is that a little generosity and thoughtfulness will be repaid in the long run.

Too many Depression-raised older people, in my opinion, are overly worried that their money will run out before their days are done, and are, frankly, stingy. Take a chance occasionally and enjoy yourself. If you cannot afford a restaurant, make sandwiches and invite your friend to your home. If your friends are unavailable, take a picnic lunch and eat it in the park with the squirrels, birds, and fresh air.

Heating and Cooling

Every summer we read of senior citizens dying from heat exhaustion. And in the winter some live all bundled up in cold rooms to save on heating costs. As we age, our bodies do not handle heat extremes as well as before. (Babies have the same problem.) Is your thermostat easy to read? Does your house need insulation?

If you live in a hot area, install an air conditioner in one room at least. It could save your life. If you have no cool room to escape to, get a large fan, drink plenty of liquids, and eat smaller meals. (An exercise enthusiast advised me that if I wait until I feel thirsty before drinking water, I have waited too long. Drink your eight glasses a day as a regular routine.) Ask your neighbor to check on you during days of extreme heat.

In preparation for winter, have your furnace checked for operating efficiency, especially if you use gas. A utility bill averaging plan can minimize the difference in payments between summer and winter bills. If you cannot pay heating bills, apply to your local area agency on aging for help. Or ask your children to pay the winter heating bills as a Christmas present; you did it for them. If, during a cold wave, all else fails, move into a motel or move in with friends. Swallow your pride and tell them, "I am cold and don't know if I can survive."

Pets

It is a fact. People do better if they keep household pets. Midland Life Insurance Company has recently started giving up to an 8 percent discount on life insurance premiums for pet owners. Dr. James Lynch of the University of Maryland showed that people live longer after a myocardial infarction (heart attack) if they have a pet than if they do not have a pet. The presence of a friendly animal can decrease one's blood pressure. People who have service dogs testify to the worth of these excellent animals, who are trained to help their owners live independently and with a higher quality of life,

Even if you are not ill, it surely is comforting to return home to find your pet faithfully waiting. A pet gives you a living creature to talk to and care for. It focuses you outside yourself, whereas being too inwardly focused tends to cause depression and anxiety.

Some people believe that a basic sensitivity to animals and to the natural world makes them better prepared to base decisions on a larger picture. A view that includes only human interests is narrow and may be dangerous.

It is worth the expense to keep a pet even if you have to fence in your yard or hire the neighbor's child to walk it. If you cannot pay the full cost of veterinary services, tell your veterinarian you need a discount or an extended payment plan. Recycle a pet from the local pound, after checking it out first with the vet. In the case of a dog, if you intend to take it outside and can afford the cost, have it obedience-trained for you by a professional trainer. Or, if you are up to it, go with your dog to training classes and train it yourself. If you want some of the benefits of a pet without much responsibility, ask your neighbors if you may borrow their bird, cat, or dog when they are away, or walk their dog on a regular basis. All will benefit.

Neighbors

As we age, we find it increasingly difficult to take care of ourselves and our homes in the manner to which we have been accustomed. A friendly, helpful neighbor can make all the difference in the world and can be an important asset in sustaining the quality of our lives. A good neighbor will watch out for us and check in occasionally, do some grocery shopping, receive our express and oversized mail when we are absent, bring over some chicken soup when we cannot cook, replace a hard-to-reach light bulb, cut our grass, and perform a host of other thoughtful services. Just the act of sitting and listening to us when we are lonely or troubled is a very valuable contribution and is one that we can reciprocate.

If you are not now on the best of terms with your neighbors, there is still time. If there is a problem, focus on the problem, not the person responsible. Reread the suggestions on communication in Chapter Eight. Take over some cookies or invite your neighbors to tea. Act by the Golden Rule. Helpful neighbors are potential lifesavers. Just because their pet dug up your tulip bulbs is insufficient reason not to cultivate and nurture your relationship. Put a proper perspective on what is important and valuable in your life.

Most people really do want to be helpful. Try to remember several favors done for you. I think you will find it easier to remember favors you did for others. Strangely, it seems that giving makes a more lasting impression on us than receiving.

Some people are not good at receiving help. However, it is wrong to continue the habit of automatically rejecting favors offered. It tells the other people that what they can offer is of insufficient value to us. In fact, it puts them down. You thought you were doing them a favor by not accepting; you did not want to "impose." Don't ask yourself, "Did they really mean it?" Take them at their word!

Sometimes I accept a favor I do not really need or could easily do myself. My purpose is to recognize and appreciate the offerer. It builds good relationships. Try it. You won't be sorry. Of course, you, also, must act like a good neighbor yourself. Peace be with you—and your neighborhood!

Area Agencies on Aging

The Older Americans Act of 1965 is the umbrella for a system of in-home and community services enabling older men and women to maintain their independence and their dignity. Services are administered through a national network of 670 Area Agencies on Aging, usually a part of a city or county government, a regional planning organization, or a private nonprofit agency. The names of these agencies may vary somewhat. Some of the services mentioned in this chapter fall under their jurisdiction. Look for "Senior Information and Assistance" or related listings in directories, or telephone Elder Care Locator, 800-677-1116, to learn the telephone numbers of appropriate agencies in your local area.

Home Helpers and Visiting Nurses

The director of an in-home care service offers the following advice: "Most people we serve tend to wait until the very last moment before asking for help or before making a move to an assisted-living or nursing care facility. We encourage you to research your options before a crisis occurs." Begin now to collect useful information, agencies, and telephone numbers. Some local, free publications contain directories of available resources and articles on how to live at home, or how to move.

If you finally come to the point that you must have outside help in order to live, you will have joined a large club. Sooner or later almost everyone comes to this point. You will not be alone. There are 34 million people age 65 or over. Seventeen percent of them need help with everyday activities such as bathing, shopping, and cooking. Some reluctantly leave their homes; others dig in and accept help.

Understand the terminology so that you may communicate effectively with the local agency on aging and care providers. Activities of Daily Living (ADLs) are bathing, dressing, toileting, eating, and moving in and out of a bed or chair. Instrumental Activities of Daily Living (IADLs) are cleaning, cooking, laundry, and housekeeping.

If you want housekeeping help, ask for referrals from people you can trust, for example, friends, fellow worshippers, neighbors, and senior centers. Advice on hiring help is free from your area agency on aging office. Special help programs are available for low-income households. One such program is called CHORE and provides in-home services for people who might otherwise be in nursing homes. As a last resort place a newspaper ad. Interview carefully, asking about training, past work experiences, and whether or not there is a backup person available. Check references; checking on candidates' honesty and reliability is essential. Get the phone number, address, driver's license, and Social Security number of the person you hire. Put in writing and in priority order the duties you expect done. Nothing is more demoralizing and destructive of good relations than: "You didn't tell me to do that." "Yes, I did tell you."

If there are several acceptable candidates, pay each one to spend a day with you, and then choose the one you like best. Make it clear that the first month is a trial period on both sides, after which a decision will be made whether or not to continue. Be gracious. Avoid nitpicking. In an assertive but nonaggressive way express your satisfaction and dissatisfaction. But remember, the job that is done will never be as perfect as when you used to do it yourself.

At a minimum, a bath aide is a good way to start. Bathing is potentially dangerous because of the possibility of a fall. It is therapeutic to have someone bathe you and give a shampoo. You may be more comfortable with a trained stranger doing this than with any of your own children. It is not uncommon for a bath aide to do a few household chores to round out one or two hours' work.

Nurses, physical therapists, and social workers can also be employed by you. Medicare will pay for their service if the doctor has ordered it. Otherwise, you pay, unless your insurance covers it. If your financial resources are tight, you might try to hire those helpers directly. Going through an agency can easily double the cost. But remember that your direct hire could call in sick, whereas the Visiting Nurse Association would always have someone to send. Also, if you hire someone directly on a long-term basis, you could be liable for paying Social Security taxes and for withholding income tax.

Neighborhood-Based Programs

A variety of neighborhood programs exist so that the elderly can postpone or avoid going into nursing homes. The Block Nurse Program of St. Paul, Minnesota, sends nurses to regularly visit the elderly who live in the same neighborhoods as the nurses. A similar program supplies volunteers to run errands and do housework for the elderly. Some services will check by telephone on whether or not medications have been taken. For seniors in crisis, the Geriatric Regional Assessment Team (GRAT) is a service available in some communities. A team of registered nurses, geriatric mental health specialists, occupational therapists, and psychiatrists—who together specialize in crisis assessment and intervention—are available to visit, determine needs, and find remedies. Anyone may initiate the phone call.

Builders' associations in cities and counties build free wheelchair ramps for low-income, wheelchair-bound persons to get to and from their homes. Churches, synagogues, mosques, temples, and social service agencies create volunteer networks that currently serve a million older persons. The federal government funds the Corporation for National Service, which employs Senior Companions to do chores for seniors and the homebound. These services are cost effective, since isolated older people are less healthy and use more medical care than older people who are socially engaged.

Adult Day Services

Centers are available in many communities to care for adults during the day. In this case you must go, or be taken, to the center. Inquire about transportation by calling local community services and agencies. This option is especially useful for adult working children when elderly parents who are living with them require some food service and care during the day. Also, if you need help caring for a spouse or roommate, having that person attend a center during the day will give you a rest. Adult day services are called the direction of the future for delaying placement in a nursing home.

"Rescue Alice" Project

Here is an actual story of getting temporary help for four weeks at no financial outlay. My widowed mother, Alice, then 89 years old and living alone three hours distant from me, fell and incurred multiple hairline fractures in her pelvic bone. She could not leave the house and had to move about with a walker, in great pain. The most comfortable thing for her was to sit and be waited on. This, of course, required help. Being the stubborn person she is, she would not consider hiring outside help, particularly someone she did not personally know. But the need was urgent.

I knew Mother had lots of bridge friends, all 10 to 20 years younger. I called eight women and explained the problem; no one refused to help or made excuses. The result was a four-week program in which one friend visited on the same day and at the same time each week. Often they would choose mealtimes and bring enough food for both of them. Others visited and left prepared food to be eaten later. I remember that one recent widow chose Sunday, usually a difficult day to be alone or to get help, and always came with a wonderful taste treat. The eighth woman could not visit but telephoned mother every morning to check on her and to chat.

After obtaining their concurrence, I mailed copies of the schedule to all eight people and listed all telephone numbers, including my own. No one missed her turn. Some phoned in advance to bring mother's grocery order. Others did the laundry. Toward the end I sent thank-you letters, making clear that the project had officially terminated. I did not want her friends to think that we would abuse our agreement and continue indefinitely. If mother needed help after that, we would just have to hire it. In fact, she was then able to manage by herself.

One woman, having gotten into the routine and enjoying it, continued coming for a year after the project ended. Then she joined with two others to form a regular Saturday bridge-playing group at my mother's home, enabling Mother to get back into playing bridge again but from the comfort of her own home.

Mother is able to go out again, and we had a thank-you lunch for the "girls" at a local restaurant. Don't underestimate the generosity of friends and neighbors when you need help. But you must be willing to request it, state clearly what you need, and accept with gratitude.

Reassembling

When I was growing up we did not know what "reassembling" meant. Young people stayed at home until they got married or became financially independent. Then they left to establish their own homes and never lived with their parents again. Now we have the phenomenon of formerly separated family members getting back together under one roof. In 1980, 48 percent of people 18 to 24 years old lived at home; by 1995 that figure had risen to 53 percent. Among people 24 to 34 years old, the percentage increased from 9 to 12 percent; that is a 33 percent rise! Such arrangements can make good sense if all parties are happy about them.

Problems arise when expectations are not discussed in advance. For instance, you could have a situation where junior has moved back in with his girlfriend and her teenage son—the stay has lasted well beyond what you expected, rooms are messy, music is loud, and hours are different. There is too much coming and going, and no one has contributed a dime toward groceries and utilities or lifted a hand to help. This is a worst-case scenario, but it does happen. Good relationships need structure.

You could suggest reassembling for a number of good reasons: You want to share your large home. You need to have a live-in handyman/woman and chauffeur. You want supplemental income. You are lonely. You want to improve your children's life. You need security. You want to see your grandchildren more often. You would like someone to do the cooking and housekeeping. You need help in caring for an ill or disabled person.

AN INTELLIGENT APPROACH TO REASSEMBLING

- First, make a list of your conditions, including length of stay; financial arrangements for rent, groceries, telephone, and utilities; use of rooms; use of cars and other property; quiet hours; quiet places; meal times; menus; division of housework; pets; and so forth.
- Second, decide which conditions are not negotiable; that is, decide what situations you could not tolerate, no matter what.
- Third, present your proposal. Be flexible and reasonable. Make compromises on less-important points. Put the agreed conditions in writing and give each person a copy. You may be embarrassed to do this, but I guarantee that, otherwise, a misunderstanding will occur later.
- Fourth, discuss problems in a nonthreatening way as they arise, and seek solutions.

- Fifth, set a trial period of a couple of months, after which time either side can cancel with no reasons or excuses necessary. For example, "It's just not working out as I had thought" is reason enough.
- Sixth, if you decide not to continue the arrangement, allow a preset period of three weeks for your relatives to find another place and move out.

Taking In a Housemate

For any of the benefits mentioned above, or for other reasons, it may be beneficial to you to take in a housemate who is not a family member. The same conditions as for relatives would apply. (If the reason is romance, clear thinking is especially needed and, unfortunately, sometimes not available.)

In the case of a housemate, you have the option of specifying your needs. For example, you may need a handyperson, nurse, musician, or reader of stories. A variation on this is to hire someone to live in for a temporary period, perhaps during your recuperation from a stroke or surgery.

Again, sources of referrals are health care associations, senior centers, places of worship, schools, friends, associations, and, lastly, newspaper ads. For a second opinion, invite a friend to interview prospects with you. Require and check references. Put expected duties and compensation in writing. Experts say that, after about six months in close proximity, it is not unusual for live-in help and the employer to grate on each other. A change, then, may be good for both sides.

Is there anything better than living in your own home? Do everything within your power now to make it possible to continue the joy of living there as long as you can. By acting now, before an adult child or someone else suggests it, you will be showing yourself and the world that you are still capable of making decisions and taking action for your own secure future.

If we want things to stay as they are, things will have to change.
—GIUSEPPE TOMASI DI LAMPEDUSA, THE LEOPARD

185

Out of intense complexities intense simplicities emerge.

WINSTON CHURCHILL

CHAPTER ELEVEN

Understand Your Financial
and Legal Options

THIS CHAPTER FOCUSES on controlling your assets to your best advantage, passing them to your heirs or charities in an effective manner, and making health care decisions now to be ready for whatever the future holds.

Financial Planning

America badly needs a boost in private retirement savings. The 1997 update of the Merrill Lynch *Baby Boom Retirement Index* (prepared at Stanford University) showed that baby boomers as a group are saving at only 38.5 percent of the rate needed to maintain their standard of living in retirement. Only about half of U.S. workers have pension coverage.

Prime timers require less risky investments than when they were younger and could expect a future of employment earnings. However, this does not mean that all savings should simply be banked in ordinary savings accounts. If inflation is only 3 percent annually, in 10 years it will cost 40 percent more to enjoy your current standard of living. Assets that do not grow with inflation are high risk in the long term. Stock ownership is not just for the wealthy. Forty-three percent of American adults now own stock and/or mutual funds. There is a right combination of security and earnings to safeguard your future.

Free basic financial-planning advice is available at your bank, an investment brokerage, and senior centers. Or engage a paid financial planner for good advice tailored to your exact situation. About 250,000 people call themselves financial planners. There are differences. A Certified Financial Planner (CFP) must pass a tough 10-hour exam and abide by a code of ethics. A Personal Financial Specialist (PFS) is a Certified Public Accountant with financial planning training. The PFS must pass an exam and have at least three years of personal finance experience. Members of the National Association of Personal Financial Advisors (NAPFA) are fee-only planners with at least three years of financial planning experience. They take 60 hours of continuing education every two years. Lastly, there is a Licensed Independent Network of CPA fee-only Financial Planners (LINC). If you find your routine financial, legal, and medical paperwork to be a big headache, you may hire a company to manage this for you. Be sure to interview the service provider, compare prices, and check with other clients.

Some seniors transfer legal ownership of their homes and other assets to their children. (Warning! Capital gains taxes could apply since gifts are not the same as inherited assets.) This might work well in some cases. However, doing so could result in a feeling of powerlessness, loss of control, and other negative emotions. Also, older people may be viewed as of less importance and even find themselves "invisible" when they are without control of their assets and themselves.

The Gender Gap in Retirement Investment

The U.S. General Accounting Office reported in 1996: "[W]omen tend to invest their pension funds in safer and lower-yield assets than do men." Since stocks historically generate higher annual rates of return (about 10 percent) than bonds (about 5 percent), savings accounts, certificates of deposit, or even real estate, women end up with considerably smaller assets. America's 60 million working women earn more than a trillion dollars in total. Those women who save put away 1.5 percent of their income on average whereas men save 3 percent. For both sexes this is well short of the 10 to 15 percent savings level recommended by financial advisers. Women are less likely to have retirement savings or a pension than are men. One third of women say that they are depending on their husbands to do their saving for them.

When a marriage breaks up, the woman's net worth drops an average of 43 percent while the man's goes up an average of 23 percent. *Working Woman* magazine found that 80 percent of widows now living in poverty were not poor when their husbands were alive.

Barbara Stanny, the millionaire daughter of the co-founder of H & R Block, said that the only advice her father gave her about money was, "Don't worry." Using that advice, at one point in her life she found that she was broke. Eventually, she divorced and began managing her own money. Stanny has written a book, *Prince Charming Isn't Coming: How Women Get Smart About Money.* She advises: "Each day, read something about finances. Each week, have at least one conversation with someone who knows more about money than you do. Every month, transfer money from checking to savings, where you are less inclined to withdraw it." Men, also, can profit from this advice.

Telemarketers and Scams

The median net worth of older households in the USA is $86,000, a figure much higher than the net worth of younger households. Americans lose $40 billion a year to con artists, and more than half the victims are 50 years or older, according to the National Consumers League (NCL). The chief weapon used by thieves: the telephone. Research by the NCL and Los Angeles County consumer officials found that the reasons older people are vulnerable to fraud are that older people tend to be polite and curious, and they give others the benefit of the doubt.

From a flyer in the mail or a telephone call, there is no way you are going to receive something of value for nothing. If not interested, simply say so up front and promptly hang up without waiting for a reaction. If interested, have the caller mail information to be studied by you at your leisure. If they will not provide this courtesy, regard them with suspicion. Do not make financial commitments based only on telephone conversations. The Telephone Consumer Protection Act of 1991 requires companies to cease calling you for a period of 10 years if you ask to be put on their do-not-call list. Simply say, "Please put me on your do-not-call list." You are entitled to receive $500 for each violation.

Selling Your Home and Assets

The time may come when it makes good sense to sell your home and major assets. This would be true if you are moving from independent to group living, if you simply need additional funds for one reason or another, or if you decide to scale down. (Remember that, in selling your home, you and your spouse may now keep all of the profit tax-free up to $500,000 and that this exclusion may occur every two years.) If you are considering such a move but have not talked about this with an estate lawyer, an adult child, or a good friend, do so now. A sounding board will help to confirm your thinking or cause you to look for another way. Sometimes simply hearing your own words said aloud to another will cause you to see something in your plan that you had not previously seen.

If you have dealt happily with a real estate agent in the past, it makes sense to use that person again. However, obtain the opinions of one or two other agents to confirm your findings on value, marketability, and timing. Begin early to make your home appear appealing to potential buyers. Cut down on belongings, clean out closets, basement, and garage so that buyers can see the house, not the clutter. Put your yard in good shape even if you have to hire someone. Many buyers will not even enter a house that does not have good street appeal. Remodeling a kitchen or bath is usually not worth the effort and cost, but a coat of neutral paint makes a home appear clean, fresh, and ready to live in.

Reverse Mortgages

The federal government realizes that many elderly Americans cannot live adequately on their Social Security pensions. Therefore, reverse mortgages were created to enable people to mortgage their homes in return for a lump sum payment and/or a monthly income. Generally, both spouses must be age 62 or older and have a fully owned residence or one with a low remaining mortgage balance. Applicants do not have to meet employment or income qualifications. Reasons for wanting a reverse mortgage include the need for supplemental income, home repair, property taxes, insurance, health care, travel, debt repayment, or to help out family members. If both spouses have to move into nursing homes, the reverse mortgage ends. If one spouse continues to live at home, the mortgage remains in effect. Sixty percent of reverse-mortgage borrowers are women living alone, and 12 percent are men living alone.

You continue to live in your home until you die or move out. Then the home is sold and costs settled. If any money is left, it goes to you or your estate. You may end the loan at any time by paying it off; there is no penalty. You pay no income tax on the loan income, and it does not affect Social Security or Medicare. (It could affect Medicaid.) Moreover, if you choose lifetime payments and outlive what the actuarial tables say is your life expectancy, you could actually receive more total income than the evaluation of your home. You will not be kicked out.

Some unscrupulous salespeople are pushing seniors to borrow lump sums through reverse mortgages to invest in annuities, for which the salespeople get paid commissions. It is best to make inquiries to the FHA (Federal Housing Administration, 800-569-4287) for its "Home Equity Conversion Mortgage," which, also, is federally insured. Or contact Fannie Mae (800-732-6643), the congressionally chartered company that offers the "Home Keeper Mortgage." Rates are competitive. You may eventually do business with a different company. Free counseling is available locally. Contact your banker or your senior assistance officer.

A variation is the deferred payment loan, for which your home's equity is used as credit, allowing you to draw cash as needed. Still another variation is the sale-leaseback, in which your home is sold, but you retain the right to continue living in it for the rest of your life.

Cash and Viatical Settlements on Insurance

If you have life insurance on yourself, there is a cash value to it, even if it is not fully paid. ("Term" life insurance is an exception to this.) You may cash in your policy, which effectively cancels your insurance. In my opinion, continuing to pay premiums on life insurance when there are no minor or disabled children is rarely the best use of your money, unless you view it simply as a burial policy for yourself or a mechanism for your heirs to pay inheritance taxes when you are gone.

You may, instead, designate as beneficiary of your policy a viatical settlement company, which will pay you a lesser cash amount now and collect the face value of the policy when you die. (*Viatical* is Latin for "provision for the journey.") A new law in effect from 1997 makes viatical settlements tax-free for ailing people with life expectancies of 24 months or less or who meet specific criteria covering chronic illness. Consult your insurance agent or financial planner.

Beware of the sales practice known as "churning," in which an agent sells you new or additional life insurance and drains the cash value of your original policy to pay for it, pocketing a huge commission in the process. A replacement policy may sound good, but later on there will be lost benefits and negative tax consequences.

Spousal Impoverishment Provision

A person does not want to be forced to sell the family home to pay for nursing home costs of a seriously ill spouse. A current provision of Medicaid allows differing levels of assets and income for each member of a married couple. This provision allows the "home spouse" a relatively generous income and retention of considerable assets. At the same time, the spouse in the nursing home qualifies for Medicaid benefits because of low assets and income. State legislatures are permitted to increase federally set levels up to certain financial limits. Welfare reform is changing current regulations in this area.

Charity Begins at Home

Suppose you have little of value to sell, but you need money to live. Is it wrong to ask your adult children to consider contributing to your livelihood, just as you provided for their childhood? I believe not, if all of your life you yourself have been a good example of modest living, good health habits, saving, and frugality. Call a family conference to explain your needs, either in dollars or in services. These could be one-time payments for home improvement or monthly income for the rest of your life. Explain that by comparison the financial need might be even greater if you were to have to move into a nursing home.

Include distant children as well as nearby children. Find out how much each child can contribute in money or in help. Afterwards, send copies of the agreement to all, along with your gratitude. In most countries of the world, families band together to help each other. Americans in the twentieth century have come to put themselves first to the detriment of the extended family. Remember, another word for charity is "love." Consider also, however, that if your children are financially hard-pressed and/or just not accustomed to giving, they may advise you to spend down and go on the public dole.

A word about lending money to family members. Some people believe that they can treat their creditor relatives or friends less well than their bankers. If a family member or friend wants to borrow $100 or more, and if you can afford to part with your savings without hurting your living style, get the loan in writing with signatures and a repayment schedule. (If the would-be borrower has a history of unpaid debts, say from the start with no reasons given: "I cannot afford it.") If the loan is to be $1000 or more, or is for the purpose of the borrower's business investment, consider getting advice from a financial planner and a lawyer. Absolutely refuse to extend a second loan to the same person until the first is repaid. You will not be doing your relative or friend a favor if you permit financial irresponsibility. And, you will ruin your relationship. Shakespeare said it: "Neither a borrower nor a lender be."

Social Security

About 44 million Americans now receive Social Security benefits. These benefits are the primary source of income for 66 percent of elderly Americans. The retirement of 77 million baby boomers starting in 2012 will severely strain the system. You are entitled to receive from the federal government monthly Social Security retirement benefits at the age of 62 or 65 if you have earned them, or at the age of 65 if you are the spouse of one who was covered. As we are living longer, these qualifying ages are going to rise. Social Security and Medicare are very important benefits. Try to qualify even if you have to take temporary work to do so. Contact your local District Office of the U.S. Social Security Administration for answers to your questions. I have found my District Office to be helpful.

The Original Medicare Plan

Medicare is the nation's largest health insurance program. Administered by the Health Care Financing Administration (HCFA), Medicare provides health care insurance to persons age 65 and over and to certain others with disabilities. Nearly 39 million Americans are currently covered. Twenty-one percent of all Medicare spending is for treatment in the last six months of life for those 65 and over. The traditional pay-per-visit (also termed *fee-for-service*) plan is now called the Original Medicare Plan.

Medicare Part A helps pay for the following:

- Care in a hospital
- Care in a skilled nursing facility for a limited number of days following and incident to a hospital stay
- Home health care
- Hospice care
- Blood after the first three pints

Medicare Part B picks up where Medicare Part A leaves off. It pays for the following:

- Doctor bills
- X-rays and laboratory tests
- Mammograms to screen for breast cancer
- Specific other prevention screenings
- Outpatient mental health services
- Many other medical services and supplies

You are eligible for Medicare if you or your spouse worked for at least 10 years in Medicare-covered employment and you are 65 years old (Congress is currently considering age 62) and a citizen or permanent resident of the USA. If you meet these conditions, there is no premium for Part A. The 1999 monthly premium of $45.50 for Part B will rise to $97.67 by 2006. (On average, Medicare beneficiaries annually pay $2600 out of pocket for coinsurance, deductibles, and premiums.)

The HCFA assigns a private insurance company as a Fiscal Intermediary to process bills for Part A services. Similarly, the HCFA contracts with a Medicare carrier to process bills for Part B services. Keeping up with paperwork is a continuing job. If you find it overwhelming, you can hire a consultant to do this work for $20 to $75 per hour.

Unscrupulous claim processors, home health agencies, and doctors are responsible for billions of our tax dollars being misspent. If you suspect such a crime in your case, inform the authorities by calling the Fraud Hot Line: 1-800-447-8477. If your information bears out, you stand to receive 10 percent of the recovered funds up to $1000. You will be doing a favor for all of us.

Medicare does not pay for everything and does not cover everything. You must pay a deductible amount for both Part A and Part B. In addition, you must pay a portion of the approved charges as coinsurance.

Services not covered by the Original Medicare Plan include these:

- Routine physicals (except those related to mammograms, Pap smear and pelvic examinations, diabetes monitoring, colorectal cancer screening, bone density measurements, and vaccinations)
- Dental care and dentures
- Routine foot care
- Hearing aids
- Most prescription drugs

Some doctors will not accept as payment in full the Medicare-approved amount. Always ask if your doctor will accept this amount. Otherwise, you may have to pay from your pocket up to 15 percent above Medicare's approved amount.

It Pays to Persist

Frail, elderly Medicare beneficiaries with severe illnesses such as Alzheimer's or Parkinson's are being improperly denied coverage for home health services. Government data in 1998 indicated that 39 percent of the people who contested the denial of such benefits—18,500 people—won coverage at the first level of review. Of those who pressed their claims beyond the first review, 81 percent won on appeal. The problem is that, under pressure to crack down on fraud and abuse in Medicare, the government sometimes denies care that doctors and patients see as medically necessary. It is true that some people make claims for "chore services" and are not strictly home-bound. But, by denying legitimate claims, Medicare deprives patients of the very services that allow them to attain a measure of independence in their own homes. The key is to be educated about what Medicare rules allow and to be persistent.

Medicare Supplement (Medigap) Insurance

To plan your future health care budget, you should anticipate that health costs will rise at least 3 percent faster than general inflation.

Medicare usually pays 80 percent of the total cost of covered items and services. You are responsible for paying the balance. In the case of hospitalization or a serious illness, even 20 percent could be a large amount. To cover the "gap" between what Medicare pays and the entire bill, many people elect to take a Supplemental Insurance Policy. These plans are offered by commercial or nonprofit insurance companies, which charge you a monthly premium. This extra insurance applies only to the Original Medicare Plan.

All Supplemental Insurance Policies issued since 1992 must match one of ten standard benefit plans, regardless of the insurance company (except in Wisconsin, Minnesota, and Massachusetts). The plans can cover deductibles, longer hospital stays, copayments for doctors' services, and a portion of prescription drugs. A disadvantage is that if your doctor charges more than the Medicare-approved amount, or if your supplemental insurance charges a deductible, you could be responsible for additional expenses as well as for your monthly premium. Get help picking the best plan for you. Objective ratings of various companies can be found. Your state insurance commissioner has information.

Medicare Health Plan Choices

Congress in 1997 passed the Balanced Budget Act by which it expects to reduce Medicare spending by $116 billion over a 5-year period. In the past, when Medicare recipents were enrolled in managed care organizations, the HCFA paid 95 percent of the average cost of treating a patient. This 5 percent savings over the pay-per-visit system, when multiplied by millions of patients, is a huge amount of money. Currently, 15 percent of Medicare-eligible seniors are in managed care plans. The goal is to double this figure by the year 2002. (Most still use the traditional pay-per-visit system.) In November 1998, the federal government began offering the attractive opportunity to change to a Medicare Managed Care Plan popularly called "Medicare+Choice," which includes more benefits and certain limitations.

A Medicare Managed Care Plan is a contract between a health plan and the HCFA. The health plan is a Health Maintenance Organization

(HMO) with or without a Point of Service Option (POS), a Preferred Provider Organization (PPO), or a Provider Sponsored Organization (PSO). When you enroll in such a health plan, HCFA agrees to pay a fixed monthly amount to the plan. The plan then both pays for and provides health services through a single business entity. It arranges for your health care and handles most of the paperwork required for Medicare benefits.

HMOs usually assign a primary-care doctor to you and will pay for specialists only if referred by your primary-care doctor. HMOs will not pay for a physician who is not in the plan. PPOs and PSOs give their members lists of participating primary- and specialty-care physicians from which to choose. If you go to a physician not on the list, you will be charged an extra fee or suffer a reduced reimbursement or coverage amount.

Choices also include Private Fee-for-Service Plans, Medicare Medical Savings Account Plans, and Religious Fraternal Benefit Society Plans. A thorough reading of the HCFA free publication "Medicare & You" is a must for anyone who wishes to understand the system. The Web site **http://www.medicare.gov** offers information as well.

ADVANTAGES OF MEDICARE MANAGED CARE PLANS OVER THE ORIGINAL MEDICARE PLAN

- Wellness programs and preventive services are often offered.
- Routine care—such as regular physicals, foot care, eye exams, eyeglasses, hearing aids—is often covered.
- Most plans provide 24-hour access to services.
- Many plans offer paperless administration with few or no bills or claims forms.
- There are few out-of-pocket expenses (except for per-visit/per-service copayments).
- Services and care are coordinated.
- Enrollment cannot be refused based on health or preexisting conditions during specified enrollment periods (with a couple of exceptions).
- Quality assurance standards for facilities are monitored by the federal government.

LIMITATIONS OF MEDICARE MANAGED CARE PLANS

- Subscribers must use the plan's staff of physicians, except for emergency or urgent care.
- Treatment by a specialist is usually not covered unless you have been referred by your primary-care physician.
- Subscribers must obtain all services within a defined service area. It is important for people who travel a great deal or move frequently to consider this.
- A plan's service area may not include your home.
- If you move out of the plan's service area, membership is automatically canceled.
- A plan may be canceled, or care providers may leave the plan.
- The state insurance commissioner's office may have no regulatory authority over the plan.

America's annual health care spending is predicted to double to $2.1 trillion by the year 2007, driven up by the demands for better drugs and technology. HMOs are making a big advertising pitch to lure new customers. An AARP survey showed that one-third of Americans have no knowledge of the difference between HMO benefits and traditional fee-for-service benefits. More than half of the respondents reportedly got their information from HMO ads, while only one in ten used a Medicare publication. National rankings, by state, of managed care plans are available. One is published annually in *U.S. News & World Report.* Or you can go to U.S. News Online at **http://www.usnews.com** and click on HMO *rankings.*

Medicaid

Medicaid is a joint federal and state program that provides medical help for certain individuals with low incomes and limited resources. It is for people of any age who meet a minimum income and minimum asset test. In addition to the usual medical help, Medicaid also includes nursing home care and outpatient prescription drugs. In the past, some people have "spent down" and/or transferred title of their home to an adult child to qualify. Laws have gotten stricter. Now, transfer of a home must occur three or more years before health care costs are paid. A bill before Congress, the Medicaid Community Attendant Services Act, would let eligible people remain in their own homes and receive attendant care rather than move to other facilities. Watch for other changes. If you think that you might qualify, contact your state, county, or local medical assistance office.

Long-Term Care Insurance

This is private insurance that covers the cost of nursing homes and other long-term care not covered by Medicare. Formerly, the average age of people buying this insurance was mid to late seventies. Recently, the average age is early to mid sixties. The younger you are when you start it, the lower the premium. Getting an objective, well-informed opinion is difficult—from an agent, almost impossible. Understanding the many options requires considerable study. Long-term care insurance is offered by more than 130 companies, but the best ones probably are the large, well-established companies such as Travelers, CNA, and John Hancock. They have been in the business for a long time and are not apt to close down.

There are three reasons to consider this insurance. One is that it serves to protect your assets if you require long-term treatment. Another is that, in addition to nursing homes, it includes home health care and assisted living. Still another is the fear of having to compete in our old age to get good treatment; this is the supply and demand argument.

Of those who reach age 65, it is estimated that 43 percent will enter a nursing home at some time in the future. Ideally, it would be good if everyone had long-term care insurance. However, current thinking is that this insurance makes best sense for the upper middle class. For example, someone in a higher socioeconomic class, who has money enough to set aside $160,000, or enough to cover four years of care, probably does not need the insurance. (Most people who enter a nursing home after age 65 stay less than five years.) And, for those in the middle class or lower, with assets less than $75,000 ($150,000 for couples) or retirement income less than $30,000 annually, the insurance is too expensive. If your gross income is below $15,000 and your assets excluding your house and car are less than $75,000, Medicaid will probably pay the bill for your long-term care.

A good long-term care plan will offer a pool of benefits that you can use for home health care and nursing home care. A rider for inflation is essential, increasing the value of the benefit by about 5 percent per year. (By 2030, living in a nursing home is projected to cost $97,000 a year.) An inflation rider is costly, probably doubling the amount of the premium; however, since you may not need to use the benefits for 20 or 30 years, the insurance could be of limited value if inflation is not factored in.

You should understand the restrictions on the types of nursing homes for which your insurance company will pay, and choose your plan accordingly. Benefits received may not be taxable. Part of the premium is tax-deductible as an itemized medical expense.

Wills

Everyone should have a will or a living trust disposing of his or her assets. Yet most people do not. Of course, people do not want to confront their own death, but that, in my opinion, is not the main reason for procrastination in making a will. We think, it seems to me, that it is too difficult to plan ahead and that whether or not we die without a will makes little difference to the distribution of our estate. That is where we are wrong. Take the following case.

Two prime timers with previous families got married. In his will he left everything to his new wife, thinking she would take care of giving something to his children if he died first. He did die first. When she died later, her will left the entire estate to her children. His children got nothing. Put your good intentions in writing with a will. Every year on your birthday, reread your will and make revisions when significant changes have occurred.

Some states allow you to write in your will that you reserve the right to leave separate written instructions at a later time for disposition of tangible assets. This statement does not need to be notarized.

A nice touch is to leave a letter to your heirs in addition to a will. In it you can tell them your feelings, how much you love them, the principles you have tried to live by and pass on, and how you expect your children to care for the spouse who outlives you.

Federal Estate Tax

A person dying in the year 2000 may pass on $675,000 free of federal tax. (A 1997 law provides for this amount to rise gradually each year until it stops at $1 million in 2006.) No estate tax is levied on assets left to a spouse. But when that spouse dies, whatever remains over the exempt amount can be taxed. Thus, if the husband dies first and leaves everything to his wife, the benefit of his lifetime tax-exemption of $675,000 is lost. When she later dies, she can pass on tax-free only her own tax-exempt amount. This provision will not be a problem if her estate does not exceed $675,000. With a larger estate, however, it can result in a federal estate tax that could have been avoided if her husband had left his assets in a credit-shelter trust (also called a bypass trust) for her benefit.

To leave to heirs free of taxes the entire amount to which each spouse is entitled, you must create two trusts. This is usually done either in a will or by creating a living trust. Credit-shelter trust "A" (the husband's eventual gift to the children or to others) can pass on his death to the wife, who can use the income during her lifetime and have limited access to the principal. That is, while she may use some of the principal, if necessary, for such things as medical expenses or to enable her to maintain her standard of living, she is not free to use it in any way she wishes, such as gambling trips to Las Vegas. On her death, credit-shelter trust "A" passes free of taxes to the children or to whomever her husband has designated. Similarly, her credit-shelter trust "B" passes free of taxes to whomever she has designated. The ownership of all major assets is transferred to the name of the trust, which may be revoked by you at any time if originally set up as a revocable trust. Various other arrangements for avoiding or minimizing estate taxes are possible; a lawyer can advise you on how best to organize your trusts.

Please remember that the federal estate tax rate starts at 37 percent and extends to 55 percent. Unless you agree completely with every way in which the federal government spends our money, why not, instead, pass your own on to your children or to a good charity? A good source of both legal and investment information is *Making the Most Out of Your Money* by Jane Bryant Quinn.

Community Property

A community property law says that everything a husband and wife accumulate during marriage belongs equally to both. States that have community property laws are Arizona, California, Idaho, Nevada, New Mexico, Texas, Washington, and Wisconsin. (Wisconsin uses a different terminology.)

You might be okay without a will in those states if your estate is small, if there is no property owned by only one spouse, if there are no children by previous marriages, no minor children, no property in other states, and if you want your spouse and children to inherit according to the laws of your state. However, if your estate (husband and wife included) exceeds $675,000, your heirs will face the same federal inheritance tax problem described earlier. Also, the community property law will not provide for distributing the estate of the surviving spouse after he or she dies.

Living Trusts

Living trusts are more complicated and expensive to set up than wills, but they avoid probate and, therefore, are cheaper and easier to administer after a death. Once the trusts are set up, all property goes into them. Living trusts can do no more than wills to avoid federal inheritance tax.

Since living trusts are not subject to probate review by the court, your trustee (for example, an adult child) can administer it without subjecting the division of property to public scrutiny after a death, as would be the case with a will. (For example, it has been said that the entire contents of Jacqueline Onassis's will was made public and published in a book.)

Powers of Attorney

1. Power of attorney is a legal document by which you empower another person to act in your behalf in specified types of transactions. It terminates if you die or become incapacitated or incompetent.
2. A durable power of attorney remains valid and enforceable despite incompetency or incapacity but terminates when you die. Powers may include selling properties, making gifts, managing bank accounts, and making insurance decisions. However, it cannot do more than your state laws allow.
3. A durable medical power of attorney allows you to designate someone you trust to make medical decisions on your behalf, effective either immediately or in the future should you become incapacitated. It eliminates the necessity for you to know in advance all the medical problems that may arise. But it is important to talk to your family and doctor in advance about your feelings and intentions.

A friend, Mrs. Carter, was ending her days in a nursing home. She had given her son power of attorney. One day she said to him, "George, take me home. I want to die at home." George replied, "Mother, you have no home. I sold it." According to reports, Mrs. Carter did not last long after that. Be careful whom you appoint to this important position. An agent who has a reason to want your estate might act against your wishes. In all cases, the above documents must be executed while you are mentally competent.

Advance Medical Directives

Advance medical directives, also known as health care directives, include (1) durable medical power of attorney, (2) health care proxy, and (3) living will. A health care proxy has the same effect as a durable medical power of attorney, described above. If your state has this law, you may obtain a form and execute it yourself without a lawyer. Again, you must make sure that the person you designate has a thorough understanding of your wishes. The living will (not to be confused with a living trust) is easy and inexpensive to make. It lets you retain control over how you die when you no longer are in direct control. You sign a statement now, saying, for example, that you are not willing to be hooked up to life-support machines if your doctor attests that you have an irreversible terminal illness. Many people do not want to be kept alive by artificial feeding (by tubes) or artificial hydration (fluid given intravenously). Some people in fragile health do not want to be revived by cardiopulmonary resuscitation; they reason that they do not want to live if their body tells them it is time to go. Therefore, they wear "No CPR" bracelets on their wrists so that emergency room staff, 911 paramedics, and others will know their wishes without being told. Discuss this with your doctor, with family members, and with staff if you live in a nursing home. Be certain there is an understanding.

With any of these options, you are, in effect, exercising your power in advance, while in full possession of your faculties, to cover a time in the future when you may be in a comatose state or cannot speak for yourself. In a *Los Angeles Times* article on May 29, 1994, Neil S. Wenger and Martin F. Shapiro advised: "Decide now how you don't want to die: by signing an 'advance directive,' Mr. Nixon and Mrs. Onassis spared their families incalculable heartache."

In truth, even though these directives are legally binding, they are sometimes ignored by medical personnel. A study reported in the November 1995 *Journal of the American Medical Association* found that attending physicians in hospitals often were not even aware of their patients' preferences. Two thirds of them did not look at treatment requests on file in the medical records of hospitalized patients. There are several reasons. One is that in an attempt to remain relevant, treatment requests use vague language that has to be interpreted. For example, "terminal condition" and "incurable illness" are vague. Physicians must later interpret what the patient really meant. Another reason is that most living wills are completed by the patient without the benefit of medical counseling or their doctor's advice. Therefore, it is *necessary* to talk over your wishes with your doctor in addition to giving him or her a copy.

A study published in the *Annals of Internal Medicine* urged spouses, siblings, and adult children to discuss what treatments they would want, and not want, if terminally ill. When making a decision, fully one third of close relatives would not have made the choice that the patient actually wanted. The living will document without sufficient discussion is not enough. There are plenty of cases where family members have tried to get court orders to countermand these directives. It is important that you have a clear understanding with your children and others. Since families cannot be objective about the life and death of a family member, it could be helpful to use someone experienced in group dynamics when parents talk with children and/or relatives about this. The legal aspect is one thing, the emotional aspect another.

Guardianship

Suppose that you do not have any of the three advance medical directives or a durable power of attorney, and you can no longer make your own decisions. A court will determine your competency and, if you are found to be incompetent, will appoint a guardian, who could be a relative or a friend. The guardian can be authorized to make decisions about living arrangements, financial matters, and medical care. A conservatorship is different from a guardianship in that the former takes care of your finances but not your person. In the past, guardianships tended to transfer complete decision-making power. Nowadays there is a trend by the courts to confer limited, decision-specific authority for cases in which people are competent to make some of their own decisions but not others. Executing a guardianship can be costly and will be paid from your estate. If you have no family members nearby, the court-appointed guardian may be a complete stranger to you. Marshall B. Kapp, a professor of law and author of the article, "The Law and the Elderly," which appears in the book, *The Practical Guide to Aging,* wrote: "Unfortunately, the majority of people who become incapacitated in decision making have failed to take good advantage of the available advance planning opportunities."

Different Money/Legal Styles

If you are living with a mate, you may have realized that you have different styles of dealing with money and legal issues. Too often, mates do not share in decision-making and, after a death, the surviving mate has had insufficient financial experience for a smooth transition to solitary life. Here are some pointers:

- Consider that your assets have been built up together and you both have an equal right to manage and use them, even if one of you did not produce income.
- Periodically (quarterly or annually) share information on the state of finances, that is, income, expenditures, savings, and investments. Both of you should have free access to money files and have no secrets from each other.
- Plan life goals and any anticipated large transactions together, as a team.
- Accept your basically different money/legal styles and acknowledge that neither is wrong. Learn each other's style.
- Realize that the need to control—and the money itself—is not as important as warm human relations in your home.
- Consider what financial information and experience you would want for a smooth transition if the other partner were to die first.

If married, take care of your financial and legal matters while you are both alive. If your mate shows no interest, do it for both of you if possible. At least do it for yourself. If alone, do it for the sake of your heirs. It is enough that your children will be grieving your loss without the added complication of sorting through matters with which they are unfamiliar, matters that should have been properly cared for in your lifetime.

Everybody thinks of changing humanity and nobody thinks of changing himself.
—LEO TOLSTOY

Nothing is more difficult, and therefore more precious, than to be able to decide.

NAPOLEON BONAPARTE I

CHAPTER TWELVE

Is It Time to Move?

THIS CHAPTER PRESENTS the alternatives to living in a single family home, starting from the most independent mode and continuing to the most dependent mode.

Do Your Research Now

A friend, Mary, is a survivor of breast cancer but still has multiple problems, mainly connected with never-ending back pain. Her loving husband, John, provided much emotional and physical support, including back massages and doing all of the driving and lifting. It seemed that she was totally dependent on him. Although older than Mary, John was seemingly in good health and would always be there for her, or so their friends thought. Imagine our shock and consternation when John died from a sudden, massive heart attack. Overnight, Mary's world was turned upside down. The lesson to be learned is that sometimes the apparently healthier, caregiving mate dies first. Also, it is not uncommon for both mates to incur major, debilitating illnesses at the same time and not to be able to help themselves, much less each other.

Decisions on a change of residence often must be made suddenly, within days or even hours. Crisis takes away our sense of control and makes for an unproductive move. The number of appropriate facilities from which to choose will be fewer in a crisis situation. Furthermore, many placements in nursing homes are made directly from hospitals, where those who have fallen or are ill are recuperating. A hospital bed is no place from which to do research on your future home. Advance preparation is like having money in the bank—it gives you power. Start off with a thorough inward look at your attitudes about a different living style. Add to that a realistic appraisal of your physical capabilities, both now and later, making an honest estimate of how they might change in the next two or three years. Use a workbook such as AARP's *Your Home, Your Choice* to help you get started. Be aware that terminology differs from place to place in the USA.

Most people, as they age, give some thought to moving. The following point is very important. If the suggestion to explore alternative living arrangements should first come from your adult child or caregiver, thank him. Do not react with, "I'm not ready for that yet! Are you trying to get rid of me?" Be appreciative of the concern shown and enlist the help of your children.

Urban and suburban areas offer many more choices than rural areas and small towns do. The Internet offers a wealth of housing information. The site of the National Association of Realtors is **http://www.realtor.com**. You may be able to take a "virtual tour" right from your own computer.

Visit those places high on your list. Make appointments to visit one or two places each week. Seeing more per week may be confusing and cause you to give up before a thorough study is completed. Make a party of it. Go with your spouse, roommate, adult child, or best friend. Accept a luncheon invitation if meals are provided. Otherwise, visit a restaurant or shopping center in the local area as a part of your day's outing. Take pad and pencil and a list of questions you have prepared in advance. Ask lots of questions and record the replies for later review. Talk with anyone you know who lives in that facility. Otherwise, speak with strangers you see living there. Ask them how they like it. Most likely they will have opinions and be happy to tell you. Don't be shy about your investigation. This could become your home. Return for a second visit (at a different time of the day) if you are not sure. Discuss your reactions later with your spouse or a friend.

If you intend to buy into a residence with your mate, ask yourself if you would like to live there later by yourself. It is not an uncommon situation that after a husband dies, the wife decides that the residence they had selected together no longer fits her solitary living needs. You can incur very large financial losses, particularly in continuous care communities, when you buy in and then sell.

Independent Living

APARTMENTS

"The fellow that owns his own house is always just coming out of a hardware store," according to Kin Hubbard. An apartment is the simplest living arrangement and the most carefree. You get a self-contained unit with one door. Lock the door, leave, and you do not have to worry about it. Some form of security probably exists. Most things you need are on one floor and served by an elevator. You call the supervisor for repairs.

Neighbors are close, but only as close to you as you care to have them. You may choose an apartment building for adults only or one that allows families with children, according to your preference. There is no financial investment to worry about. You pay rent and utilities but no property taxes. Some apartments have no services; others may offer food service. With 30 days' notice you may move out, unless your lease states otherwise. Inquire about smoking and pets. Test for soundproofing.

CONDOMINIUMS

Approximately 85 percent of seniors live in homes (freestanding or condos) that they own, or in apartments. Condominiums have many of the advantages of apartments. But since you own your unit, you have a financial investment, and you have a say in how it will be managed. If property values go up, your investment will increase in worth. True, you must pay local property taxes, but those may be deducted from your adjusted gross income by itemizing on Schedule A of your Internal Revenue Service tax return.

There is an upside and a downside to owning a condominium. Instead of rent you will pay a monthly mortgage and/or a maintenance fee. The fee is determined by the homeowners themselves. And that is the rub. If you have homeowners who want expensive landscaping and frequent painting and renovation, the cost will go up. You must share the cost. If you wish to sway the others to your view, you must become active in the condominium association and/or the elected board of directors. If the monthly fee does not include a funded reserve for major repairs, all owners will pay a special assessment if, for example, a new roof is needed. It is best to obtain a copy of the condo declaration and the monthly financial report as well as information on the dates and amounts of the two previous maintenance fee increases and special assessments.

Is there any restriction on renting in the condominium? Renting means turnovers in residents and people not showing the same care that they would show for their own investment. Some condo rules restrict rentals. If possible, talk with your potential neighbors before you decide.

Finally, if you buy any residence, make your purchase conditional on a home inspection, which will cost $250 to $400. Inspectors will point out defects that might become problems later and that can give you leverage for a better price or for requesting repairs by the seller. You will also receive tips on home maintenance, such as how to change the air filters. This is a wise investment.

AFFORDABLE COOPERATIVE HOUSING

The federal government has established a Section 42 tax code making it profitable for corporations to construct and rent reasonably priced housing. This relatively new system caters to old and young, families and singles, and requires about 10 hours per month of work such as planting flowers or participating in the neighborhood watch. There is a sense of community and sharing. One single-parent resident said, "We are more than neighbors."

SENIOR HOUSING

This is subsidized housing for low-income seniors. Criteria for such housing relate more to income than to assets. Sponsors are federal, state, county, and city governments, and nonprofit organizations and churches. Construction methods make this housing accessible to disabled residents. An on-site supervisor usually is present, but normally no services are provided, except possibly a van for shopping. Seniors prepare their own meals and care for themselves. (There may be regional differences in services and in length of waiting lists for entry.)

CO-HOUSING

Co-housing takes us back to the time when people lived in small towns and watched out for each other. In co-housing communities, small houses are usually built around a shared courtyard and common community building. These owned houses have their own kitchens and patios, so there is plenty of privacy, but if you feel like getting out, you can stroll a few yards to a bench in the courtyard or visit the community building.

The community building usually has shared laundry facilities, a child-care facility, and a shared library. Most communities have group dinners three or four times a week. The mindset of the residents, more than the architectural design, is the main difference setting co-housing apart from the typical condo.

RETIREMENT COMMUNITIES

These are for seniors who like the advantages of living in large communities. They offer a variety of multiple-unit and single-family accommodations, with social programs, security, communal dining rooms, and shops. Some may also offer health services, but the focus is on seniors who can care for themselves.

MANUFACTURED HOMES

These are an outgrowth of mobile homes but are nicer looking. They are less costly and more quickly built than conventional homes of similar sizes, though they are very well made and as big or as small as you wish. Manufactured homes are built in a factory and placed or

213

assembled in a home park (or anywhere you choose). Once placed, they are as permanent as any individual home. Manufactured housing accounts for about 20 percent of all new residences.

As with a condo, you buy the home and pay a fee for maintenance of the common areas such as streets, fences, and entrances. Larger home parks have perimeter fences and guards. You have a small yard, which you may maintain yourself or hire someone to maintain. Cost of living should be somewhat less than in a house; ease of living is greater.

ELDER COTTAGE HOUSING OPPORTUNITY (ECHO)

ECHO homes are small units designed to be placed on the same property as a family member. They conform to city zoning regulations.

ACCESSORY DWELLING UNIT

This is an "in-law" apartment, that is, a living unit added to an existing home, perhaps in a basement or garage, and sometimes built by the owner's own hands.

HOME SHARING

You could move in with another adult, someone you enjoy being with. You would each have a bedroom and share the kitchen and living room. The two of you could make any arrangement you like with regard to the amount of work you do, if any. Or choose a young family with children, which would give you the role of a surrogate grandparent without many obligations. Your local senior information and assistance office can advise on matching services.

Think carefully about what you want and consider the applicable suggestions made in "Reassembling" in Chapter Ten. However, unlike reassembling, where you are dealing with blood relatives, sharing another's home is much easier to terminate if you should later become dissatisfied.

Living with Assistance

MOVING IN WITH THE KIDS

Formerly, this was the most common arrangement for taking care of the "old folks." In 1962, 28 percent of American elders lived with their children. Today that figure is 15 percent. It is still an arrangement that can bring satisfaction and blessings, or unhappiness and discontent, depending on you and your family. In all likelihood, you already know whether or not such an invitation would be forthcoming from your children and whether or not you would like to accept it. Considerations applicable to "Reassembling" in Chapter Ten apply here, also.

If, after careful reasoning, you believe in your heart that it is workable, don't wait to be asked. Ask first. If they won't do it for love, perhaps they will do it for money, if you do have money and would like to spend it in that way. However, before asking, consider how you will feel if the answer is "no."

If the children are willing to take you, be sure that you are paying your way in money and/or services insofar as your resources and energy permit. In addition to reviewing the "Rules of Effective Communication" in Chapter Eight, following these hints will help to make your welcome last.

- Stay clean and neat.
- Give your children plenty of privacy.
- Try to make your own friends and develop interests outside the home.
- Provide information about your arrangements for hospitalization, burial, and so on before being asked.
- Don't get involved in family arguments or comment on how your grandchildren are being raised.
- Even if asked, don't give advice—simply reply with, "What do you think is the best way?"
- Clarify what you are free to do and at what hours.
- Try your best to find solutions to your own problems.

ASSISTED LIVING

"Assisted living" is a name given to a wide variety of facilities bridging the gap between your own home and a nursing home. From 1990 until today, the number of residents in this arrangement has increased to one million. Assisted living facilities are attractive because they can offer a home-like environment and a wide variety of accommodations from modest to luxury and from room-with-meals-only to personal and, sometimes, health care. The level of services may increase as the ages, or needs, of the residents rise. Residents pay a monthly rent and then pay additional fees for extra required services. Social activities and transportation are usually provided. In size, assisted living facilities tend to have more residents than do the adult family homes described below.

ADULT FAMILY HOMES

These are sometimes termed *adult foster homes* or *adult care homes*. They are private homes, licensed in some states, usually caring for four to six residents. Rooms may be private or semiprivate. All meals are prepared centrally for residents. Other care may include assistance with activities of daily living, that is, help with eating, bathing, dressing, and monitoring medications. Doing laundry might be extra. Residents have use of the living room and, perhaps, a recreation room.

Sometimes couples go into these homes to remain together when one needs help that the other cannot provide alone. Adult family homes operated by families with children can offer a satisfying social setting.

It may be possible to negotiate the price for such care. You should visit several times and ask lots of questions. Get recommendations from social workers and nurses who visit there and from hospital discharge nurses. Ask your state or county ombudsman for a report and advice.

DIFFICULTIES WITH ASSISTED LIVING

The following remarks apply to assisted living, board and care homes, adult homes, congregate facilities, residential care facilities, domiciliary homes, personal care homes, and other boarding houses under one name or another that cater to the elderly.

216

- States are not uniform in regulating assisted living facilities. However, ask to see the state license and the last survey report if applicable. What are the qualifications of the administrator?
- Medicare usually will not pay for any assisted living services. An exception would be skilled nursing care in an accredited facility.
- Medicaid might pay in some states if a resident meets income eligibility requirements.
- What are the emergency and safety policies and procedures?
- The written contract is all-important. Wording in a brochure or promises made on a tour mean nothing if the commitments are not in the contract.
- The contract should include designation of a specific room, the right to return to that room after a temporary absence, rules governing who can come to live or visit, approved room furnishings and modifications, details of any transportation provided, what specific services are included, how many staff are on duty and their training, assigned responsibility for scheduling medications, and provision for 30 days' or less prior notice for canceling the contract.
- Get copies of the contract and the rules and policies, and have them reviewed by a lawyer with appropriate experience before signing.
- Arrange to be visited periodically by a caregiver who will be your ombudsman. Compliment the staff when you see that they are doing well. Complain and follow up where justified.

Nursing Homes

Twenty-four hour supervision and skilled care are available in nursing homes, described here, or through continuing care arrangements, described in the next section. Entry to nursing homes often occurs not after a long period of decline in personal functioning but with a sudden loss of faculty because of injury or illness, followed by a spell in the hospital to receive acute care. Moreover, the person who makes the selection of a particular home is usually a family member but not the person who will live there or pay the cost.

THE FACTS

Consumer Reports published in its August, September, and October 1995 issues a comprehensive report on the condition of nursing homes across the USA. (Conditions may or may not have changed much since then.) For the report, Senior Investigative Editor Trudy Lieberman visited 53 nursing homes and 27 assisted living facilities; these first-hand reports were combined with the results from 60,000 inspection reports required by the Health Care Financing Administration. (The HCFA certifies about 16,000 nursing homes receiving payment from Medicare and/or Medicaid, which accounts for about 86 percent of the industry. The federal government requires inspections every 12 to 15 months.) The report's findings follow.

- Thousands of nursing homes provide care that is of poor or dubious quality.
- About 40 percent of all HCFA-certified facilities repeatedly violated federal standards over four inspection periods.
- Federal and state laws are enforced erratically, even for homes with repeated violations.
- Useful information to help decide on specific homes will not be provided by government agencies.
- The best advice comes from state and county ombudsmen, of whom there are more than 800, usually contacted through state agencies on aging.
- Reading recent state inspection reports is the only objective measure of life in a nursing home and is a *must* in making a decision. Homes sometimes conceal their reports or fail to provide them, which is against the law. If you have trouble obtaining a copy, do not consider that home.
- Almost 70 percent of nursing homes are run for profit. For-profit homes and homes with religious affiliations were almost equally represented in the top one third of quality.
- Individually owned for-profit facilities seemed to have the poorest records; the few government-owned nursing homes were above average.
- Sixty percent of the bills are government paid.

- Homes' brochures do not match reality.
- Amenities such as matching furniture, coordinated color schemes, ice-cream parlors, etc., are misleading and are not a reliable indication of quality.
- When visiting facilities, sniff for urine odors or air fresheners; observe safety hazards, understaffing, interaction between staff and residents, and the hygiene and grooming of residents.
- Eat a meal at the home, if possible. Many facilities fail such food inspection, provide substandard nutrition, and do not follow their posted menus. (The nonprofit Research Triangle Institute found that 25 to 30 percent of all nursing home residents are underweight. Some are at risk for premature death.)
- Observe planned activities, personalization of rooms, the use of restraints, failure to respect residents' dignity (45 percent of homes were found deficient), bedsores (25 percent deficient), range of motion activities (25 percent deficient), and development of sufficient care plans (60 percent deficient; almost 30 percent of homes were cited twice).

HISTORY

Nursing homes were unknown until the late 1930s and 1940s. It was Medicare and Medicaid in 1965 that caused the sudden burst in their availability. With inflation, growth in the elderly population, and increasing staffing costs, there will be greater pressure on nursing homes to operate more cost-effectively. This will lead some homes to reduce the quality of care further. Most nursing homes are operated for profit, and the number affiliated with large chains is increasing. Some nonprofit homes are operated by religious organizations. This does not mean that they will be less expensive, although some may provide better care.

Some homes or units now specialize in transitional care or rehabilitation. These are skilled nursing facilities that aim to return patients to their own homes as soon as their condition permits. Transitional care units also exist within some hospitals.

FUNCTIONAL ABILITY OF RESIDENTS

Although a majority of nursing home residents are functionally impaired and unable to live independently, a number of residents have no medical reason for being there; they simply have nowhere else to go. Among all Americans over age 65, only 5.4 percent live in nursing homes and other institutions, a smaller percent than a decade ago. Even among the disabled elderly, 80 percent live in the community with the help of caregivers or a social support network. The nursing home administration periodically will consider new plans of care for residents. It is extremely important that family members or representatives be present at those meetings unless residents are completely competent to represent themselves. Otherwise the plans of care will be decided without any input at all from residents. Personal possessions are inventoried at the time of admission. A copy of the inventory should be kept in the administration's safe, and possessions acquired later should be added to the official inventory. Otherwise, there is no recourse if a valuable item is missing. Residents may be asked to sign a "hold harmless" statement to free the administration of liability. Residents are well advised not to sign, nor can they be forced to do so.

COSTS

Prices for a one-year stay often exceed $50,000, $60,000, or even $70,000. People who can pay privately receive priority for admission and, in effect, subsidize those covered by government programs. However, do not assume there is a relationship between cost and the quality of care.

The daily rate for a semiprivate room is often $100 to $200. To that base can be added extra charges for such items as incontinence or bedsore care, laundry, hand-feeding, and turning and positioning. There is a big markup for supplies such as diapers, rubber gloves, and catheter tubes. Where medications are marked up two or three times, residents' families should insist on purchasing them outside. Physical, occupational, and speech therapy are extra. Some homes have "special-care units" (for example, for Alzheimer's and dementia patients) at extra cost, which were found by the Consumer Reports article to be no better than regular care at a good nursing home.

MEDICARE FINANCIAL PROVISIONS

Many infirm elderly people enter nursing homes for help with bathing, dressing, eating, and toileting. This is termed "custodial" care, for which Medicare pays nothing. When a patient enters a nursing home directly from hospitalization for illness or injury, a 100-day benefit period begins for those eligible for Medicare, which pays for the full cost of skilled nursing for the first 20 days. After that, a co-insurance period begins for which Medicare will pay up to about $100 a day. Since that amount does not cover the full cost, Medicare Supplemental Insurance is essential.

In nursing homes, rehabilitation therapies are reimbursable by Medicare only if ordered by a doctor for at least five times per week. Payment stops when no further improvement in function is made.

Medicare patients entitled to skilled nursing care get high preference for admission to nursing homes. However, Medicare patients not coming directly from a hospital may face a wait of six months or more.

MEDICAID FINANCIAL PROVISIONS

Medicare and Medicaid together annually spend over $42 billion on health care and benefits for elderly Americans. To qualify for Medicaid a patient must meet an income and asset test, which varies from state to state. When a patient is accepted for Medicaid, most of the individual's income, for example, Social Security and pension, goes directly to the nursing home. Residents can keep $30 per month or more for personal expenses. Spouses of Medicaid residents with no income of their own can keep a monthly stipend. To meet the asset test, some residents, for whom nursing home care was formerly reimbursed by Medicare, must "spend down" their assets to qualify for Medicaid. Spending down one's assets often happens in less than 12 months. Laws change, and it is good to get advice from an elder-care attorney to effect a "spend-down." But first, complete the files discussed in Chapter Nine.

Approximately 11,000 facilities are certified for both Medicare and Medicaid; about 1100 are certified for Medicare only. Some people going off Medicare and onto Medicaid may have to find a different nursing home. Since homes prefer Medicare patients (for the greater income), it may take several years' wait to be admitted for Medicaid. Sometimes Medicaid patients have been sent to hospitals for treatment of conditions requiring acute inpatient care, only to find when they are discharged that no bed has been kept for them in the nursing home. It is important to know the rules. A knowledgeable lawyer may be useful. Think of Medicaid as a safety net for the poor.

PLANNED SOCIAL ACTIVITIES

For most people, entering a nursing home is considered the last stop in their lives. Look for one that provides social contact, planned social activities, and intensive rehabilitation, in addition to nursing care and all of the care necessary for everyday life. Currently, provisions are being implemented to allow residents a say in decisions about their daily lives. More attention is being paid to involving family members, friends, and volunteers from the community in the residents' care and social lives.

STAYING CONNECTED AND IN CONTROL

If the nursing home has a residents' council, join in and participate actively. Councils have been known to produce good changes on behalf of the residents. (Food preparation concerns are always high on the list of dissatisfactions.) If there is no council, start one. Don't accept that it is impossible to make improvements. The nursing home administration is interested in receiving input from residents. It is in their best interests to keep residents happy and all rooms filled.

If you see or suspect abuse of an aging adult, notify the Adult Protective Services office in your city or state government. If the instance took place in a nursing home or other long-term care facility, notify your county or state ombudsman. Your action may prevent further abuse.

In his book Full Catastrophe Living, Jon Kabat-Zinn describes the work of two psychologists, Ellen Langer and Judith Rodin, who studied elderly patients in a nursing home. One half of patients in the test group were given plants and encouraged to care for them and also to do more for themselves instead of letting the staff take over all responsibilities. Patients of similar age and disability in the second group were given plants and told that the housekeeper would take care of the plants. The second group was not encouraged to do more for themselves. Within three weeks there was a significant improvement in the health and vitality of the first group. Eight months later, the death rate in the first group was one half that of the second group.

THE EDEN ALTERNATIVE

This is the name of a program, now used in more than 100 nursing homes, that integrates plants, animals, and children into the nursing home life. Dogs, chickens, and llamas may be full-time residents. Some locations maintain barns and gardens or share space with kindergartens and summer camps. Dr. William Thomas, founder of the Eden Alternative and author of *Life Worth Living*, believes that the biggest ailments facing nursing home residents are helplessness, loneliness, and boredom. The residents are "bloated with therapy and starving for care." In one study, he found that residents living responsibly and interactively with plants and animals had 15 percent fewer deaths and used fewer medications. Drug costs decreased by 38 percent. There was a 26 percent reduction in turnover of nurses and aides. One nursing home resident, formerly so depressed that she remained silent, now wanders the hallways chirping a duet with a songbird on her shoulder. Look for this philosophy in your search. Visit **http://www.Edenalt.com**.

TIPS FOR RESIDENTS

The transition to a nursing home will be made easier by short-term respite visits to nursing homes or even to adult day care centers before you make a permanent move. Otherwise, the adjustment to being moved "cold turkey" could be a shock.

If you are in a nursing home, there are some things you can do to make life fuller. Eat all of your meals in the dining room. Instead of remaining silent or talking mainly about illnesses or grandchildren, at the end of each meal assign an intellectually stimulating topic for discussion at the next meal. Rotate discussion leaders at each meal. Move to other tables sometimes, to meet new people.

Insofar as you are physically able and have the time, participate in every social activity. Get out at every possible opportunity. Ask your friends and relatives to visit you on a schedule so that you receive at least one visitor each day or several each week. Write letters and talk by phone every day. Do everything possible to stay active and happy, to lead a normal life, and to maintain control of your present and future.

SENIOR REFERRAL SERVICE

Senior referral service agents may help to address your physical, emotional, and spiritual needs and your financial situation. They are familiar with the senior housing alternatives in your area. They will match your priorities to the housing profiles and recommend two or three places for you to see. If you select one of them, the agent receives a commission from that home. You pay nothing for the service. There is some criticism that since they receive their commission from the facility, they may be less than objective. You may prefer to call the National Association of Professional Geriatric Care Managers, which represents more than 1000 professionals who charge you, rather than the facility, for their services. Their Web site is http://www.caremanager.org and their national telephone number is (520) 881-8008.

Do your utmost to assure a good fit on your first move. "Transfer trauma" is extremely stressful and expensive. The National Citizens' Coalition for Nursing Home Reform, located at 1424 16th St. N.W., Suite 202, Washington, D.C. 20036, sells the publication Nursing Homes: Getting Good Care There for $17. Nursing Home Compare at http://www.medicare.gov is a new Web listing of all Medicare and Medicaid certified homes. It includes data on the most recent inspections and on the severity of any deficiencies found. AARP has a Web site at http://www.aarp.org/getans/consumer/rights.html that is titled Rights of Nursing Home Residents. Start early to educate yourself and to build a network of friendly and supportive people to help you and your caregivers make the right choice.

Continuing Care Communities

Continuing care communities (also known as life care communities or continuing care retirement communities) run the gamut of services and costs. There are more than 1200 in the USA. At one end of the continuum they offer completely independent living. (Most require that you be able to live independently at the time of admission.) Then they can carry you through a progression of health stages, offering assisted living, then skilled nursing care, and finally, completely dependent living in a health care center—all within the same community. A less-perfect form of such a community would have you go elsewhere when there is a medical crisis. Continuing care communities are like towns; they have clinics, stores, banks, libraries, transportation, and recreational and educational facilities. They can be an ideal solution if one spouse needs nearby medical assistance and the other is well.

Naturally, the cost of such communities is high, and therefore, they tend to be peopled by those with financial means. These communities may require a substantial entrance or endowment fee and a monthly maintenance fee. Newer ones may operate on a straight rental basis. Some enterprises have gone bankrupt due to poor management.

What happens if, after the death of a husband, the wife decides she does not want to live there anymore? It can happen that less than half of the entrance fee would be refunded. You might be financially trapped. Therefore, when you shop for such living arrangements with your spouse, ask yourself if you would also like to live there alone. If you are considering the purchase of long-term care insurance, try to check out several of the kinds of facilities discussed in this chapter before making a decision.

Holding a Garage Sale

Scale down on what you intend to keep by holding a garage sale on a weekend. Especially salable items are furniture, exercise bikes, appliances, books, baby toys and furniture, camping gear, clothing, and jewelry. (Provide an electric outlet to prove that appliances work.) But no item is too insignificant. One man's junk is another's treasure. Make sure that clothing is clean, tag it for size, and hang it on pipes. Men's clothing does not sell well because the mostly female customers are unsure of their mates' sizes. Have plenty of card tables and doors or planks on blocks so that people can inspect small items without bending down to the floor. Stack books with the spines up for easy reading of titles.

You will gather valuable ideas on pricing and selling by visiting in advance a few garage sales, swap meets, and second-hand stores. A newspaper ad listing your most valuable items is worth the investment. Post signs in large letters at the local supermarket and throughout your neighborhood.

Consider pricing merchandise at about 25 percent of the current new cost. Put price stickers on everything and be prepared to drop the price to make a sale, especially at the end of the day or weekend. Price in even dollars or, for small items, in even quarters. (One expert does not price anything and prefers, instead, to dicker with customers to get the best price.) Do not accept checks. Have plenty of change on hand and keep money in a fanny pack or pocket, not in a box on a table. Lock your home doors and do not let anyone in to use the toilet or phone. Get your friends to help. Be ready an hour before the stated time. Have plenty of bags for customers to carry away small things. Make sandwiches for yourself and your crew on the previous evening.

Preparing for the Mover

Moving is a very stressful experience and deserves forethought. Make a moving plan six weeks in advance from advice found in library books. Get recommendations on movers from family and friends. The Interstate Commerce Commission (ICC) can send a report on customers' complaints against the nation's largest carriers. Obtain written cost estimates from two or three carriers.

Ask for a free copy of the ICC's *When You Move: Your Rights and Responsibilities*, which moving companies are obliged to provide. A binding estimate means that that is the amount you will pay. In a nonbinding estimate, the company can charge you up to 10 percent over the estimated cost. Consider buying insurance for added protection and for binding pickup and delivery dates. Find out who insures the company. Claims up to about $2000 can be settled in small claims court in cases where the carrier has not given satisfaction.

Schedule your utilities to be disconnected on the day after your move. Set up a bank account in the new city in advance of your move so you will have money available immediately. Don't forget to pack telephone books from the area you are leaving. Get help to inventory items being unloaded at the destination.

Moving with Fido

One woman said she would rather live in a cardboard box than give up her pets to live in a good place. Depending on your choice of a new residence, you may be able to take your pet with you. The following suggestions may help you to obtain acceptance of your pet from a prospective landlord. Be up front about the fact that you want to move in with your pet. Prepare a pet résumé including the pet's age, breed, weight, behavior traits, housebreaking and spay/neuter status, health, training, and so on. (The San Francisco Society for the Prevention of Cruelty to Animals distributes a sample pet résumé.) Bring a letter from a previous landlord, veterinarian, or groomer. Schedule an interview that includes your pet and during which you demonstrate its good behavior. Negotiate in the contract for a pet damage deposit and a shorter lease period. With advance preparation and conscientious responsibility, you may be able to move with your pet. Some people ask that their pets be "put to sleep" when they die. Another alternative is to plan in your will for their continued care when you are gone.

Closure

If you have lived in your home for a long time, or even for a short while, you have become a part of each other's spirit. Yes, even a house has a spirit, partially derived from what you have put into it. There are memories of raising your children there, of birthdays and holidays experienced there, of hot summers and cold winters, of pets and flowers, of delicious food and happy mealtimes, and of some sorrows, frustrations, and disappointments.

Leaving a home connected to so many memories is an important transition in your life. Recognize it as such and honor it. Before finally vacating your home, visit each room. Remember what part of your life that room has been to you. Thank that room for serving you well over the years, and tell it "good-bye." Don't forget to invite your children who have also lived there to join you.

It is important to remember that adequate advance preparation for a change of residence, as opposed to no preparation at all, can make an immense difference in the degree of control and happiness you experience in the new setting.

Part Five

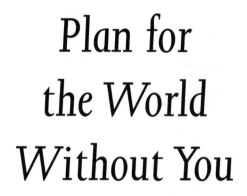

Plan for
the World
Without You

Write your own obituary. If you are dissatisfied with what you read, think about what you want that obituary to say, then reset your goals to accomplish it.

ROY MENNINGER

CHAPTER THIRTEEN

Build a Legacy

THIS CHAPTER IS ABOUT life completion tasks. As you come to terms with your mortality, you naturally turn to the task of healing your relationships, enjoying your achievements, and leaving a legacy for the future. Paraphrasing Erik Erikson, you are what survives of you.

Writing Your Own Obituary

You were born into this world with a clean slate. Everyone loved you and said, "How cute." You did not have an enemy or an accomplishment to your name. Now, after living the majority of your life, is the world a better place because you have passed through?

As Roy Menninger suggested, try to write the obituary that will appear in your local newspaper after your death. Does it contain all of the details you would desire? Does it exhibit the love and warmth by which you want to be remembered? Where does it show that you have given something back to the world, not merely taken from it? If your obituary does not satisfy you, rewrite it as you would want it to read. Be reasonable. Then start living in such a way as to become that person. Even if you are 90 years old, there is still time.

Gratitude

It is so easy to say, "Thank you." And it sounds so nice when you hear it said to you. Most of us ought to say it twice as much as we now do. Saying "I love you" is a little bit harder. If said about 100 times more often than we say it now, the frequency would be about right. I believe the world would be a much better place. We would feel the difference.

Does your gratitude show? We could not have gotten this far in our lives without the help of a lot of people. Perhaps there was an aunt who helped raise us when one parent died. A high school principal may have encouraged us to stay in school. Finally, we graduated or even went to college. An employer hired us, taking a chance on an inexperienced newcomer, and patiently taught us. A neighbor was warm and friendly and baby-sat our children. A nurse took such good care of us in the hospital and promised we would get well. The list could go on and on; yours will be different from mine.

Do you need help finding one or more of the people you want to thank? Norma Mott Tilman was a private investigator for more than 10 years and is the author of *How to Find Almost Anyone, Anywhere*. She has located more than 1000 missing persons. If you have patience and access to the Internet, you may be able to accomplish the task yourself. If not, you may hire an "information broker," also available on the Internet.

It is not too late to express your gratitude, even to those no longer in this world. Make your own list of people who have had a positive influence on your life, or who really helped you out when you needed it. Send notes or cards to them expressing your gratitude and telling how much their actions helped you.

If the person has died, send the note to a relative with a brief explanation. Or, if you can't find where to send it, give it to yourself. Make it an exercise in your appreciation, and in commemoration of their spirit. But use "I" and "you" words, just as if you were talking with them.

I wrote such a note to my deceased father. It was an emotionally moving and satisfying experience. I had not completely grieved my father's death, nor even had a chance to say good-bye. Sixteen years later I was taking a course in preparation for hospice work. One exercise was to write a letter to a deceased relative. I wrote to Dad. In that letter I wrote the things I would like to have said to him face to face. The truth is, I had plenty of opportunities earlier to write or say those things. Dad and I had been the correspondents in the family. We exchanged letters often. But I had written about the weather or my job, giving those things a preference over my gratitude for his role in my life.

When I finished that letter, with the important things finally said, I had a sense of closure and peace. When you finish your letters, you will know that feeling. And the world will be a little better because of your thoughtfulness.

Forgiveness

Forgiving is a tougher job than expressing gratitude. But do you want to shackle yourself to the painful past? Remember, if you don't forgive, you are giving the person who hurt you permission to keep on hurting you. Forgiving is spiritual surgery on yourself. Your positive action could prevent a negative pattern from being passed down to the next generation. We are all models for good or evil.

> There is no greater disaster
> Than enemy-making
> For then you lose your treasure,
> Your peace.
> When conflict arises,
> Compassion always prevails.
>
> —Tao 69

Don't confuse forgiving with forgetting. You will never forget. But if you forgive, the painful memory will grow smaller. Do not forgive people for being what they are. Forgive them only for what they do. Or visualize that person and see if there is at least one commendable characteristic. That is a start. Open yourself up to the possibility of a new relationship.

Make a "grudge list" of those people against whom you hold a grudge or from whom you parted with enmity. Write a note to each person; write, "Please forgive me." You will feel a lot better later. Avoid going into a lot of background detail. Some things are better left unsaid unless they are crucial for forgiveness.

If you cannot write, have someone write for you, or use the telephone. Use "I" statements, not "you" statements. For example, don't say, "You made me mad when you didn't attend Mom's funeral." Instead, do say, "When I did not see you at Mom's funeral, I felt sad." Say these two statements aloud and notice the difference. Phrase your reconciliation in the way you would like to hear it if you were in the other person's shoes.

If it is too late for a new start or you cannot bring yourself to say the words, reclaim what you can. Just start behaving pleasantly when in the presence of that person and make no negative comments.

If you have the courage to "bite the bullet" and finish this job, you will have made a significant step in building your life's legacy. "Just do it!"

This Is Me: A Scrapbook

What do you want your unborn grandchildren to know about you? Is there a useful document you could leave, to which heirs could refer from time to time for information about you and for the pleasure of reminiscence? One way is to make a big scrapbook. You can title it "Grandmother Alice" or simply "This Is Me." See the book *Joy of Scrapbooking* by Lisa Bearnson and Gayle Humpherys.

Start with a family tree going as far back as you can remember. If you don't do it, it will be lost forever. Include your birth certificate, high school diploma, marriage license, and any other certificates of accomplishment. Sort through your old snapshots and include a generous number depicting the various stages and important events in your life. Include your prize ribbons for your apple pie or swimming race or your Girl Scout awards. Include newspaper clippings mentioning you, programs of high school plays in which you participated, and photos of your needlework or your arts and crafts creations. Use a copy of your employment résumé. Save one page for a list of

"Accomplishments That Gave Me Pleasure." (For example, I climbed to the top of Mt. Hood.)

Include a reminiscence and life review. What was it like before television? Describe your typical school day. Talk about family activities. How did you get your first job, and what was it? How did you and your spouse meet and marry? What is the source of your inner strength? There is no one who can do this job as well as you. Believe me, it will bring a lot of pleasure later to your heirs. It will also be a wonderful reminiscence and therapy for you. You will confront the significance of past events, examine how they shaped your life, reexperience your good feelings, and reaffirm your sense of identity. What gifts have come from age and experience? What is your unique version of successful aging? Do not simply list facts but also feelings, choices, and decisions.

An AARP pamphlet entitled *Reminiscence* has this to say: "In fact, research has shown that older people who undergo life review are less withdrawn and apathetic. Reminiscing promotes mental and emotional well-being and combats isolation, loneliness, and depression." Finishing this project will give you a sense of power, accomplishment, and contentment.

Sight and Sound

WRITING

Depending on your talents and inclinations you may wish to write some vignettes of your life. Take a creative writing course and write the story of how you and your spouse first met. Or send your written autobiography to older grandchildren, one chapter at a time.

A wonderful guide on how to get started writing about life experiences is Bob Greene and D. G. Fulford's book, *To Our Children's Children*. If you cannot hold a pencil to write, ask a relative or friend to help you. Or dictate your comments into a tape recorder.

AUDIO MEMORIES

My father had remarkable recall of poetry and Shakespearean lines that he had learned 60 years earlier. As we sat around the evening bonfire on camping trips, he would sometimes be persuaded to recite for us. Those are fond memories. One of my prized possessions is a cassette tape of him reciting from memory Robert Service's *Cremation of Sam McGee*. It brings tears to my eyes. You might consider taping a poem or a favorite song, or just telling how life was in your childhood days.

VIDEOTAPES AND SNAPSHOTS

Transfer old home movie camera film to videotape. Or use a camcorder to film yourself. If snapshots are plentiful, you could create a photo album in addition to the shots included in your scrapbook. Write in names and occasions or approximate dates. The alternative, unfortunately, is for your children, after you are gone, to attempt to sort through a box or album of photos and wonder what they are seeing. You stay in charge. You decide what you will pass on and what you will throw out.

A Family Reunion

Sometimes the idea for a family reunion is born at a funeral when family members get together from near and far. Wouldn't you like one more opportunity to greet and hug your family members while you are still able? Could you and/or your children carry out a reunion? About 200,000 family reunions are held annually in the USA. Pick a significant date one or two years in advance, for example, some member's 90th birthday. Once the date is selected, don't change it. Invite *all* family members. This is a time to heal old wounds. Get a travel agent to help with favorable air fares and hotel discounts. Have backup plans for bad weather, and have plenty of activities for children. Prepare a souvenir such as a T-shirt or family photo. If some distant members cannot travel, make use of videoconferencing or a camera on your e-mail. For additional advice, contact one of the several specialized reunion services or consult *The Family Reunion Planner* by Donna Carter.

Memorializing Your Name

In my boyhood church there is a restored stained glass window with the names of the benefactors, my father and mother. The restoration did not cost much and will give pleasure for a long time. Worshipers will remember my parents long after they are gone.

Other ways of memorializing your name and doing a good turn are limited only by the amount you can give. Endow a university chair. Establish a charitable trust. Make gifts to charity. Donate real estate to make a city park. Start a scholarship fund for bright students in financial need. Make gifts to build or expand a hospital, church, school, or museum. Buy a bench in the park. You decide. How would you like to be remembered?

Meaningful Presents Need Not Be Expensive

As we age, we accumulate lots of presents and treasures. On the other hand, we might not have an abundance of ready cash. One senior I know is having the fun of presenting gifts back to the people from whom she received them. Usually, we give gifts that we ourselves would like to receive. This person cannot spend money on purchasing new gifts for Christmas and every birthday that comes along. Therefore, she selects, wraps, and presents gifts received over the years. As far as I know, her relatives and friends understand and are happy to receive them. If wrapping is difficult, use gift bags.

Consider that each person you love will value some possession that was intimately a part of you. It will become deeply meaningful and comforting after you are gone. One woman enjoyed handling a book that had been her mother's and still had a hint of her mother's old perfume. I value my father's large pocket watch, which he purchased in his teens when he had dreams of becoming a railroad engineer. These are tangible memories of our past and continuations of the lives of those now gone.

Who Gets What?

Make a will that treats all children equally. Have a loving get-together with your children and tell them the provisions of your will. Don't make an unequal division of your property and keep them in ignorance until after your death. That only makes business for lawyers and therapy counselors.

We have all heard horror stories about the difficulty heirs have in dividing among themselves their parents' personal possessions and treasures. Even worse, siblings have fought over this process and incurred ill will. Save them from a tough job. Enjoy the fun now of presenting your treasures to the ones you want to receive them. Merely writing a name on the back of a painting does not mean that person will get it. You do it. Then you will be sure. These gifts can include family heirlooms, jewelry, chinaware, silverware, and artworks. If you need ideas, at your next family reunion simply ask, "Who wants what?"

Divesting

In addition to the treasures and jewelry mentioned above, over a lifetime we have accumulated a lot of furniture, sheets, towels, empty canning jars, books, unfashionable clothes, hats, guns, fishing tackle, golf clubs, bowling balls, tennis rackets, and so on. Did you know that you can take a deduction on your federal income tax for used clothing and other items of value donated to charity?

A great number of unused possessions can actually be a burden on us in several ways. If they are of value, real or sentimental, we may be concerned about what will happen to them when we are gone. That is why I recommend giving them as gifts. As suggested by William Morris, "Have nothing in your houses that you do not know to be useful, or believe to be beautiful." If we live in a clutter of possessions, they are a daily reminder that we are suffocating in "things," including the contents of our drawers and files. They make it harder to quickly find the items we really want. By the way, your bank will shred and dispose of your confidential papers at no cost to you.

Finally, consider the probability that someday you will have to "downsize" to another residence and get rid of much of what you now see. It cannot all fit into a compact apartment. Do you want to complete the difficult job of hurriedly getting rid of half your possessions in a few weeks or a few days? Do you want someone else, who may not know what is of value, to do it for you?

Start now! Choose the possessions that will continue to bring you much pleasure, those you "could not live without." Over time, give away or dispose of the rest. Ask your children to have a garage sale or join one in the neighborhood. Recognize trash for what it is. Don't be offended if your daughter-in-law does not want the crystal bowl with a chip in it.

"The job is too big," you say. "I don't know where to start." As the King in *Alice in Wonderland* advised, "Begin at the beginning . . . and go on till you come to the end: then stop." Take the contents of one drawer per week. Surely you have time for that. Before you know it, the energy of the project will grab you and propel you. You will actually begin to look forward to the challenge, and enjoy it. When you undertake this job, you will be exercising your control, your decision-making. The resulting feelings of contentment, accomplishment, and peace will astound you.

> Since it is not granted us to live long, let us transmit to posterity some memorial that we have at least lived.
>
> —PLINY THE YOUNGER

If you don't go to other men's funerals,
they won't go to yours.

CLARENCE DAY

CHAPTER FOURTEEN

Help Others Celebrate Your Individuality

AFTER YOUR DEATH there are various ways of celebrating the fact that you have lived in this world. Consider exercising now your choice for the style of event that is most appropriate to you.

Reasons for a Funeral or Memorial Service

Ernest Morgan, in his book Dealing Creatively with Death, has compiled examples of actual services that offer food for thought. In connection with one example, the Reverend Roy Phillips gives us "Reasons for a Funeral or Memorial Service."

> The words of a memorial service should strive to evoke remembrance, thanksgiving, a sense of the uniqueness of the person's life, a sense of the privilege of having known that person, a sense of loss, of sadness, a feeling of emptiness, of unsureness and a hint that the ending of this life is a rehearsal of what is to come for every one of us. The words should evoke a sense of trust in the slow, but steady grace of healing and the affirmation that we can live on and will live on, blessed by that

life and by the memory of the one who once was and is now gone, but who is and will be present in the world, and in us in mysterious and hidden ways.

A funeral or memorial service is also an occasion for relatives to see each other for the first time in years and to share stories about marriages, divorces, births, and how the kids and grandkids are doing.

A Good Funeral

Frank and I had been in the same cancer support group. When I entered the church to attend his memorial service, I was greeted by the sounds of live jazz music—you know, those good old tunes of the '30s, '40s, and '50s. A three-piece combo of senior jazz musicians was holding forth at the front of the church, just to the side of the altar. No solemn organ music was going to send Frank off.

The church was packed with Frank's friends. I took a seat toward the back and began looking around. "Why so many silver chalices on the altar?" I wondered. Then after a closer look I couldn't believe my eyes! They were not chalices but Frank's collection of 14 chrome toasters decorating the altar. The walls on both sides of the church were adorned with beautiful enlarged photographs of nature scenes. Frank had been an amateur photographer. I had not known that. During our Monday meetings over a two-year period together, I had learned about Frank's cancer, his wife's support, and their wonderful spirit. Now I was learning how he had lived and what had been important and significant in his personal life. Why do we have to wait for a funeral to experience this?

The preacher spoke well and not too long. The music was great. Friends were invited to relate their personal, warm experiences and memories of Frank. Afterward, we approached the altar and examined the toasters, toys, photographs, and other memorabilia that was Frank.

Downstairs a delicious buffet lunch had been laid out. People, in no hurry, ate and talked and laughed and cried and remembered their beloved husband, father, and friend. Frank, in my opinion, went out in style. I will never forget that wonderful funeral service. It was an inspiration for me.

An Inadequate Funeral

Twenty years later I am still sad when I recall my father's funeral. Many people knew him. His job with the electric power company took him all over the county, meeting people every day, and he did it for 40 years. He was a regular churchgoer, a member of two fraternal organizations, and an avid sports fisherman. Dad was a "people person," outgoing and friendly. He was noted for assigning interesting nicknames to people he was fond of, and for a deep bag of humorous expressions. As an adult, he had lived and worked in the same town for 55 years. Inevitably, many of the local people could relate interesting stories about Dad and about how they had touched each other's lives.

Looking back on it now, I believe I should have talked with the parish priest in detail about what he planned to do and should have more effectively indicated the wishes of our family. Unfortunately, I did not do so and assumed too much. Because of his age and background, the priest was experienced only in the more traditional liturgy. During the ceremony my father's body lay in the casket in front of the altar. Sadly, there was hardly anything else that was a reminder of who, in life, he had been.

To my surprise, the priest asked no one during the ceremony to relive any memories of Dad. It was as if the priest was the only one who should speak. He talked mostly about death and heaven and the church's position on those things. No one, I am sure, came to the church that day for the purpose of receiving theological instruction. At the end of his talk, the priest mentioned, almost in passing, that my father was a good man, had provided for his family and helped the church. That was it! Afterward, people left the church and returned home, without any transition time to talk and remember. The immediate family and relatives went to the cemetery and, later, got together at home.

In the church there was no mention of the thousands of people who enjoyed electricity in their homes and workplaces because Dad had strung the wires. No tribute was voiced to his working through stormy nights to restore service after an outage so that customers could have hot coffee at breakfast. There was no mention of his hours spent visiting elderly war veterans at the local veterans hospital. Nothing said about his warm personality or hobbies.

I grant that ritual is important, and that many people will be comforted by a traditional religious funeral, but surely God does not need any of the human's ritual before accepting his servant to the next life. The ritual is for us, the living! Even in a traditional service, most clergy will now suggest that words from family and friends are welcome. Properly, a funeral or memorial service belongs to everyone who is present for it. We gather to remember the person who has just died, to celebrate that person's life with us. It is a time for tears and laughter, for saying how much the person will be missed, for stories of the funny things he or she sometimes did. Our mourning process will be helped if we are able to speak in a leisurely fashion and to show our feelings about the person we have lost. For some, this can better be accomplished in the less formal structure of a memorial service. Others may wish to have both a traditional funeral and a memorial service.

"Dad, I sure dropped the ball on your service, but I often and deeply cherish my memory of you."

My Memorial Service

Coming back from Frank's service, I was really impressed with what I had seen and heard. In contrast, I was directly confronted with the utter absence of any real-life emotion at my father's funeral. I had already had a few thoughts about what I did and did not want to happen when, eventually, people came to remember me. Considering what I had recently learned, I put into writing a plan for a final party. I term it "party" because, at the minimum, I want everyone who makes the effort to attend to go away with a full stomach and a lighter heart. I gave copies of the plan to my wife, my children, and my minister. No two individually crafted plans for a memorial service and distribution of remains will be the same. What could be more personal? I, also, will keep my plan personal.

The reactions of my family, however, were interesting to me since we had never discussed it before. My wife said, "My, how egotistical you are, wanting to be in control even after you're gone." It seems that she could not care what happens after she leaves this world. That is a feeling shared by many. My son said, "Sounds like a great party, Dad. Too bad you won't be there." Pondering that comment, I think he is right. Perhaps I will revise my plan and attend my own memorial service at age 80. Why shouldn't I have fun, too?

Consider Your Plan

Visualize your friends and relatives assembled to memorialize you. After that, think about how and where you want your remains to reside permanently. With those pictures in your mind, what would please you? If some ideas emerge, put them in writing and give copies to your family. "This is what I want to have happen. Please honor my wishes." Do not depend on a will since wills may not be read until after the memorial service.

However, it is wise to leave some things to the discretion of the family. Some very strong-minded men and women have insisted they wanted no service of any kind. In some cases the surviving mate or children have countermanded those instructions. Without such a ceremony, family and friends may experience a sense of incompleteness in the mourning process that can last for years.

One woman reported that over 15 years after her mother's death she still has frequent dreams of receiving a telegram announcing that her mother has finally been located, and had not died after all. It seems that out of respect for what she assumed her mother would have wanted, the daughter had not permitted an open coffin and, in fact, had not herself seen her mother's body.

As you formulate your plan, there are many possible considerations. I will raise only a few.

COST

How much of your estate should your heirs use in getting you to your final resting place? After all, there is hardly a limit. Americans spend about $25 billion a year in the funeral industry. In some countries people quite comfortably plan and prepay in advance. In Belgium and the Netherlands for example, 70 percent have a prepaid funeral plan. For the USA, experts advise that prepaying is more costly and not entirely safe. Rather, they suggest designating a bank certificate of deposit or a life insurance policy for the future cost of funeral and interment. In America only one in four persons has planned some details of the funeral or burial in advance. In a lifetime, most people arrange only one or two funerals and have little knowledge about what they are doing. Also, often they are not spending their own money. After a death has occurred, it is unlikely that the survivors will walk out of a mortuary to compare prices elsewhere. It is almost too late to start investigating options.

PLACE

Traditionally, we use a church, synagogue, temple, or mosque, even if we have not set foot in one for 30 years. Recently, there is considerable flexibility in religious services. Talk with your clergy about the range of possibilities. Think about the size of the place of worship, and the number of friends and relatives who might attend.

I attended a memorial service at a golf club. It had been important to the deceased in his lifetime. There was no minister or prayers; the deceased's children officiated, and they and his closest friends spoke. Others might consider a fraternal lodge, yacht club, union hall, sports club, or funeral home. Or would a tavern be more appropriate?

A hospice center can be a good alternative memorial service site for people who have died with hospice care. Often hospice centers will have chapels or reflection rooms appropriate for smaller services. The hospice will be a familiar and comfortable place for relatives and friends who have made many visits to you there. The hospice chaplain can officiate. He or she may be the member of the clergy who knew you best toward the end of your life.

Will you have a second service in a distant city? Or do you expect everyone to attend the one? For $39.95 you can purchase PreNeed software from PowerSolutions for Business. You can contact them at **http://www.funeralsoftware.com**. The software will walk you through the funeral planning process.

Content of Service

The March/April 1996 issue of the AARP magazine, Modern Maturity, carried an article by Roger Rosenblatt. "In Memoriam" discusses his plan for his own memorial service. Two things he wrote struck me. "I would use [my will] to design a memorial service that would give pleasure to those in attendance." Regarding his choice of religion he adds a bit of humor: "I would like the ceremony to be led by a priest, a minister, and a rabbi. This would prove that the three clergymen could get together in something other than a joke about golf."

Consider the music you have enjoyed in life. At one friend's funeral I was surprised to hear sung a popular song of my youth, "I'll Be Seeing You." In New Orleans they use a walking jazz band. Or you may prefer a church organ, guitar, or bagpipes. One Seattle man, an operatic baritone in his youth, sang at his own funeral. His recording of "The Lord's Prayer," made 10 years before his death, was played at his funeral.

One person recorded her own eulogy on video. Her friend reported: "It was both hilarious and uniquely comforting when we played it at the memorial service." One professional photographer took his own picture, which appeared later with his obituary.

What religious readings or poetry would be appropriate? Who should read them—the minister or your best friend? Do you want your family to participate, or just attend? For example, if you want your granddaughter to talk about memories of Grandmother, why not ask her now? An interesting idea is to have friends and relatives write letters telling what they remember best about you. You could have them do it in advance so that you, too, may read and enjoy them. I recommend incorporating a family touch. At the end of the service and before adjourning for refreshments or leaving for home, your surviving spouse or adult child can say "thank you" to all for having come to honor you.

A printed program distributed to all is an opportunity for providing biographical data about you that may be unknown to many. Or you may include your own poem or a photo of your artwork or your own photo.

For people who like the idea of an open casket, one person I know had her father attired in a jogging suit and a T-shirt that read, "I'd rather be skiing in Aspen." My elementary school chum asked to be buried with his deceased mother's scarf wrapped warmly around his neck, as she had wrapped it in his childhood. If you do not want to be viewed in your casket after you are dead, now is the time to tell your relatives.

Interment, or What?

Charles N. Barnard wrote an interesting and humorous article, "Shop Before You Drop," in the July/August 1996 issue of *Modern Maturity*. He visited a crematorium, an undertaker, and a cemetery, and interviewed many workers in that trade with a view to arranging his own end. This shopping experience was amusing to him, still alive and well as he was, but he thought how painful it would have been for his family. He reasoned that death was "simply another of life's events" for which he should be responsible. A bereaved family does not want to seem cheap and, therefore, is vulnerable to sales pitches for expensive caskets. He wrote, "The best way to make those wishes known was to make some decisions and arrangements while I was still my unsentimental, frugal, living self."

"Preplanning" is the trade term for shopping and making decisions about what will happen to your body after death. Undertakers are quite accustomed to those kinds of shoppers. There is no charge for consultation. Before visiting any undertakers, you should consider a basic question. Do you want to be cremated, buried, or have your body turned over to a medical institution for science or organ donation? If cremated, an option used by 21 percent of Americans, an expensive coffin is unnecessary; you can still be buried, kept at home in an urn, or spread to the four winds or seven seas. One person reported he wanted to be in three places simultaneously after death (much as he would have liked in life), and cremation was the only way to do it.

Cremation urns are now available in a variety of shapes: a ceramic golf bag, a Volkswagen bug, eagles, dolphins, and whales. Survivors have been known to take Dad's favorite silver cocktail shaker to the funeral home for his ashes. Even coffee cans and cookie jars have been utilized. About 30 percent of Roman Catholics choose cremation, but not all dioceses in America will allow cremated remains in the church for the service. Orthodox and Conservative Jews do not accept cremation, while some in Jewish Reform congregations do. Buddhists often choose cremation and want to witness the procedure.

If embalming with burial is your wish, an economy coffin starts at about $500. A pine box would be cheaper. The U.S. Patent Office issued a patent in 1997 for a burial coffin arrangement including a decorated ceremonial casket that can be used a number of times. It can be placed over a disposable inner casket that is made from a material not detrimental to the environment.

On the higher end there is scarcely any limit. In recent years, funeral prices have risen three times faster than the cost of living. A very modest funeral will cost about $3000. The USA average now is $6000 to $7000. Cemetery items add another $3000 to $4000. (Be aware that some small financial death benefits come from Social Security and the Veterans Administration.) Ask a relative or friend to check and see that you get what you paid for. In 1997 a commercial cemetery was fined $15,000 for substituting grave liners when customers had paid for vaults.

The Full-Service Funeral

Funeral directors can perform many services. For those survivors who do not want to do the tasks themselves, this is an easier though more expensive course. National Selected Morticians lists the following services that directors can provide:

- Arrange funeral plans.
- Assist you in notifying friends and relatives.
- Secure necessary permits and death certificates.
- Take care and custody of the body.
- Coordinate all details with the clergy.
- Arrange for the music you have selected.
- Place obituary and funeral notices in the newspapers of your community and beyond.
- Assist in arrangements for burial or cremation.
- Assist in arrangements for cemetery space, grave opening and closing, flowers, and monuments.
- Arrange transportation for you and the members of your family prior to, during, and after the funeral.
- Notify any fraternal orders or other organizations.
- Supervise and direct the funeral or memorial service.
- Notify your attorney if you are in need of legal assistance.
- Assist in securing Veterans Administration burial allowances to which you may be entitled.
- Assist in filing a claim for benefits under the U.S. Social Security Act, if applicable.
- Help in completing insurance forms.
- Contact friends to serve as pallbearers.
- Make all necessary arrangements for transportation, funeral service, and burial if the deceased is to be sent to a distant location for burial.
- Provide follow-up and practical assistance with unforeseen details and help in making adjustments after the funeral.

A recent widow wrote the following words to a funeral home/cemetery: "I was especially glad my husband and I had pre-planned our funeral arrangements. When my husband passed on, all his wishes were on file at your office. This made everything so much easier for me at a very traumatic time in my life."

Memorial Societies

Ernest Morgan's book *Dealing Creatively with Death* is an excellent source of information on planning memorial services and disposal of remains. "Memorial societies are cooperative, nonprofit consumer organizations, democratically run, that help their members to get simplicity, dignity and economy in funeral arrangements through advance planning. They are not run by funeral directors." These societies save 50 to 75 percent of usual funeral costs. Interestingly, members tend to be educated, middle-class people. Sadly, it is lower-paid workers who more often pay the full costs of memorial and funeral services.

Innovative Alternatives to Burial

Recently I returned to my home town to visit a high school classmate. His parents had been nice to me, and I asked where I could visit their graves. "Go to the Pacific Ocean," he said. He and his sibling had traveled there together and simply let their mom's and dad's ashes be intermingled with the waves.

One Minnesota man had always wanted to take the trip down the Mississippi River to New Orleans; he was fascinated with the river. Unfortunately, there had been no opportunity during his lifetime. However, his daughter carried out her father's wishes. After cremation, she loaded him into a 2-liter, plastic, soft drink jug and sent him off down the river. He got his wish! (Nowadays there may be rules about disposing of human remains. Check with your local authorities.)

At one time I was sure I wanted my ashes scattered in Olympic National Park; I love the place. (With park ranger approval, it is legal.) However, the mourning process of one's survivors might be better served if they had the comfort of an occasional visit to a cemetery. Yet, if they have no interest in visiting, burial might just be a guilty weight around their necks for life. Recently, I obtained valuable insight by raising this question during a family gathering. To my relief, my children did not at all mind stating their preferences about "old Dad's" earthly remains. They want me, whole or incinerated, at a grave site. What they want is what they will get! I am grateful for their candid comments and so happy that I took the opportunity to get their feedback.

In this age, when family and friends are likely to be scattered wide-ly across the USA, World Gardens offers the opportunity to make a virtual cemetery visit on the World Wide Web. For $35 you may place on the Web a story of the deceased, with photo and information about the funeral service. It can then be accessed by anyone, any-where. As I write this, Forever Enterprises of St. Louis claims to be putting 10,000 digital biographies on the Internet in 1999. It has gone a step further by installing small video monitors in seven ceme-teries whereby photographs and videos of the departed may be viewed by touching the screen.

Make Your Wishes Known

A woman, known to be very humorous in life, asked that her head-stone read, "See, I told you I was sick." Talk with your family mem-bers about your wishes and get their reactions. Then confer with your minister if you plan a religious rite. If you do not have surviving fam-ily members, ask a friend to be your funeral representative after your death and let others know of your choice. If, while living, you do not indicate your preferences for a funeral or memorial service and inter-ment, you are telling your survivors that you do not care. They, then, will make the decisions for you based upon what they think is proper and considering the advice of the clergy and the mortician. Chances are that they will spend more money than you would have if you had made a preplanning arrangement.

Planning ahead can be stimulating and interesting. You will be in control, and you will make the decisions. Looking ahead to your own demise is not a morbid pastime. On the contrary, it is regarded by experts as a sign of being mentally healthy. Refusing to consider a time when you will not be around is unhealthy. Besides, death can be sudden and is always sad. Your mate and children will thank you for making your wishes known beforehand and for saving them this investigation and decision-making at a difficult time in their lives.

There is no death, only a change of worlds.

— CHIEF SEATLH

Part Six

You're
in the
Home Stretch

Dying is close to the experience of birthing. No one can do it for you, but there are some people who can help.

A SPIRITUAL COUNSELOR

CHAPTER FIFTEEN

A Time to Seek Inner Peace

THIS CHAPTER HELPS to prepare patients, families, and caregivers for end-of-life emotional and spiritual peace.

Emotional and Spiritual Needs of the Dying Person

It is said that every illness is a spiritual as well as a physical crisis. Each year as many as 250,000 people learn that they have a terminal illness. And yet no one can imagine his own death. It follows that no one in this world can provide to us the certain answers that we all crave at this difficult time. However, even though complete answers may not be forthcoming, keeping quiet and worrying alone is of no help either. The problem is that even in times of health most of us are not accustomed to supporting each other spiritually outside the context of our religion. It follows that giving the sick spiritual, not only moral, support may require some courage, something akin to being a pioneer in a new world.

Talking about our fears and concerns is one way to help us achieve a peaceful death. Through discussions with a sensitive and trusted listener we will discover or reaffirm our own answers. Commenting on dying patients, Carol McEvoy, chaplain with St. Peter's Community Hospice in Helena, Montana, said, "They may believe cognitively in

God and an afterlife, but they still have doubts. That's where growth can occur, in the dialogue, in being able to live with unknowingness. That's where a person truly becomes real—being able to say: 'I don't know for sure but that's okay.' "

A famed expert on death and dying, Rachel Naomi Remen, MD, said, "Healing may not be so much about getting better as about letting go of everything that isn't you—all of the expectations, all of the beliefs—and becoming who you are. Not a better you, but a realer you."

Kenneth J. Doka and John D. Morgan, editors of *Death and Spirituality*, list three significant spiritual needs of a dying person: the search for the meaning of life, to die appropriately, and to find hope that extends beyond the grave.

THE SEARCH FOR THE MEANING OF LIFE

Yes, even at this time, or we could say, especially at this time, we wonder why we are here. Some are very angry at God. But that is okay; God understands.

TO DIE APPROPRIATELY

Dr. James F. Fries, author of *Living Well*, wrote: "Psychologists have shown that death is feared less than isolation, infirmity, sickness, depression, and increasing pain in the final days, months, or years." We hope to die with peace of mind and with the feeling of relatedness, that is, surrounded by our loved ones in a comfortable place, preferably at home.

TO FIND HOPE THAT EXTENDS BEYOND THE GRAVE

Most of us want to believe that we have a spirit particular to us that will survive our mortal bodies in some form or another, in some place or another. To whom or to what do you commend your spirit?

Death is not an isolated medical event but a natural process that often includes experiencing the completion of a life well lived. Even those who do not believe in an afterlife of the body or spirit hope that they have accomplished something in the world that will live on after them: perhaps children, work, or art. We call it our *legacy*.

Who Will Want Religious Help?

Generally speaking, we die as we have lived. Lifelong worshipers will probably feel comforted talking with their rabbi, pastor, or other spiritual leader and with fellow worshipers even after attending services becomes physically impossible. They are at ease with their faith. Talking about it will make them even more accepting of their situation and at peace.

A former attendee might want to reestablish contacts with his or her place of worship. A woman dying in a hospice center told me that even though she had not been in a Catholic church in 10 years, she wanted her funeral in the church. I asked, "Wouldn't you like to meet the priest who will officiate at your funeral?" She did meet him and later died, I believe, more at peace.

Some persons who have never committed to organized religion might want to talk with a member of the clergy. Perhaps they have considered doing so for a long time and are at last ready. I ministered to one such man in a hospice center. Not knowing anyone in the clergy, he had contacted a "fire and brimstone" type who did not provide the understanding the patient needed. In fact, the patient was more confused than before as to which branch of Christianity was the best one for him. On the matter of the many divisions of the Christian church I assured him, "God is looking down on that situation and laughing. Select the church that does good and pleases you. God will be with you."

A person who has not been a worshiper, who does not want to talk about spiritual issues, and who is comfortable that way will probably make no changes at the end. That does not mean that person desires no comfort and companionship.

Doctor-Patient Communication

Leanna J. Standish, ND, PhD, LAc, a naturopathic physician and licensed acupuncturist, lists "the purposes of medicine" as articulated by various physicians and health care organizations she has encountered. While all these purposes can be considered correct, Dr. Standish's evolving position is the last listed.

- To cure disease
- To prevent death
- To prolong high-quality life
- To facilitate healing
- To provide excellence in patient care
- To assist human beings to expand consciousness through the experience of health and illness and to live, suffer, and die well

Apparently not many physicians consider it a part of their responsibility to help patients die well.

In a lecture on June 27, 1998, Dr. Joseph E. Pizzorno, Jr., president of Bastyr University, described a survey that asked 300 medical doctors what they thought was the most important *alternative* therapy. Prayer was the answer given by 54 percent, yet only one in nine doctors recommended it to their patients. Spiritual healing was the answer of 24 percent. None recommended it to their patients.

Many doctors feel uncomfortable when they can offer no cure. When a physician offers intellectual analysis and technical jargon rather than discussing dying, patients may find this a barrier to communication and become reluctant to voice their most important fears and anxieties. Bedridden patients sometimes tell me, "I don't know what's going on. My doctor does not see me." Some patients may be in denial about their terminal condition. However, I tell all of them that they have the right to know and may ask their physicians.

On the other hand, doctors may decide to begin life-prolonging procedures when patients merely desire pain control. Patients are most satisfied when they can receive frank and full information directly from their physician. For example, is the treatment effective or not? This information will permit them to plan their final days. Patients receive much needed final support from doctors who are genuinely interested, empathetic, and informative. The American Medical Association has stated: "Physicians have not been taught to manage their dying patients." Families and caregivers may have to intervene when end-of-life medical information is not forthcoming.

Family-Patient Communication

Some families try to protect the patient from the knowledge that he is dying. They ask the clergy or friends not to discuss it or, worse, they keep the clergy or friends from visiting. Research shows that most patients know when they are approaching death imminently. An open discussion at this time will relieve tensions. Not courageously facing this fact deprives the family and patient forever of the chance to show love and gratitude. It also deprives the patient of the opportunity to make peace with someone if there has been a rupture in relations.

Some patients do not bring up the topic of death for fear that the family does not know and that the knowledge will upset them. This is wrong. Of course, the families know as much as the patients. Doctors or the clergy can help to clarify this issue.

Primary Caregiver-Patient Communication

A primary caregiver is usually a mate, adult child, sibling, or other relative, or a very close friend with a history of interrelationship and communication with the patient. Even if the patient is hesitant to broach the subject of end-of-life issues, the primary caregiver should suggest that the remaining time is precious. To offer, instead, false hopes of getting well and going home is inappropriate. Patients usually welcome open and honest communication. This open approach may be maintained until all of the important issues have been discussed. The patient may be the only one who knows what outstanding issues are significant and worthy of attention.

The caregiver, then, may be the catalyst in effecting communication between the patient and all other important persons in the family. Or the caregiver will seek the assistance of others, such as clergy and doctors, in helping the patient to reach a place of spiritual and emotional peace in his or her relationships. This scenario between caregiver and patient is ideal and good. However, sometimes it does not happen in those cases where past communication has been inadequate, closed, and superficial. Old habits die hard.

Medical Social Workers

Social workers in a hospital or other health care facility are trained to facilitate discussions of impending death. Attitude and acceptance will vary among family members, as will communication between the patient and various members of the family. By talking with all principal persons, the social worker will assess the situation and see that the facts are shared. A social worker can also be a link between doctor and patient when adequate communication is lacking. Sometimes patients will be more open to personal questions from an experienced social worker, even though that person may be a stranger, than to identical questions from a friend or acquaintance who knows all of the players in the drama.

The opportunity for life review by the patient is said to be an important and helpful process in preparation for peacefully leaving this world. Hospice social workers know how to do this. The family can help by posting above the patient's bed some biographical information. For example, "Grandma emigrated from Ireland as a child of six years with her parents and four brothers and sisters. She worked hard, married a Boston policeman, and raised three children. Grandma is an accomplished oil painter and has exhibited in several galleries. She especially enjoys a neck massage and likes orange sherbet, which you will find in the freezer. Please read from the Bible for her if you have time." In this way, rather than simply being the "Lady in Room No. 9," Grandma takes on a definite character, which makes it easy for staff and visitors alike to have conversations of significance with her.

What Can Clergy Do for You?

Patients, family members, and friends receive much comfort and hope from participating in familiar rituals. Spiritual healing can take place even though physical healing is impossible. Some people are reluctant to ask clergy to visit them, thinking that they are undeserving of such visits and that clergy are too busy. I assure you, they want to be of help at this time. It is perfectly all right to call a minister, priest, or rabbi to visit you in a hospital, nursing home, your own home, or wherever you may be, for any of these services:

- To receive prayers and anointings, to make a confession of sins, and to receive absolution
- To admit that you are frightened and to request help
- To receive affirmation of your faith, understanding, strength, and resources
- To question church doctrine on which you are troubled and need clarification
- To frankly admit your disagreement with some points of church teaching and to elicit clergy's reaction
- To question the appropriateness of certain medical treatment options
- To request clergy to be advocates for you to the medical team and to the family regarding your treatment and other wishes
- To question what happens to your body and spirit after your death
- To discuss memorial/funeral services
- To support, listen to, and console you and your family members

If you should encounter a member of the clergy who is not comfortable dealing with death and dying, ask for someone else. Put your need for peace and reconciliation before their need to avoid straying onto uncomfortable ground.

The Role of the Chaplain

Hospitals, hospice programs, and some nursing homes employ full-time chaplains to assist patients with spiritual and counseling issues. Often they are ordained ministers, priests, or rabbis. Usually they do not represent their own particular religious denomination in their work unless a patient requests it. They are open to everyone in a supportive and confidential way. Such chaplains, whether or not they are ordained, have generally received specialized education and training to help the sick and dying and their families.

Chaplains and spiritual counselors can perform most of the services listed above. They are versatile and adaptable. Chaplains have good working relations with clergy in the local community and will call them in for patients when requested. Because their work focuses on issues of health, sickness, and dying, chaplains can be expected to have an understanding of patients' physical, emotional, and spiritual end-of-life concerns, as well as the concerns of patients' families.

Chaplains work in medical institutions and with doctors, nurses, social workers, and others. They can be expected to understand the institutional care system, to be an unflappable presence, to represent the patient's wishes, and to actively intervene when necessary. Chaplains can talk about advanced medical directives, for example, living wills, durable powers of attorney for health care, nonresuscitation directives, and organ donation.

In the end, the patient's wishes and decisions should be the chaplain's chief concern. One woman approached the chaplain with the worry that her mother was not approaching death with the correct mental attitude. The chaplain replied, "When you die, you can do it your way. Now let your mother have it her way."

If you should encounter a chaplain with whom you are not comfortable or who is not helping you, do not feel limited to consulting only with that institution's chaplain. Ask for a member of your own clergy, or ask that another spiritual counselor be called in for you.

Euthanasia

"Mercy killing" is practiced in the Netherlands. Although there are no laws permitting it, since the early 1970s there has been an informal understanding between physicians and the government. Polls there consistently show that about 80 percent favor euthanasia, up from 44 percent during the early 1970s, but only to avoid "useless suffering" where death is a virtual certainty.

The Northern Territory of Australia legalized euthanasia for the terminally ill in 1996. A doctor there devised a computer-controlled hypodermic needle that four of his dying patients used to end their lives. Then, in 1997, the Australian Parliament invoked a federal power to quash that territorial law. That same year the Constitutional Court of Colombia in South America ruled 6 to 3 that no one can be held criminally responsible for taking the life of a terminally ill or grievously injured person who has offered clear and precise consent.

As a people, Americans are troubled by mercy killing. Most of us have been raised with the church's teaching that God put each individual on the earth, and therefore only God can determine a time and place for each person's death. It is not humanity's right to control our own death. People are concerned, too, about what might motivate a mercy killing.

One day in the hospice center where I work, a woman named Greta appealed to me. "My husband, Alex, is just languishing here. He has no quality of life. I feel sorry for him. Can't you do something to hasten his going?" It is true that Alex's grave condition had not changed much since his admission two months earlier.

"This is not the Netherlands," I replied. "Nothing can be done to put people away." This interested Greta and, after hearing about the practice of euthanasia in the Netherlands, she said in her no-nonsense way, "Let's put Alex on the plane! He's not doing any good here." It seems we grow impatient for change if the patient is neither improving nor getting worse.

In the USA in 1997, 21 state legislatures considered bills dealing with pain treatment for dying patients. That year, the U.S. Supreme Court rejected the notion of a constitutional right to physician aid in dying. However, Chief Justice Rehnquist noted that the Court's ruling permitted the debate to continue. Justice O'Connor was confident that the right balance would be struck among all parties concerned. To be sure, the issue will come up again in the future.

Thanks in part to modern medicine, humans are living longer, sometimes longer than desirable or natural in certain unhappy circumstances. Perhaps those in dire physical and emotional pain should have the prerogative of controlling the time of their death if they wish. After all, dying and death are a natural process in the God-ordained life cycle.

Physician-Assisted Suicide

I had to reconsider the information I had given Greta when a feature story appeared in the *Seattle Times*. It previewed a 1996 article in the *Journal of the American Medical Association* reporting on replies from 828 physicians in Washington State on the question of physician-assisted suicide. Even though this action is illegal, doctors had provided a potentially lethal prescription of pain-killing medicine to a quarter of those patients who had requested it and a lethal injection to another quarter. A third of those receiving the prescription did not use it.

The survey showed little difference between the Netherlands and Washington State in the number of euthanasia requests received and granted by physicians. When asked the reason for the requests, 35 percent of patients said they were experiencing severe pain and 25 percent were worried about medical costs. It is interesting to note that 77 percent feared future loss of control, 75 percent feared being a burden, and 74 percent said they feared being dependent. Dr. Anthony Back, an oncologist and the study's lead investigator, concluded that pain does not seem to be the paramount driver for these requests.

Dr. Back proposed that doctors need to improve their end-of-life care. I understand that to mean: "Get to know your patients better emotionally and spiritually, as well as physically." However, in ten interviews with physicians it appeared that the doctors "were reluctant to assess nonphysical suffering."

This study tells us that it is possible to obtain our doctors' help in ending our lives, even though it is technically illegal. Further, it says that doctors cannot be expected to be very helpful in easing some of the nonphysical fears we face at the end of life. These would include fear of exhausting our estate or even of leaving our medical bills for heirs to pay. In the USA, surveys show that 50 to 70 percent of Americans favor laws permitting physician-assisted suicide. The cry for dignity, even at the end of life, is strong. We fear becoming dependent or a burden. It is our humanity that speaks to wanting to retain control to the end.

Oregon's Death with Dignity

Oregon voters, after twice passing the Death with Dignity Act, finally got court approval in 1997 to begin using physician-assisted suicide. The law allows doctors to prescribe a lethal dose of oral medication to terminally ill Oregon residents who have less than six months to live. The patient must make two requests orally and one request in writing. A second physician must confirm the diagnosis and confirm the patient's mental competency. More than 10 people have since died in this way. Nearly twice that number were turned away as being ineligible. An additional small number received the lethal prescription but died of their diseases. Thus, there has been no large surge of patients to use the new law. But patients would be well-advised to ask their doctors, before their illness becomes advanced, what help would be provided if suffering becomes severe. Dr. Peter Goodwin, medical director for Compassion in Dying, said, "One always regrets the death of anybody, but if this was the patient's wish . . . and the patient had an easy death and was spared a lot of suffering and loss of dignity, then obviously it was a good thing." Oregon also leads the nation in physician prescriptions of morphine to relieve pain.

Preparing Ourselves

Helping others can be a great aid in coming to terms with our own fears of dying. One of the most important ways we can prepare ourselves to cope with terminal illness is to welcome being close to someone facing terminal illness with inner peace. Extending ourselves to help others will repay us not only in the present but also in the future. Are you preparing for your future? Or do you think your future will never come?

The key to immortality is first living a life worth remembering.

—INSCRIPTION AT TOMB OF MARTIAL ARTIST BRUCE LEE

The biggest disease today is not leprosy or tuberculosis,
but rather the feeling of being unwanted.

MOTHER TERESA

CHAPTER SIXTEEN

Home Hospice— the Way to Go

THIS CHAPTER DISCUSSES the several options for how and where, with the support of family members, friends, and experienced personnel, a person can leave this world. Of all possibilities, only hospice offers skilled staff trained to focus solely on comfort and pain control for terminally ill patients. For this reason, the chapter gives special attention to the hospice experience.

In the Beginning

The following is a too-familiar story. At some point in your prime time years, you and your mate are both in reasonably good health, you are living in your owned or rented home, and your quality of life is good. Then an illness hits and slowly drags you into a downward spiral. You never give up the hope of a miracle cure. But it is also possible that finally you are facing a life-threatening illness.

As you are forced to relinquish doing things for yourself, your mate provides more than her normal support. You feel sorry that she is giving up activities she enjoys in order to help you. You have thought of going to a nursing home, and you suspect that your mate has been thinking of it, too. You are relieved that she has not mentioned it. But how much longer can it be avoided? This, also, could be the story of an aged parent and her adult caregiving child. Many diseases follow this course, though heart attack and stroke victims may be taken suddenly, without any preparation time.

The Quandary

When a person who is ill requires more care than can be provided by those with whom he or she lives, then relatives, friends, and neighbors are often recruited to help. However, this response cannot usually be sustained. As the patient's needs increase, lay caregivers may be less able to satisfy them adequately. The patient may think that more could be done to make the situation tolerable. Patience on both sides becomes frayed. As much as the patient wants to die at home, the time comes when the disadvantages of being cared for by friends and family at home outweigh the advantages. What is the next scenario?

Scenario One: Managing Professional Help in Your Home

The principal caregiver, usually a mate or adult child, must look for professional help. Going through an agency offers more security than placing a newspaper ad, but it may be more expensive. An overnight nurse costs about $200 per night, an aide, less. Other special help may also be needed: a bath aide to help with a large patient, nutritional information when the diet needs to be changed, a social worker and spiritual counselor to handle depression and end-of-life issues, a physical therapist to teach mobility or improve muscle tone, or a daytime hourly caregiver to permit some rest for the principal caregiver.

Selecting, managing, and coordinating these various specialists and services requires time and skill. If this is the first such experience, how does the caregiver know what is needed, or even what is available? Fortunately, professional consultants may be hired to assess such a situation and make recommendations. Contact your local Senior

Information and Assistance office or a registered member of the National Association of Professional Geriatric Care Managers (520-881-8008 or http://www.caremanager.org).

Scenario Two: Institutional Outplacement

If it finally comes to leaving your own home, the choices offered are usually an adult family home, an assisted living facility, or a nursing home, depending on the level of care required. Indeed, it is not unusual to try more than one if the first does not work out well. Sometimes a patient goes unwillingly to a care facility, and the caregiver may suffer guilt feelings for insisting on this solution. However, this may be the only all-around adequate arrangement. On the positive side, there will now be full-time caregivers on the scene.

Custodial care and assisted living are the philosophies practiced in these facilities. Patients will require varying levels of assistance with personal hygiene, meals, medication, and other needs. Some may require occasional hospitalization but often are in rather stable condition for months or even years. Some die soon. Therefore, the staff must care for a variety of situations; they must possess more custodial than end-of-life expertise.

A close relative or friend of the patient will want to monitor care frequently through unscheduled visits, discussions, and observations. Some families can perform this ombudsman-type function well. Others, for various reasons, cannot. Here again, consultants are available to serve as overseers or private ombudsmen for the patient and the family.

Scenario Three: The Hospice Complement

When a physician advises that, if the disease runs its natural course, the patient has less than six months to live, the hospice program may be enlisted. This program introduces a whole new level of specialized end-of-life care. The patient may choose to reside wherever he or she wishes—at home if there is a primary caregiver, in an adult family home, an assisted living facility, a retirement home, or a nursing home. Increasingly, even hospitals are designating some beds for hospice patients. Hospice care complements whatever services otherwise exist, concentrating on quality of life, on keeping the patient pain-free and comfortable. A number of free-standing hospice centers accept inpatients and provide all hospice services in the hospice center.

What Is Special About Hospice Care?

Today about 80 percent of older people die in institutional settings such as hospitals, nursing homes, and other long-term care facilities with conventional medical care. Since we do not often see death, for most of us death is a distant and frightening event. This pattern is changing. More families are experiencing the death of a loved one in the same habitat where they shared nurturing and happy events.

Hospice in America has more than 25 years of experience in helping patients and their families in this sacred, final period of living and dying. It is not involved with invasive technology or heroic measures to artificially extend life or treat illnesses for which no cure exists. The hospital atmosphere is absent. There is less emphasis on technology and more emphasis on people. Hospice's methods and professional personnel can be finely focused on the patient's comfort and the quality of remaining life. Where I work in hospice, the staff are superb. It seems that this exceptionally important activity attracts a particularly devoted, loyal, and caring type of person.

Hospice Philosophy

The National Hospice Organization states the following as its philosophy:

> The purpose of hospice is to provide support and care for persons in the last phases of an incurable disease so that they can live as fully and comfortably as possible. Hospice affirms life and regards dying as a normal process. Hospice neither hastens nor postpones death. Hospice believes that through personalized services and a caring community patients and families can attain the necessary preparation for a death that is satisfactory to them.

For people in the last phases of an incurable disease, hospice provides the most up-to-date knowledge and support. Staff are experts in pain and comfort management. Indeed, it is not uncommon for patients to feel that their condition has improved after receiving the benefits of hospice care for a few days. Hospice is unique in giving patients and family the opportunity of focusing equally on physical, mental, emotional, and spiritual needs. Neither are patients' financial needs ignored. Hospice is also unique in including supportive services to the family after the death of the patient. Bereavement services are offered to survivors for one year after the loved one's death. Costs are covered by Medicare and Medicaid for those eligible.

Before the advent of managed care, the traditional purpose of hospitals was to cure patients and send them home. Given the high level of medical education and technological advancement in America, no hospital-generated expense was too much as long as an insurance plan or patient paid for it. Patients with reasonable expectations of being cured still come from all over the world to be treated in American hospitals, the best available. Despite this, the hard reality is that most Americans die in hospitals, witnessed by silent sentinels of high-tech equipment, and too often isolated and in pain. Hospitals could do a better job of accepting, on behalf of their patients, the idea that death is natural and inevitable. The best and most expensive health care is not necessarily the best end-of-life care.

Some of the services offered by hospice may be available elsewhere, but only Medicare-certified hospice programs must provide all of them. Since hospice care is, by nature, "high touch" rather than "high tech," Medicare has implemented the Medicare Hospice Benefit to provide more effective and less costly care for patients with terminal illnesses.

Hospice Past and Present

Hospice in medieval times was a place of rest, comfort, and hospitality for travelers or those on pilgrimages. The word seemed appropriate when, in London in the 1960s, the first modern hospice opened to offer comfort, pain-free care, and death with dignity to those at the end of their lives. The first American hospice opened in 1974 in New Haven, Connecticut. Now more than 3000 hospice programs operate in all 50 states. The National Hospice Organization coordinates, sets standards, and supports ongoing education and new developments. While hospitals have a periodic surplus of beds because of extremely high operating costs and the subsequent need to move patients out as soon as possible, the number of hospice programs is increasing. A special need exists at this time in America, and hospice is filling it.

Hospice treats 400,000 dying patients each year, up from 100,000 patients in 1983. The median period of care is 36 days—half of all hospice patients die within that period, and half live longer. In the beginning, hospice cared almost exclusively for terminal cancer patients. Now, however, about 20 percent have other fatal conditions, such as lung and heart disease, AIDS, and Alzheimer's (for which the timing of death is harder to predict). Some 85 to 90 percent of all hospice patients die within six months. One hospice patient insists that she has lived longer than the predicted six months primarily due to the tender, loving care she has been receiving from hospice staff.

Twenty-nine percent of hospice patients die within two weeks of entering hospice. These late enrollees miss the full benefit of hospice. They probably spend much of their last months in more expensive hospitals. Some doctors seem slow to recommend hospice care to their patients. (A 1997 study by Dartmouth Medical School epidemiologist John Wennberg showed that at the end of their lives, residents of New York and New Jersey spent three times as many days in the hospital as those in Salt Lake City and San Francisco.) Therefore, don't wait for your doctor to recommend hospice. Ask, "Doctor, if my situation does not improve, should I start thinking about hospice?"

Ninety percent of hospice patients are cared for at home, the rest in institutional facilities. Originally, hospices were independent community organizations and depended primarily on volunteers. However, with funding from Medicare in 1983, most are now divisions of hospitals, home care agencies, or regional hospice chains. For-profit hospices now make up about 15 percent of the total. Hospice providers have been growing by 17 percent per year. Almost one in five deaths (apart from sudden deaths) now take place under hospice care.

Relationship to Medicare, Medicaid, and Private Insurance

Three fourths of patients receiving hospice services are insured by Medicare and pay no out-of-pocket costs. Patients not eligible for Medicare may have hospice coverage through private insurance. About 12 percent of all hospice care is funded by private insurance without Medicare. Medicaid covers hospice care in 42 states. Also, like hospitals, many hospices will accept some patients regardless of ability to pay.

Although Medicare rates vary from locale to locale, Medicare reimburses the hospice program about $100 per day for patients cared for in their homes, in nursing and adult family homes, and in assisted living facilities, with a higher rate for in-hospital hospice care. Usually the insurance reimbursement does not cover all of the actual expenses. Therefore, hospice programs rely on some volunteer services and on donations and fund-raising activities, which are funneled through nonprofit foundations. When a patient dies in hospice, grateful family members often request that any donations be sent to the hospice program. Some programs receive start-up funds from local governments, private foundations, and grants.

Electing the Hospice Medicare Benefits does not mean renouncing all other Medicare benefits. For example, it could happen that a hospice at-home patient might fall and break a bone. Regular Medicare benefits would be activated for treatment of the broken bone, even to the extent of hospital admission, if necessary. This would have no effect on the patient's Hospice Medicare Benefits. Therefore, electing hospice care for a Medicare-eligible patient at home, in a nursing home, adult family home, or wherever, adds nothing extra to the patient's financial responsibility. Where medications or hospital-bed rental were being paid for by the patient, Hospice Medical Benefits can sometimes decrease the cost to the patient. Usually, hospice patients are relieved of the fear that they may be draining their own or their caregiver's financial resources.

Benefit Periods

Hospice benefit for the individual patient covers two consecutive 90-day periods and a subsequent period of 30 days. A review takes place at the end of each benefit period. There is a fourth, indefinite period of care for people who survive beyond these 210 days and whose condition is still appropriate for hospice care. A Medicare respite benefit permits a patient to spend up to five nights in an inpatient setting, as needed, to give rest to at-home family caregivers. Some private insurance plans cover at-home respite.

Requirements for Hospice Care

The patient must have a physician-certified illness with a predicted life expectancy of six months or less. The patient, family, and doctor must concur that hospice care is desirable. A family member or close friend is required to assume the responsibility of primary caregiving when the patient lives at home. Medicare Hospice Benefits or some other funding source must be available. Patients actively seeking a cure will not, of course, enter the hospice program. Hospice provides comfort and freedom from pain but does not work toward a cure or life-extending treatments or surgeries. That is, a patient does not seek both a cure and hospice services simultaneously.

Admission to Hospice

When the patient, the caregiver, and the doctor think that the patient is ready for hospice, a hospice nurse and a social worker visit to explain the program and the patient's rights and benefits. They ascertain and honor the wishes, concerns, priorities, values, privacy, and lifestyle of the patient and family. The patient signs a statement to elect Hospice Medicare Benefits and agrees to the hospice plan of care designed in consultation with his or her own doctor. Hospice care begins immediately wherever the patient is residing at that time. A patient who chooses not to remain at home but to reside in a nursing home, an adult family home, or a hospice-provided residential center is responsible for room and board costs there. (Room and board in a hospice center could cost $175 per day in some locales.) Only the hospice program complement to room and board is covered by the Hospice Medicare Benefit.

The Hospice Team Approach

Mary Skalandaitis was a hospice patient and the grandmother of Chip Hanauer. Chip, as a champion hydroplane driver, is accustomed to working with highly skilled support teammates who are the best in the world at their individual duties. Chip observed that the kind of support teamwork he takes for granted in his sport is seldom available in the everyday world. But concerning his grandmother's hospice care, Chip said, "Hospice shared my philosophy of keeping my grandmother comfortable. They alleviated any pain quickly and worked closely with doctors and nurses at a local nursing home. Her death turned out to be a very positive experience. I have no doubt it wouldn't have been so positive without hospice."

A decided strength of the hospice program is the team approach concept, with the team consisting of the following people:

- Your doctor and the hospice medical director
- Skilled and supportive nurses to assure physical comfort and relief of pain, nausea, and vomiting, and to provide case-management services
- Medical social workers to provide counseling to patient and family, to help with insurance and financial concerns and with case-management services
- Staff to instruct caregivers on administering home care
- Chaplains to provide spiritual support as desired
- Physical, occupational, and speech therapists whose goal is comfort rather than cure
- Nutrition specialists and pharmacists as needed for consultation
- Volunteers to provide assistance, companionship, and massage therapy, and to give at-home caregivers a few hours of free time
- Bereavement staff to work with anticipatory grief and after-death grief

The most active members of the team meet weekly to discuss each case and any new developments or special needs. This coordinated effort ensures that each patient is treated individually and with an up-to-date care plan.

Former first lady Rosalynn Carter wrote *Helping Yourself Help Others* based in part on her personal experience of caring for a terminally ill father and grandfather and her then 91-year-old mother. "All caregivers feel guilty, even if they are available 24 hours a day. But if caregivers don't watch out for themselves, they'll lose the ability to truly help their loved ones. The best thing a person who is devoted to a dying family member can do is to be involved in a support group. The other members of the group can detect when someone begins giving too much, and can help point it out." Hospice staff are on call 24 hours a day for emergencies and during the day for less-urgent questions a caregiver may wish to ask; they constitute a true support group for the caregiver.

Hospice in a Nursing Facility

If you move from your home to a nursing home, hospice can follow. Or hospice care can be initiated in a nursing home or other treatment facility. Hospice would support you by providing specialized care and expertise suitable for a terminally ill patient. Hospice works with the nursing home staff to keep the patient pain free. In consultation with nursing facility staff, hospice addresses the patient's physical, emotional, social, and spiritual care needs. It provides ongoing training, education, and support for nursing facility personnel. Nursing homes, adult family homes, retirement homes, and other such facilities welcome this extra help. This service is at no extra cost to those who are covered by Medicare, Medicaid, or private insurance.

The Hospice Center

Some free-standing hospice centers exist in the USA, and these are probably at the top level of end-of-life inpatient care. There may come a time when the needs of a patient can most beneficially be met in such a center rather than at home or in a nursing home. Here the patient will receive specialized comfort and care around the clock from experienced hospice staff. Increasingly, hospitals also are setting aside some beds for this purpose. Even though the setting may be a hospital, curative care is not pursued.

Patients are transferred into hospice centers from homes, from hospitals without hospice-designated beds, from adult family homes, from nursing homes, and from wherever else they may be. Hospice coordinates these transfers. Some patients come into the hospice program for the first time when they enter hospice centers. Medicare or Medicaid will pay the full inpatient cost if the necessary requirements are met, which usually means that the patient cannot be effectively treated elsewhere. In other cases, the patient will be financially responsible.

A hospice center nurse told me, "We provide the patient with what we do best, giving comfort and freedom from pain. That leaves the family free to do what it does best, giving undivided love and attention."

A Revocable Decision

A minister asked me, "I wonder if hospice is moving people into nontreatment too soon?" A member of his church went from hospital to hospice care where, eventually, the suggestion was made to withhold tube and intravenous feeding and artificial hydration. The nearby family concurred in that decision, but out-of-town relatives were not comfortable with it. The minister suggested leaving plenty of time for decision-making. Of course, this action should receive careful discussion by all affected. However, a patient already admitted to hospice who comes to believe a cure is possible may drop out of the hospice program at any time and pursue curative therapy. Later, the patient may stop the curative plan and again enter the hospice program.

Nontraditional Hospice Care

Traditional hospice care requires that patients be within six months of death and give up curative treatments. This rules out patients not expected to live long who have not given up aggressive treatments, as well as those expected to live several years. Now, two large health maintenance organizations, in Minneapolis and Los Angeles, offer hospice-style home care and counseling to this latter group. Experts think more HMOs soon will offer this kind of service through hospice and home care agencies.

The Bottom Line

Our government and legislators have endorsed the hospice program by favoring it through legislation and through provisions for federal reimbursement. Most adults with terminal illnesses, regardless of financial means, are eligible to benefit personally from hospice. Patients and their families know that with hospice they will receive continuous support and never be alone. No better program exists for end-of-life quality care. Fortunate are those who make use of it.

A Word to Family and Friends

Is there anything to be done or to be learned at this sad time? Those people close to the dying person should, insofar as they are able, actively participate with him or her in the dying process. Of course, this will help the patient. But also it will help those left behind to value their own participation in this rite of passage, which will assist them in their grieving process. This experience will also help them to face their own death more easily when it comes. How will we adjust emotionally to receiving a diagnosis of a terminal illness? Previous close contact with a dying person is a key factor. Talk frankly about death and dying. You will feel better for having been involved.

Discovery is not only finding new things but looking at old things with new eyes.

—SIGN AT MYSTERIES OF EGYPT EXHIBIT, CANADIAN MUSEUM OF CIVILIZATION,
OTTAWA, CANADA

The experience we call death occurs when the body completes its
natural process of shutting down, and when the "spirit" completes
its natural process of reconciling and finishing. These two processes
need to happen in a way appropriate and unique to the values,
beliefs and life-style of the dying person.

HOSPICE OF HILLSBOROUGH, INC.

CHAPTER SEVENTEEN

What You Should Know About Systems Shutdown

THIS CHAPTER EXAMINES what dying is like from the perspective of both the patient and the caregiver.

No Previous Experience Necessary?

Dying can be done with no previous learning; thousands do it every day. However, that is not the ideal, nor is it necessary. Before the days of nursing homes and hospices, sick people often died at home, unless hospitalization was required. Grandparents were helped into the next world by adult children, private nurses, ministers, neighbors, and caring friends and relatives. All of this was observed by the grandchildren as a part of normal adult life. Now, because most sick people die in hospitals and nursing homes, we have raised generations with little previous firsthand experience with the dying, and little knowledge of what to expect. For many, death represents a failure of medicine and technology rather than a natural process of being human. We are without knowledge of how to help our loved ones face their end, nor do we know how to face our own end.

Knowledge is power. Although no one can be completely prepared for his or her own death or that of a loved one, does that mean that we should enter this important experience blindly? If you were preparing for a long trip, would you do so without reading a travel guide, without packing your bags, or without giving a hug to your family and friends and saying good-bye?

Preparation for Birth and Death

Birth and death are two events in which the principal character is not in control and cannot refuse to participate. However, in both cases we trust that those assisting us, our caregivers, are gently guiding us through these difficult times to the best of their abilities. It is now recognized that a child in the womb will be greatly influenced for good or bad by the actions of the expectant mother. To protect and nourish the unborn, the mother will get proper nutrition, abstain from the use of alcohol and drugs, and avoid traumatic experiences. Perhaps she will sing soothing tunes and engage in pleasurable pastimes for the favorable outcome it will have on her infant.

An adult near the end of life may have already planned to receive tender, loving care, to be in the midst of loved ones, and to have pain adequately controlled. Ideally, he or she will have indicated in clear terms what medical interventions are wanted or not wanted. At our death, as at our birth, we are dependent on others to "do the right thing." But we must first know, "What is the right thing for me?"

Where Will I Die?

To gain a better understanding of the place of death for older Americans, I used the vital statistics for mortality from the U.S. Department of Health and Human Services. The percentages I quote in the three categories below are derived for people 65 years and older and are rounded to the nearest whole number.

HOME

Nineteen percent of older Americans die at home. If you are dying at home it probably means that you have remained there all along the way, or that you have returned home from a stay in a hospital or nursing home. It also means that someone in the house has been ministering to your needs, may be exhausted, and perhaps hasn't had a good night's sleep in weeks. There may have been a lot of coming and going of other helpers, medical specialists checking on you, and relatives and friends making a last visit.

The inside of the house may have taken on the appearance of a makeshift hospital with lots of containers and medicine bottles on tables and other flat surfaces. The furniture has been rearranged to accommodate a special bed or a wheelchair lane. Various pieces of medical equipment stand near your bed.

Although you are not completely comfortable about the unknown future and may be concerned about the health of your caregivers, right now, at least, you are home where you most want to be. If your care is good, you are blessed.

NURSING HOME

Twenty-three percent of older Americans will die in a nursing home, what registered nurse Patricia M. Haynor referred to as a "managed death." If you are dying in a nursing home, in all likelihood you will have been there quite some time, perhaps years. It has taken on many of the characteristics of your home. Interrupting your stay have been several, short inpatient visits to the hospital.

Finally, you understand the doctor to have said that you will probably not return to the hospital again. Nothing that the hospital can do will add meaningful days to your life. You receive hurried attention from the nursing home staff. You would always appreciate more visits by loved ones, but you are consoled that they are not forced to take care of you 24 hours of the day. You are thankful that they appear rested when they do visit.

HOSPITAL

A majority of older Americans, 57 percent, will die in a hospital setting. In your hospital bed you are surrounded by all of the latest technology, perhaps tubes for oxygen and hydration and machines to massage your legs and monitor your heart. Maybe someone has also made the decision for you that you should be kept alive by every possible means. There is a bustle of activity as staff enter your room to administer medicine or otherwise check on you, and then leave. (A hospital patient who was not terminally ill counted 56 instances of people entering her hospital room during one average day.) The setting is not as comfortable for receiving visitors as is your home. Conversations filled with deep meaning are more difficult to carry on because of the hospital atmosphere. Fortunately, this is becoming a less-frequent hospital scenario.

Will I Suffer?

On the way into this world you cried at the separation from your mother and at the unfamiliar world around you. On the way out you probably will not cry; few people do, but that does not mean that you are perfectly comfortable.

Everyone wants to escape pain. However, you will probably experience some pain until the dosage of your pain medication is properly adjusted. Then you may have periods of time when you are relatively pain-free. Increased pain may signal the need for further changes in dosage or medications. Nurses familiar with pain management can assist patients in setting up a comfort assessment journal so that pain control can be tracked.

In 90 to 95 percent of all terminal patients, pain can be successfully treated. That leaves 5 to 10 percent of patients whose pain is intractable, that is, not easily controlled. Unfortunately, not all physicians are well versed in pain management, especially in terminal cases and especially in the elderly, who do not react to medicine in the same way as do younger patients. In his book *Denial of the Soul: Spiritual and Medical Perspectives of Euthanasia*, M. Scott Peck, MD, writes: "Across the country, hundreds upon hundreds of doctors and nurses are literally turning their backs on patients in physical agony when that agony could be quickly, easily and safely relieved." I have heard horror stories (but not in my hospice work) of doctors who undersedated because they feared the patients might become addicted to drugs. We expect our doctors to know everything about every disease and to be pain management specialists as well. Such expectations are unrealistic.

Although general awareness of pain management techniques is increasing in the medical community, this is the area in which hospice physicians, oncologists, and other specialists are the experts. They are skilled in palliation techniques—in relieving symptoms without effecting a cure. Ira R. Byock, MD, is a practicing hospice physician in Montana, President of the American Academy of Hospice and Palliative Medicine, and author of Dying Well. He wrote: "Effective therapy may require the efforts of a physician with special interest in palliative medicine and a team of hospice-trained nurses, consultant pharmacists and others. When a person is dying, pain is never purely physical. Yet I want to state again clearly in all cases the physical distress of the dying can be controlled." Sometimes sedation is the price of such control. I want to be in Dr. Byock's camp when my time comes.

We can be optimistic about the discovery of new drugs and new techniques that are coming onto the scene. Many patients are now fitted with pumps that allow them to self-administer pain medications within certain limits. Chances are that you will not be in persistent physical pain. For some patients at the end of their lives it seems that thinking of leaving their loved ones and the only world they have known causes greater emotional pain than any physical pain.

Hunger and Thirst

Dying patients are not hungry, and most of the time they are not thirsty. Sometimes they desire small sips of water, ice chips in the mouth, and lubricants applied to the lips. The beneficial effects of dehydration are less secretions and less cough. Cancer patients do not live longer with tube feedings. To the contrary, tube feeding seems to shorten life. Calories may be taken up by tumor cells, causing accelerated growth. Furthermore, tube feedings are sometimes associated with developing pneumonia. Some patients get agitated and pull their tubes out. It is best at this point to honor the body's intuitive wisdom. Let it shut down in its own natural way, without the burden of unnecessary food and liquids.

The Five Stages

Elisabeth Kübler-Ross was the first to clearly detail the progressive stages in the mindset of patients hearing a diagnosis of a terminal illness: denial, anger, bargaining, depression, and acceptance.

DENIAL

"No, there is some mistake. It can't be me." That is the initial reaction to first hearing that you have a terminal illness. We cannot bear to be suddenly confronted with such devastating news. We have to put it away for a while and bring it back gradually in order to process it. Family members may be in denial even longer than patients.

ANGER

As rational humans, we cannot continue to deny the truth. Eventually, we accept the diagnosis and then react with anger. Not only are we angry at others; we are angry at God for letting this happen. It is particularly difficult for family members and medical staff to deal with this anger, since very few people are able to put themselves in another's shoes and feel the same emotions.

BARGAINING

We may promise God to improve our life in return for being cured of our illness. Or perhaps we ask to be able to live until our daughter graduates from college or marries. This is a request for postponement.

DEPRESSION

After the truth of the diagnosis sets in, along with progressive worsening of the illness and mounting medical costs, there is a deep sense of loss. We gradually become aware of the real consequences of our illness and grow depressed.

ACCEPTANCE

At this stage we are neither angry nor depressed. Nor does acceptance mean we are happy. In fact, we are almost without feelings. This stage is accompanied by weakness and a need to sleep often; the body is winding down. There will be less talk, sometimes just a wave of the hand, and a diminishing interest in visitors.

These five stages are not necessarily a straight-line progression. Sometimes patients move in a different order, or slip back to previous stages, for example, to bargaining. Other experts on dying have questioned the accuracy of Elisabeth Kübler-Ross's five stages but have acknowledged that, generally, they are useful for helping the family to understand what is going on with the patient.

For Caregivers: Unfinished Business

Dying people sometimes hold on for longer than expected because something additional is needed in order to complete their stay on earth. This might be as straightforward as the arrival of a distant sibling or friend for a last farewell. It might be a long-anticipated wedding date for the last unmarried child. Or it might be something more subtle.

There may be a need for forgiveness, or for gratitude, not previously expressed. An alert caregiver will listen to everything said in order to help the dying person clear this obstacle. Politely ask the patient to explain anything you did not understand. A caregiver can keep a notebook beside the bed so that whoever is in the room can record observations on the patient's gestures and verbal communications. Do this especially if what you observe does not make sense to you. Share observations with other caregivers.

Encourage the patient to consider his or her life's accomplishments and disappointments as a way to help uncover any problems. Be a good listener. Frequently ask, "What do you need?" Say often, "I am here for you." Help the patient feel safe and you will learn more. Later, ask yourself what you have learned from this visit.

Whose Business?

Do not assume that a problem related to you by another, even a family member, is an accurate representation of the patient's state of mind. I had been visiting Helen, a patient in the hospice center. One day her adult daughter expressed concern that her mother was not working through unfinished business and that this was causing her mother to linger. When I asked what those issues were, the daughter told me that there had been a poor mother-daughter relationship. She believed that her mother had mistreated her as a child and that her mother needed some help in asking forgiveness before she could die in peace. The daughter asked for my help.

In subsequent personal talks with Helen, I asked if there were any people with whom she needed to make peace. Every time she answered in the negative. Finally, I become more specific and asked about her children. Helen replied that she was definitely satisfied with her relationship with her children. Later I learned that the daughter had approached other hospice workers with the same request. This was a problem in the daughter's mind, and I am not sure it was ever resolved. But as far as I could tell, it did not seem to be a problem for Helen.

Advance Directives in Action

Dr. Linda Emanuel, the American Medical Association's vice-president of ethical standards said, "Physicians have not been taught to manage their dying patients." The patient's living will serves as a written directive as to what heroic measures, if any, should be employed to keep the patient alive. Medical personnel tell us that, in fact, few living wills are written to fit the exact way in which people die. The health care proxy (see Chapter Eleven) can take over to allow decisions on questions that are not neatly addressed by the living will.

Even so, some health care personnel and family members may attempt to impose their own wishes. For example, hospitalization may be suggested so that some modern technology can keep you alive for a few more days. Or a concerned relative may insist on cardiopulmonary resuscitation, which may only delay the progression of a normal death. The outcome will depend on how well you have instructed your relatives, doctors, and other caregivers weeks, months, or years before. You have a right to control what others do with your life, right up to the end. Be sure that they know your wishes and can be trusted.

Please Do Not . . .

Besides pain management, another factor affecting a dying person's comfort is quality of care. As a hospice worker over the years, I have developed some instructions to hand to my own eventual caregivers of actions I do not want:

- Do not speak loudly or shake me if I appear unresponsive. My sleeping time will gradually increase. Just sit and wait, or come back later.
- Don't play games such as, "Do you know who I am?" I may not know.
- Do not term my gurgling sounds a "death rattle." I am too weak to clear my throat and to cough up normal secretions. Gently turn my head to one side and the fluid will drain by gravity.
- Don't attempt to restrain me if I am restless and picking at my bed covers. A change in metabolism and decrease of oxygen to my head are causing it. Just speak to me calmly or tune a radio to my favorite, soothing music.
- Do not become alarmed that I am not eating or drinking. My body does not crave food or drink, and that is as it should be. My weight loss will be great, but that does not mean you are starving me. Forced feeding may cause me to vomit. Keep me supplied with small chips of ice, or my favorite juice drink, to moisten my mouth.
- Don't imagine my breathing has stopped before it has. Probably I am in an irregular breathing pattern with shallow breathing and then no breaths for up to one minute. To make sure, hold a small mirror in front of my nose and mouth to check for vapor.

- Do not imagine I cannot hear. Hearing is the last sense to go and is working even when a person cannot respond. Identify yourself by name, speak normally, and refrain from saying anything in my presence you don't want me to hear. I am here; don't talk as if I am not.
- Don't deny what I tell you I have seen and accuse me of hallucinating. I know what I saw; you don't.
- Do not misunderstand me if I am talking about getting ready for a trip. I am speaking indirectly. Look for other meanings in what I say.
- Do not try to tell me I will get better. We both know that is untrue. The charade is too tiring. Admit the fact of my impending death and act on it, for both our sakes, while there is time.
- Do not stop my pain medication if I fall into a coma. I can still feel pain even while I am unable to respond.
- Don't go against my wishes and give me artificial feeding and artificial hydration to prolong my life if I have indicated my objections to them. Don't make my transition time any longer.

Please Do . . .

Here are some of the things I plan to tell my caregivers that I do want:

- Do visit me often. I might desire almost constant companionship. Perhaps it is a reminder that life continues. If you want me to respond to conversation, choose a time when I am alert. Otherwise, just wait and be there when I awaken. Hold my hand. Yours feels so good.
- Do keep me warm but not piled high with heavy blankets. The blood circulation to my extremities is decreasing in order to flow to the most vital organs. My skin will feel cool to the touch, and the color will change and become mottled.
- Do realize that I may attempt to get out of bed and, in the process, accidentally fall. Don't blame yourself. Perhaps I am only trying to begin a journey.

- Do let me retain some control of my life. Permit me some say on meals, visitors, bathing, and the like. Play my favorite audiotapes or CDs when I am alone.
- Do understand that, to me, one day is just like any other. I become confused about dates, places, names, and even faces. Sometimes I get frustrated at not being able to say what I mean. Just know that I love you and I appreciate your time.
- Do listen to me. You may be comforted by what you hear. You will learn something about me that you did not previously know. Your words in response will make me feel peaceful and recognized.
- Do realize that dying does not mean that one moment I am here and the next I am gone. Mentally, physically, and spiritually, I will enter and leave that dimension beyond life several times before the end. You will recognize those times in my speech and movements.
- Do keep my body clean and bedclothes fresh. I am sorry that you have to take care of my toilet and that sometimes it is a mess. I am grateful.
- Do understand if, toward the end, I do not call your name. That means that you and I are reconciled in my mind. I may not yet be finished with someone else. It does not mean I hold you in less esteem.
- Do accept that any seemingly strange behaviors, or utterances that are unlike me, are a part of my dying experience. My thoughts may be occupied with other times, other people, and other places. I am not losing my mind. Rest easy.
- Do, toward the end, assure me that it is all right to let go, that I need not worry about your ability to take care of yourself without me. That troubles me more than dying itself. Give me permission. Tell me, "I love you," and "Good-bye."
- Do, finally, when my heart has stopped and my spirit is freed, gather around my bed. Don't hurry. Hold my hand or shoulder, share a few memories, say a prayer, cry, or just silently think of me.

Death, the Final Stage of Growth

In their book *Who Dies?*, Stephen and Ondrea Levine say that there is no single moment of death. It takes from 20 minutes to several hours for the element of consciousness to withdraw from the body. They write: "It seems that in the last moments, for many, their experience is converted from hell to heaven, from resistance to an openhanded ease, a floating out." Physical comfort or discomfort no longer has any meaning.

I quote the words of Elisabeth Kübler-Ross from her book *Death: the Final Stage of Growth*:

> It is the denial of death that is partially responsible for people living empty, purposeless lives; for when you live as if you'll live forever, it becomes too easy to postpone the things you know that you must do.
>
> . . . Death is the final stage of growth in this life. There is no total death. Only the body dies. The self or spirit, or whatever you may wish to label it, is eternal.

Part Seven

Life Is
(Now)
for the Living

Sometimes, when one person is missing, the whole world seems depopulated.

ALPHONSE DE LAMARTINE

CHAPTER EIGHTEEN

Immediate Needs After the Death

PART SEVEN IS WRITTEN for the benefit of the survivors after the patient has left this world. This chapter explains options, starting from the time immediately after death, through placing the loved one's earthly remains in final rest, and finally, disposing of personal possessions.

A Time of Calm, or Bedlam?

You, the survivors, will be sad when your loved one dies. At the same time, initially it could be a time of great relief and thanksgiving if the death was peaceful and if preplanning had been completed.

If the death was sudden and if you and the deceased had not discussed his or her wishes, you will endure a nightmare of planning, conferences, and decisions, even while receiving a torrent of inquiries and condolences from friends. This time could hardly be busier, or sadder.

Organ Donation

The following is quoted from the Associated Press, December 16, 1997:

> The Rev. Dalton Downs stood before his congregation and told the sad truth: His arteries were twisted, and he'd need a heart transplant to survive. "I told them I was dying and I needed their prayers," he said. On the way out of the church, Dawn Alexander put her arms around her minister and whispered: "If I had two hearts, I would give you one." Dawn died of an aneurysm a year later, and her heart was donated to Downs.

About half of Americans who want organs donated have not told their families, according to the Department of Health and Human Services. More than 55,000 people are on the transplant waiting list, up from 16,000 in 1988. Additionally, the number of people awaiting a cornea, bone, skin, or tissue averages 3500 monthly. About 20,000 Americans receive organ transplants in a year, but some 4000 die waiting for a donor. Decisions on organ donation must be made in advance. This is a beautiful way for a part of you to continue living in the body of another who might die if it weren't for you.

Doctors and medical institutions have a lot to do with whether or not organs are donated. William De Jong of the Harvard School of Public Health co-authored a 1998 study showing that donor families are more willing to cooperate if they think that their loved one received good care and that everything was done to try to save him or her. Many families that did not donate were angry at the medical establishment. About half of the families said that organ donation was not brought up at the right time; for example, doctors or nurses approached families for organ donation without telling them the patient had died. Another barrier to organ donation is the lack of understanding by a family that brain death is real death, even though the heart may still be beating.

The federal government is trying to provide an equitable means of apportioning donated organs nationally to those with the greatest medical need. One problem is that those patients most in need are usually the sickest and have the worst chances for survival and for leading a productive life; they may require multiple transplants. Another problem is that areas of the country that are more successful in recruiting organ donors may see those organs sent to distant parts of the country that are less successful in recruitment, instead of benefiting local patients.

The federal government recently changed the procedure and now requires hospitals to report every death to a local organ-procurement organization, which will contact families about organ transplants. The government also requires those people working in the local organization to get special training in how to approach families. Hospitals generally oppose the new rule but must abide by it to receive Medicare payments.

Seeing Your Loved One Off

If the death was expected, you probably contacted a mortuary and made arrangements according to the wishes of the deceased. Even if you did not want to take on this job, you would have been pushed to do so by medical staff assisting you at the end.

A van will pick up the body from the place where death occurred and will take it for cremation, embalmment, or whatever was planned. The family should not be in a hurry. This may be the last time you will see the loved one in the shape that was familiar to you for so many years. Permit yourself to manifest outwardly what you feel inside. A funeral director described what happened when the body of his own father was being picked up at the hospital by people he did not know. He asked them to stand aside while he lifted his father's limp body from the bed to the cot. He described the sense of desertion he felt as two complete strangers took his father away.

If possible, have other loved ones present as the deceased is wheeled to the van. Respectfully and tenderly say good-bye as the deceased is loaded and carried off. Indeed, chaplains and staff at some hospice facilities make it a practice to prayerfully "see off" the deceased. Self-control at this time should not prevent you from expressing your natural, human emotions but should empower you to permit without fear the outward display of how you feel inside.

Options

1. One option is embalmment at a mortuary, followed in a few days by a funeral or memorial service with the body, and an earth burial. A variation is cremation instead of embalmment.
2. A second option, with assistance from a mortuary, is immediate burial, with or without a graveside service, followed by a memorial service if desired. Embalmment or cremation is usually not necessary if burial is within 24 hours after death.
3. A third option is immediate removal to a medical school, followed by a service later. Much later the remains may be buried, or cremated and buried. This plan must be made well in advance. It is wise to have a backup plan in case the medical school for some reason is not accepting bodies. Of course, there are no costs incurred in this option except possibly for transportation.
4. A fourth option is immediate burial by the survivors without professional help, followed by a memorial service. Some religious groups use this method.

What would have pleased the deceased? Or would it have been of no concern?

Federal Trade Commission Compliance

In 1998 the Federal Trade Commission checked funeral homes in several areas of the USA for compliance with standards on disclosure of information and prices. Offenders risked being place in FROP, the Funeral Rule Offender Program, set up by the FTC and the funeral industry. In the county in which I live, 17 funeral homes were visited by investigators who were using a prescribed set of questions to "shop" on behalf of a terminally ill relative. You may benefit from knowing the points checked.

- Funeral homes are obliged to let you take their price list. Therefore, do not hesitate to ask for a copy of the price list if you would like to study prices in the more relaxed atmosphere of your own home.

- Most cemeteries in my county require either a vault or a grave liner. If you want to avoid that, check your area's laws on burial on private property.
- My state requires the funeral home to refrigerate, embalm, or cremate a body within 24 hours of receiving it.
- Caskets may not be required for cremation. Check your local laws.
- One funeral home was warned for failing to explain that some items on the list were nondeclinable, but that others could be declined and thus did not have to be paid for.

Compliance with FTC standards varies by region of the country. Compliance is high in my area of the Northwest. However, in Philadelphia, for example, 19 of 67 homes were in violation of FTC standards. Being an educated shopper applies to funeral homes as well as any other purchased item or service.

What Must Be Done When a Death Occurs

Preparations for many of the following tasks can be made in advance of an expected death.

1. Decide on burial, cremation, or donation of the body. Contact professional services and decide on all costs. Get a written, all-inclusive estimate.
2. Telephone relatives and close friends who might want to attend the service. If out-of-town relatives and friends will not be staying in your home, recommend places where they might stay. Notify any fraternal, professional, and military organizations that might want to send a representative or delegation.
3. Get friends or family members to answer telephones for you. Give them written information on what you want callers to know, such as time and place of funeral, whether or not flowers are desired at the service, and to whom charitable donations

should be made. Have them keep a call record in a notebook. Coordinate food service and child care and arrange to have someone at home during the funeral to forestall burglaries.

4. Write the obituary. Include names and locations of surviving relatives. For grandchildren and great-grandchildren, a statement on the number of them is sufficient. Include college degrees, memberships, employment, military service, hobbies, honors, and awards. Decide whether or not you also want a paid obituary notice, with or without photo.

5. Take appropriate action on the deceased's incoming mail, utilities, etc. Pay bills and/or notify creditors. Cancel credit cards. Safeguard valuables. Notify neighbors about the death if the deceased lived independently.

6. Send thank-you notes to everyone who sent flowers, made charitable donations, or assisted in a special way.

7. Get 12 copies of the death certificate. The requirement is usually greater than you initially foresee. Notify the lawyer regarding the will, or the trustee regarding the living trust. Check all insurance policies and prior employment for possible death benefits.

8. Report the death to the Social Security Administration and all other possible sources of pension income.

9. Obtain death benefits as appropriate from the Social Security Administration and the Veterans Administration, as well as any survivor's benefits. (As of January 1, 2000, if Congress approves a Department of Defense request, all veterans honorably discharged will be entitled at burial to a flag ceremony and the playing of taps.)

10. Inventory contents of safety deposit box. Look for a list of all owned assets. Get a copy of the last federal income tax return and eventually file the next one when due.

11. Within nine months of death, pay federal and state estate taxes and state inheritance tax.

These tasks will progress according to how well you and the deceased were able to prepare for the decisions and paperwork you will face. As indicated in Chapter Fourteen, a funeral home will provide some of these services for you.

Dividing Personal Property

What follows applies particularly to the situation in which both parents have died, or parents have had to leave the family home suddenly and without the likelihood of ever being able to return to their former life. The adult children, the person with power of attorney, or a court-appointed guardian, then, would dispose of the estate. The following also applies to new widows and widowers who are scaling down their possessions.

After their mother died, two brothers disagreed on how to dispose of her personal possessions. (Their father had predeceased her.) Then they found a letter addressed to them in her desk. It instructed them to give to specific family members each piece of furniture, wall hanging, and figurine to which she had attached a name. This was a big help and enabled them to empty the house and also to carry out their mother's wishes.

A thoughtful mother, diagnosed with cancer, sent typed lists to her three daughters of every personal possession she thought they might value. Her instructions were to mark the list: C for cherish, W for want, and A for will accept. After her death, the mother's master list was used by the father as the basis for apportioning her possessions among the daughters. Deviations were made only if all three daughters agreed to them. This ailing mother's thoughtful and heroic task was much appreciated.

In another family, parents died leaving 7 children, 24 grown grandchildren, and a houseful of items of interest to everyone. First, an appraiser put a dollar value on all items. A copy of this list was given to each of the 7 children, who marked what they and their own children wanted. Some ties were decided by a roll of the dice. The value of each item was deducted from the total one-seventh value of the estate so that all 7 children got equal dollar value. Spouses of the children were not invited to help with the distribution process.

Some people have the fun of giving away treasures while they are still living. There are many innovative ways to distribute personal items and retain peace in the family.

Estate Sale or Trash?

Look carefully at all items. One woman who had lost her grandmother at a young age discovered after her mother's death the diaries of both her grandmother and mother. Those treasures enabled her to get to know those women better. In a separate case, a valuable coin collection was turned in for probate and netted only the nominal cash amount instead of a collector's market value. The lesson: classify, identify, and photograph such items turned over for probate.

Don't be in a hurry to finish the job. In dismantling their parents' home, two sisters and their husbands were filling trash bags and hauling them to the curb when they got the idea of consulting the Yellow Pages for a collectibles dealer. He arrived, spent one hour, and handed them a check for $800 for items that had been intended for the trash. The best way to obtain maximum dollar value from household furnishings is to do your own research using library books on antiques and consulting antique dealers. The Internet is worth checking as a market for antiques and collectibles. However, if you do not have the luxury of time, call in a consultant/appraiser who will appraise the items at a fee of $100 per hour or less.

Consider an in-home auction. Two siblings decided to keep about 20 percent of their deceased parents' furnishings and personal items and to dispose of the remaining 80 percent. To get an understanding of how in-home auctions work, they observed one and found it to be conducted in a very professional manner. Their fears allayed, they asked a consultant/appraiser to hold an auction. It was gratifying for them to see the people who were going to use their parents' possessions. They received a check for 50 percent of sales, a greater amount than they would have realized had they used an auction house involving transportation and overhead expenses. An alternative is to sell directly to a dealer. An expert advises obtaining a signed itemized list from the dealer to avoid possible misunderstandings.

Instead of selling the items you do not intend to keep, consider donating them to charitable organizations for distribution to the homeless or for sale to raise money for other causes. Clothing, for example, may not be easy to sell but can be readily donated.

Keep It Friendly

Adult children and relatives who have always gotten along well can survive the disposal of an estate with no bad feelings. In fact, the experience can draw them even closer together as they support each other in difficult moments, have fun examining old familiar articles, and recall happy memories of growing up together. The disposal of an estate will pose a serious strain, however, on families where problems already exist. A woman reported that due to unresolved family conflicts and a will that was intended to be as simple as possible, the settling of her parents' estate five years earlier had resulted in one sister still not speaking to another, and another sister only making tentative contact. Another person was saddened because name tags on deceased parents' treasures had been switched. She recommended that to prevent this, an attorney keep a list of valuables and their intended distribution.

Two adult children of a father in his nineties and a stepmother in her seventies dreaded the task of eventually disposing of a house chock full of furniture, closets packed with clothes, and boxes piled to the ceiling. They decided to spare themselves the job by asking their father to change his will, leaving the house and its contents to their stepmother instead of to them. The father was overwhelmed by their generosity. The children simply had wanted out, and they felt a welcome sense of relief as a burden was lifted from their shoulders. The result was that the father and stepmother then became motivated to do the cleanup and disposal themselves, and they relocated, adopting a simpler lifestyle.

The lesson to be learned in disposing of an estate is to act slowly, involve as few people as possible, be fair and generous with relatives, and realize that not even a fine piece of china or furniture has more value than good family relations.

Grieving is world-oriented, and those who have entered
into this deep emotion are expressing what we all feel
and are afraid to face.

ROBERT SARDELLO

CHAPTER NINETEEN

What Is Normal Grieving?

THIS CHAPTER DRAWS on the experience of thousands of people who have suffered the grief of losing a loved one. It reassures you, the grieving survivor, that you are not losing your mind but are perfectly normal.

Experiences of Grief

Everyone has grieved, not only people who have suffered the death of a loved one. You may have grieved divorce (loss of a marriage), children leaving home, menopause (loss of child-bearing ability), retirement (end of a career), or moving to a different city or neighborhood (loss of familiar surroundings). Other losses include loss of friends, of a job, of self-esteem, of independence, of eyesight, or of physical agility. How did you get through those occasions for grief? Probably you will do about the same with the recent death of your loved one.

Your grief for the recently deceased loved one did not begin at the time of death unless that death was sudden and unexpected. If an illness was involved, your grief began when you first suspected that there would be no recovery. You began to brace yourself for a possible death. You started the grieving process when the loved one was still with you.

305

C. S. Lewis in his classic book *A Grief Observed*, written after his wife's death, described his distress: "No one ever told me that grief felt so much like fear. I am not afraid, but the sensation is like being afraid. The same fluttering in the stomach, the same restlessness, the yawning. I keep on swallowing." I highly recommend this book, both for help in grieving as well as for wisdom of life in general.

Phases of Loss

In her book *Men and Grief*, Carol Staudacher outlines three phases: retreating, working through, and resolving. I believe that her analysis applies equally to grieving women as to grieving men.

RETREATING

We protect ourselves from the harsh reality of another's death by reacting with shock, disbelief, and related emotions. This gives us time to digest the full import of the event. It is much like the patient's denial of his own terminal condition, as discussed by Elisabeth Kübler-Ross and explained in Chapter Seventeen.

WORKING THROUGH

When at last the full extent of the loss hits us, we express fear, sadness, anger, abandonment, depression, guilt, and other emotions. We think about the loved one and cry in a disorganized and sometimes unexpected way. I worked with a widower who, in the first few weeks, could not drive the freeway without crying profusely.

RESOLVING

We are ready to rejoin the world after measuring our loss and determining how we have been changed by it. We redefine ourselves and think of ourselves in new terms, such as *widowed, alone,* or *single.*

Normal Manifestations of Grief

I am indebted to two hospice and bereavement workers with whom I've worked, Gerri Haynes and Kay Kukowski, who built the following list of normal manifestations of grief, which may occur to a greater or lesser extent at any time during the three phases mentioned above. From working with recent widows and widowers I can confirm these manifestations. It does not follow that you will necessarily experience the majority of these. Share your experiences with your relatives soon after the death. You can reassure each other that you are not out of your minds.

- Nausea, diarrhea, loss of appetite
- Feeling of emptiness in the stomach
- Lump in the throat
- Tightness in the chest
- Feeling of weakness
- Palpitations
- Inability to sleep, early morning awakening, extreme fatigue
- Grinding teeth during sleep
- Dryness of the mouth
- Inability to concentrate, forgetting what you were doing in the middle of a task, forgetting what you were saying in the middle of a sentence
- Loss of time perception
- Difficulty with remembering or maintaining a schedule
- Intense sense of loneliness and feeling of social isolation
- Overwhelming sense of sadness
- Longing for life to return to the way it was
- Crying at unanticipated times
- Oversensitivity to noise
- Breathlessness, frequent sighing
- Restlessness, inability to complete normal tasks or read a book
- Experiencing occasions of resentment that "life goes on" for others
- Hearing, smelling, seeing the loved one, particularly in familiar settings
- Needing to retell the details of the loss again and again
- Experiencing a feeling of anger at the loved one for dying
- Temporarily attempting to preserve life "as it was" for the loved one

- Recurrent feelings of guilt or remorse
- Assuming characteristics, mannerisms of the loved one
- Sense of unreality about life and the death of the loved one
- Irritability, feeling "on edge"
- At approximately three-month intervals, experiencing intensified feelings of sadness and loss
- Heightened sense of sexuality
- Confusion over the appropriateness of laughter and enjoyable activities

Unresolved Grief: My Story

Sometimes something happens to short-circuit the grieving process, to keep us stuck in it. This prevents us from being whole again.

I was working abroad, half a world away from my father, when I was awakened by a call at three o'clock in the morning informing me that Dad had died of a heart attack. He was 75 years old. I knew his heart had not been good, but with medicine he had been living a normal life. His death was unexpected.

That same day, I flew to my mother's home, helped my sister to do things that needed to be done, and three days later boarded the plane again for the return flight. I burrowed into my work even though part of my mind was thousands of miles and several years away. The result was that I did not allow myself a proper grieving period, nor the opportunity to interact with other grievers. Another factor complicating my grieving was my belief that "men don't cry." Of course this belief is nonsense, but in my case it was true. In my adult life I had cried only twice. Because of my upbringing, I find it difficult even to this day to shed tears.

Many years later, and with the encouragement of a bereavement counselor, I decided to "bite the bullet." I found a time when I would be home alone. My father had recorded his voice reciting from memory one of Robert Service's poems of the Yukon, of which Dad was very fond. I played that tape and heard my father's voice for the first time in 21 years. It brought back childhood memories of sitting around the evening campfire on fishing trips with family and friends.

I cried and sobbed and cried some more, my face wet with tears. Two decades of pent-up feelings poured out. Gradually, in no hurry, I recovered my composure and dried out. The burden I had been carrying was lifted. I felt lightened and relieved. I loved my father more than ever. Why had I taken so long?

The Tasks of Mourning

This time of mourning may seem to lack purpose and organization, to lack direction. Keeping in mind the goals of healing and of rediscovering meaning in life, you will find the following tasks, which I have adapted from my co-worker Gerri Haynes's materials, to be helpful:

Acknowledge the shock and pain of your loss, and be gentle with yourself. Allow yourself to cry, laugh, rest when you can, get regular exercise, eat nourishing food, and care for your spiritual self. These self-care tasks are important now and will remain important in the months ahead.

Know the reality of your loss. When the shock of the death begins to lift, you may be confronted with moments of incredible pain. While this pain is very difficult, it can lead you to a more complete realization of the meaning of this death. Using clear language about death may help to bring this reality into focus. Talking about the time of the death and about the funeral, reminiscing about your loved one, and considering the activities of life without that familiar presence are all parts of this work.

Tolerate the emotional suffering that is inherent in the work of grief. Continuing to seek the support of understanding people, while caring for yourself emotionally, spiritually, and physically, can help you recover the coping skills necessary to continue your life.

Convert the relationship with your loved one from a relationship of the present to one of memory. This effort will help you readjust to an environment from which he or she is absent. For many, it is important to evaluate the place their loved one filled in their life—to think about the roles played by that special person and to consider who may be available to assume some of those roles. Of course, some aspects of this person's place in your life will never be filled by another.

Begin to develop a new identity, a different self, and to invest in new relationships. Relate the death of your loved one to a sense of the meaning of your own life. A new perspective will help you reconcile your loss with the reality of your living on.

These overlapping tasks may be accomplished in different ways. Remember always to be good to yourself—be patient and caring. As the weeks go by, give yourself credit for the progress you make, even the small steps.

Complicated Grief

Alan D. Wolfelt, PhD, in the *American Journal of Hospice and Palliative Care*, March/April 1991, wrote that "complicated grief is becoming more pervasive in our society." He prefers the term *complicated* rather than *abnormal, unresolved,* or *pathological.* What distinguishes normal grief from complicated grief is the intensity and duration of grieving.

Complicated grieving is prevalent because of our society's increasing rejection of rituals, such as funerals, when death occurs. Another factor is a lack of knowledge about the mourning experience. The social conditioning that occurred in our families also plays a part; for example, families may instill the idea that not manifesting emotion shows courage.

Most mourners experience normal grief. Doctors Clayton, Desmaris, and Winokur, writing in the *American Journal of Psychiatry*, vol. 125, no. 2, found that two to four months after a death, 81 percent of the mourners reported that they were improved. Only 4 percent reported they were worse. Those who were improved dated the improvement at 6 to 10 weeks after the death.

You may feel a lot better after 6 months. If you do not, get professional help. Getting help does not mean that you are either weak or crazy. Rather, it says that you care about yourself.

Family Members May Let Each Other Down

"The sentimental image of family that we present publicly is a defense against the pain of proclaiming the family for what it is—a sometimes comforting, sometimes devastating house of life and memory." This is what Thomas Moore wrote about families in *Care of the Soul*. It is natural to think that our greatest support in grieving should come from those closest to us and closest to the one who has died. Unfortunately, this is not always true. I encountered a situation in my work in which one sibling would not talk at all to the other sibling on the subject of the recent death of their father. This refusal denied a normal healing experience to both of them.

In other instances a person may prefer to grieve alone. A month after the death of Richard, a hospice patient whom I had visited, his wife's family traveled from a great distance to stay with her. She later told me, "I did not want their visit at that time. It was an imposition on me. I wanted to live alone and feel my grief by myself."

Reshaping the Family

Lewis Tagliaferre and Gary Harbaugh in their book *Recovery from Loss* say about grieving families: "When there is a loss of a family member, the entire family structure is changed. Nothing is exactly as it was before. If grief work is not completed by all members of the family, the reshaping is faulty and there will always be a hole in the family structure, left by the departed member."

Insofar as possible, family members should telephone or visit each other often to talk about their feelings and all aspects of their remembrances of the deceased—and should continue to do so for months. Speak frankly. Say "died" instead of "passed away"; trying to evade the fact is not helpful. Love and support each other and honor the memory of the one who died.

Friends and Caregivers

If you are a friend or caregiver, do not be too cautious in your interactions with grieving people. A friend may hesitate to relate an interesting tale about the deceased to the widow for fear of upsetting her. In fact, she wants you to say his name, wants you to remember him, wants your candor. Silence leaves her feeling deserted and invisible.

Several weeks after the death of someone I have known, I usually ask the widow (or widower), "Have you received any messages from Harry?" This shows that I have not forgotten him and am still interested in the memory and in her feelings and well-being. It gives her an opportunity to say whatever is on her mind. Sometimes she will reply that she has seen him in a dream or that he has talked to her or held her. This is comforting to both of us. (One recent widow replied with humor: "No messages. I think he is neglecting me again.")

Support Services

Support services for those grieving are available free at local hospitals, hospices, places of worship, and specialized agencies. Some programs may offer six-week courses of one meeting per week, with the opportunity to continue after that time. Others may provide ongoing support groups with no beginning or ending dates. Participants are grouped by type of loss. For example, surviving spouses will be grouped separately from parents of stillborn babies. They are led by experienced facilitators. No one is forced to speak. Crying occurs, and so does healing.

When I was told that I had to attend such a series for survivors as a part of my preparatory bereavement training, I reconsidered whether or not I really wanted to continue. It was difficult for me to bring myself to join a group of nine total strangers and share my feelings. Most of my group had lost spouses; I was the only one present who came with unresolved grief for a parent, and I was not permitted to reveal my trainee status. On average, spouses are ready for this about three months after their mates' deaths. In my group one woman had experienced her loss as recently as six weeks before, one man as long as six months earlier.

It turned out to be a tender and beautiful learning experience. I couldn't wait for the next week's session to begin. There is something intimate about sharing close, personal losses with other people who are concurrently experiencing the same emotions. Even the presence of old friends, with whom you have not shared that common experience, may be less consoling than new friends experiencing a similar loss.

Why should *you* get help? You wouldn't expect to be your own surgeon and remove your appendix by yourself, would you? Neither would anyone expect that you would sit home and suffer in silence. Be gentle with yourself. Realize your inexperience and vulnerability at this time in life. Put yourself in the hands of a caring, trained bereavement counselor. You'll be pleased that you did. You have nothing to lose but your grief, in due time.

Effects of Grief

It is for sure that grief will change you. *Bereavement Magazine* of January 1990 carried an article by Joanetta Hendel describing the ways in which we are changed by grief.

- We become vulnerable. Our previous safety and security disappear. But this vulnerability opens new perspectives to us.
- Grief enervates us, permitting depression and anger to temporarily enter in.
- We become aware of the limitations of family and friends, who are unable to provide the support we need. However, other people appear unexpectedly to provide help, bringing new elements to our social structure.
- Marriages are challenged. Each mate expects more than the other can give.
- Our priorities change. We come to live in the "now," and relationships are more important than ever.
- We become more spiritually aware, more connected to ourselves and to the universe.
- Grief breaks down walls between us and others. We receive compassion, and we feel compassion for other sufferers.
- Death becomes a point of reference from which we build a new future.

Your grieving may be the most shattering and difficult experience in your entire life. Let me say it once more: Treat yourself lovingly and tenderly.

What we have once enjoyed, we can never lose. All that we love deeply becomes a part of us.

HELEN KELLER

CHAPTER TWENTY

Single Again and Socializing

THIS CHAPTER EXAMINES a period that could require two years or more. It takes you from grieving to reentering the world as a single individual with normal social expectations and rights. It recognizes that you may not be the same person you were before. Indeed, you may wish purposely to change some aspects of your lifestyle and your previous manner of interaction with others.

If you are reading this chapter for the first time very soon after losing a mate, you probably will not be capable of absorbing all the information. Read it again in a few months.

Losing a Spouse

Each year nearly one million people in the USA lose a spouse. The *Monthly Vital Statistics Report* for November 10, 1998, shows that there are more than 13 million widowed people in the USA and that over 11 million are women. Widows' self-esteem often drops, and their income, too. (The Social Security Administration reported in July 1998 that the average monthly Social Security benefit for a widow[er] was $736.) Widowers move to higher risk categories for suicide, auto accidents, depression, and heart disease. Younger widows and widowers face increased health risks compared to older ones. Living alone again, after all of those years together, is probably the most difficult adjustment of your life. It is even more difficult for older people and for those who believe that now they are not *needed* by anyone.

Even three months after your loved one's death you are still in a state of shock. Is it a dream? Will he walk in the door from the office or return from his fishing trip? At the supermarket, if you crane your neck, will you catch sight of him? You might be afraid to be alone in the house at night. If you married your high school sweetheart and stayed with the same one, you may never have been alone before.

During this time do not make any big changes such as selling your home or putting all of your stocks in a cash position. The *Brown University Long-Term Care Quality Letter* advises that we need as long as three months simply to "absorb the fact of death." One widow delayed selling her late husband's pickup truck—the mere sight of it in the driveway was reassuring.

Anger and Pain

It is okay to be mad at the deceased; it's a natural reaction. She is the one who left. You didn't. Often the target is the doctor in charge or the funeral director. But that's okay, too. If the anger does not come out, it may turn inward and emerge as depression, guilt, and loss of self-confidence. Be aware, however, that anger will keep some people away from you and is exhausting. Therefore, after an appropriate time—and only you can decide what is appropriate—the open anger must cease so that you have room for new challenges.

In our society pain is a "no-no." We want to get rid of it, and by all means quickly. If one brand of aspirin claims that it dissolves faster than another, that's the one we take. The pain of grieving is going to last longer than we want. Don't try to shorten it by brushing it away. Avoid the temptation to have your doctor prescribe a drug. Instead, get right in and feel the height and depth and breadth of the pain of your grief.

Did you know that at this special time you are blessed? "Blessed are those who mourn. They shall be comforted."—Matthew 5:4. You have it on good authority.

One Half of a Couple

Some friends and family you had counted on won't be there. They do not know how to just be with you quietly and only listen. Or they think they must give advice on how to "get over it" and have no clue what to say. Therefore, they simply avoid your presence.

Previously close couples may invite you to dinner or for a drive, and those invitations are to be appreciated. However, do not expect them to include you in parties for couples. They are afraid that your conversation and appearance may be depressing to others. Some may even fear that you will steal their spouses. Some acquaintances you see in public will turn away, hoping you haven't seen them, to avoid being pressed into a conversation that they do not know how to conduct. Just being natural does not occur to them. Betty, a widow of six years, told me that the worst thing about encountering her old friends is that no one wanted to talk about her deceased husband. In conversations with friends, he had been 50 percent of her life one day and became zero percent the next day. Why did everyone avoid saying the name "Charlie"? He was still very much a part of her—why not of them?

Good Listeners

On the other hand, people not previously close may be the best listeners and the greatest comfort at this time. After all, no advice from friends is as valuable as a good ear. You need to talk! Spill out your innermost feelings. Some volunteers have been trained to listen; you can seek one out through your hospice program, place of worship, or community or senior center.

This is an opportunity to make new acquaintances, to fulfill new needs for the next chapter of your life. Mourners should voice their needs, telling friends and acquaintances what will be good for them.

When someone asks you, "Is there anything I can do?" *always* answer in the affirmative: "Yes! Please come over tomorrow and just listen to me for one hour. I need to have a good ear."

Even if you don't need anything, make something up. If you turn down an offer, believe me, it won't come back. "Well, I asked her," they reason, "and she didn't have anything for me to do. I guess she is okay." On the other hand, if you accept their offer, they will probably come back again to help. That's how people are.

Change Takes Time

Dr. Joyce Brothers, renowned psychologist and author, suffered the death of her husband, Milt. In *Positive Plus: The Practical Plan for Liking Yourself Better*, she wrote of recovering from grief: "It takes two to three years for most people."

An expert on change, Mary Catherine Bateson of George Mason University and author of *Peripheral Visions: Learning Along the Way*, said, "We expect to get through these things faster than we should. I think it is important to realize that any significant life transition is going to take at least a year, maybe three, maybe five, and during that transition, you draw on all your previous experiences of transition." Dr. Laurance Kirmayer of McGill University said that when he started his psychiatric training in the early 1970s, bereavement was a process expected to last about 13 months. However, now the symptoms of bereavement may be treated as depression after only eight weeks, and drugs are often prescribed.

Our personal history of earlier transitions in life is likely to leave us with useful experience—wisdom—to help us with this grieving. But we are not limited by our own experience. We can look at how our friends coped with change, and we can remember and learn from how our parents did it. Libraries and bookstores have many good titles on grieving and recovery.

Stay Occupied

Yes, time is important for coping with grief. But what you do with that time is also important. Again, Dr. Brothers urges that if there is only one piece of advice she could give, it would be this: "If you have a job, return to it as fast as you can. And if you do not have a job, get one." New Choices and other such federally funded programs help women to reenter the work force. (A caution: Men, more often than women, sometimes escape into work, stay busy all of the time, and never give themselves time to grieve. Examine your motives.)

Find work away from home a few mornings each week. This may be paid employment or volunteer work. It will give structure to your life and help you establish new relationships and a wider support network. It also will give you something new to think about.

To me, it is remarkable and heartwarming that so many soon-to-be widowed people I encounter in the hospice program later decide to volunteer their time in the very program in which their spouses died. Obviously, they were profoundly touched and impressed with the care their husbands or wives received and now want to do something in return to help others. These volunteers seem to recover faster.

Combating Loneliness

Evenings and Sundays are usually the worst for loneliness. If you are alone at night, find something you can do with both your mind and your body, rather than simply watching TV or going to bed before you are tired. Use evenings for paying bills, balancing your checkbook, writing letters, reading a book, doing the housecleaning, washing and ironing, sewing and mending, cleaning out closets and drawers, preparing meals to freeze and eat later, or keeping a journal of your thoughts and feelings.

Go grocery shopping or visit the mall or take an evening class. Or schedule a dinner with a friend. (Of course, talking on the telephone to supportive listeners is helpful at any hour.) That is, defer everything possible from daytime to the evening. Fill your evenings with being busy with pleasurable activities and/or things that have to be done actively.

Save the daylight hours for activities best done during the day and/or when there is a greater possibility of associating with others. This includes visits or lunches with friends, exercise and activities at fitness clubs, biking, museum tours, adult education classes, walks in the park, bird-watching, farmers' markets, volunteering at schools or for environmental cleanup, gardening, or washing the car.

Sundays, the Sabbath, and other religious holidays are when families get together, and these are particularly difficult days for those recently alone and without supportive families nearby. Start the day by going to a place of worship, followed by coffee or brunch with a friend. Surely you are not the only single person in the congregation. Look in the newspaper for community activities on weekend days such as fairs, festivals, and ethnic celebrations open to the public, and attend them, even if alone. Visit someone who is lonely or volunteer on weekends at a hospital. Schedule a regular Sunday meal with your adult children, preferably at their houses. Ask them to do this as a favor to you for a three-month period, if being with your children and grandchildren is pleasurable for you. Stop after three months, unless they insist and you want to continue.

Plan pleasurable activities with friends a couple of weeks in the future, such as clothes shopping, meals, or fishing. In that way, you will enjoy looking forward to some happy events. Always have several such activities on your weekly schedule. Make notes on the times and situations when you find yourself lonely and try to cut down on those occurrences. If you enjoy alcohol, limit your consumption to one drink, and that in the evening. What you put into this loneliness-fighting strategy is what you will get out of it. It is impossible to eliminate loneliness 100 percent, but you can put a big dent in it if you work at it.

The New Reality

You do not actually *recover* but, rather, *adjust*. After you have allowed yourself to crawl through the emotions of grief, the next challenge is reconciliation and adjustment to your new reality. You will still grieve, but you can never return to being the same person you were before. Accept that, and build something positive on a new foundation.

A widow with children and grandchildren wrote to *Parade Magazine* columnist Marilyn Vos Savant asking for suggestions on how to come to *know herself better*; it was her main goal. Vos Savant answered in part: "Take up traveling—alone. . . . When you remove yourself from everything familiar—including friends and family—you learn what you are really like. What's more, you might learn that you're capable of growth and expansion." (Don't try this too soon but after a few months or a year.)

Who Am I?

At this time you may feel broken down and dragged through the mill. Your self-confidence is zero. Now is a good time to review your assets. List five or ten personal strengths that have served you in the past when you needed them. Do it now. This is you. You have called on those strengths before and can do so again. Frequently look at this list for self-affirmation when you are feeling low.

Next, identify your current needs. Consider that previously you and your spouse complemented each other. You fit together like a jigsaw puzzle. You used your strengths to do the things you do well. Your spouse performed the tasks that you could not or did not want to do. Now there is a hole. Since you need to be self-reliant, at least for the short term, what should you learn in order to function as a whole unit? If it is an office or job skill, get it. If you need to be able to fix things around the house, take a course in home repair. It will be a confidence builder.

You may not choose to rebuild yourself just as you were before. Why should you? Maybe your deceased spouse always maintained financial control without sharing information and decision-making with you. Perhaps you resented it. This time you are in control. Take one of the courses in financial management offered at community colleges, technical schools, or senior centers. Knowledge is power.

If you are a widower who is tired of eating meals out, learn to cook the food you like. Ask your supermarket or food co-op manager where you can take cooking lessons. It will also be a socializing experience.

Loss spurs some people into creativity. Grandma Moses took up embroidery at age 67 after the death of her husband. At 78, when arthritis made embroidery too difficult, she began painting, and she painted until she was 101. There are many examples of writers, artists, and other people who have mastered new skills and excelled in new enterprises. We are limited only by our imaginations.

Remake yourself to be the individual you want to be. You are still young enough to learn and to act on new learning. You are at the helm of your own ship and can sail anywhere you wish.

Improving Communication

You are probably so devastated that you communicate like a wimp. Your voice sounds lifeless, as if you had just been awakened from a sound sleep. You avoid the discomfort of eye contact. You resent people who, though married, say, "I know just how you feel." Now is a good time to reread the Rules of Effective Communication in Chapter Eight and to take a course on assertiveness training. In the meantime, look at yourself in the mirror. Is that the look you want to present to the world?

One widow wrote of having a first date with a man she had met. They enjoyed each other greatly, but he did not call again. She decided she would call him, in a nonaggressive way. She did, and he was happy that she called. It turned out that he just needed a little encouragement. Push yourself to reach out in communication to others when you think it is in your best interest.

Socializing

At this time you need a sympathetic ear more than you need an intimate relationship, which could lead you down too self-limiting a path. Especially if your marriage contained some negative quality, you may now need to work out that problem with professional help before considering a romantic relationship.

Practice letting go. Especially when the death was sudden and your mate did not have time to say good-bye, you may have difficulty in resolving unfinished business. It would be unfortunate if a surviving mate ended up memorializing the dead spouse. On a sheet of paper write down the things you admired, respected, and liked about your mate. On the other side write what you disliked. Be objective. As difficult as it may seem, this exercise can be helpful in your adjustment.

No one can meet all of your needs completely. That was probably true when your mate was alive, and it is true now. Therefore, it is important that you expand your circle of friends and acquaintances to increase your security and to give you the confidence that you have someone who can be contacted for any need. Widows appear to have an easier time forming relationships when they have had their own friends before their mates' deaths, rather than relying only on the support of married couples. Those women who do not have such friends tend to rely on their children for emotional support. The same is probably true for widowers, since men typically have a smaller number of close friends.

Be sure to have enough same-sex social contacts. I found in my work as a bereavement worker that recent widowers told me private things they probably would not have wanted to reveal to a woman. Women, on the other hand, can provide a quality of understanding and support to a widow that would not normally be expected from a man.

Statistics on Widowhood and Remarriage

In their book *Social Gerontology*, Nancy Hooyman and H. Asuman Kiyak provide these figures: The average age for new widows is 56, and many face 20 years or more of widowhood. Most women by age 70 are widows. The corresponding age for men is 85. As more women compete for stressful high-level management jobs, and as men learn to avoid unhealthy lifestyles, this ratio may decrease. The *Monthly Vital Statistics Reports* for July 14, 1995, published by the National Center for Health Statistics, stated that for persons age 65 and above, there were 18,866 marriages for women (639 first marriages) and 34,900 marriages for men (1436 first marriages). Divorces in the same year, reported in the March 22, 1995, issue, totaled 5151 for women and 9599 for men.

H. Z. Lopata, author of *Widowhood in an American City*, studied widows with happy prior marriages. She found that as many as 36 percent said they would not marry again. AARP statistics from the mid 1980s show that 52 percent of widowers are remarried within 18 months of their spouse's death, and that about half of those marriages end in divorce. Perhaps not enough time had been invested to adequately pass through the stages of grieving a lost partner and understanding a new one. Women seem to need remarriage less than men do.

According to the Census Bureau, 70 percent of widows age 65 and older live alone. However, the stigma that was once attached to older people living together without marriage has decreased. The Census Bureau numbers for this arrangement are up eightfold since 1970. Also, Congress is reconsidering existing tax laws that make some married taxpayers pay more than they would if single. These laws have caused some older people to avoid remarrying in order to hold onto more of their money.

An Ideal Person

Widowed persons often seek someone with the same qualities as the dead spouse, but some seek the opposite qualities. If you want a more intimate relationship, first you should identify the qualities of your ideal partner. This may be someone quite unlike your deceased spouse. Your lifetime experience to date has changed you from the young married person you were 40 years ago. Your recent bereavement and its opportunity for personal rebuilding have changed you again.

In their book *Recovery from Loss*, authors Lewis Tagliaferre and Gary Harbaugh recommend the Meyers-Briggs system of locating your personality type. The ideal person will complement your personality so that there is an amicable fit. First you must know who *you* are.

Some people are put off by personality typing, thinking that they will be defined too rigidly and their actions constricted. However, I have found the Meyers-Briggs Type Indicator to be extremely self-revealing and very accurate. Get the book *Please Understand Me*, by David Keirsey and Marilyn Bates, which explains the Type Indicator. It is better to use the book with a teacher. But even without help you can probably discover which of the 16 different personality types comes closest to describing you. Another insightful and simpler personality system I have used is the Enneagram, which also helps to steer you away from selecting disharmonious mates. A book combining both systems is *Are You My Type, Am I Yours?* by Renee Baron and Elizabeth Wagele.

Learning to know yourself better and recognizing the qualities you desire in a partner will guide you in finding compatible people and help you avoid painful situations. Above all, don't drift into a relationship with the same type of personality you did not enjoy before. Pick your goals first. Then select the matching mate.

Building More Intimate Companionship

The fear of reaching out to meet someone new may be in proportion to your age. Other factors are how long you were married and whether most of your socializing was as a couple with other couples or whether you had plenty of friends aside from those of your deceased mate. Many books and services are available to help you evaluate and polish your dating skills. When you do decide to take the initiative in attempting to form an intimate relationship, you will be acting something like a teenager again. Remember how it was? In some way send out a verbal or nonverbal message of your interest.

Matchmaking friends will call with prospects. If you are not ready for a one-on-one date, agree to go on group outings. Or consider contacting an old sweetheart who is also free. Psychology professor Nancy Kalish's book *Lost and Found Lovers: Facts and Fantasies of Rekindled Romances*, claims that 60 percent of responders to her questionnaire had formed a long-term relationship with a former love. Some had been apart 60 years.

If you use a matchmaking service, be aware that the largest age pool is 35–45. If you are over 50 and/or more than 10 or 20 pounds overweight, you may not be accepted by the service. Look for a specialty service that fits your interests, for example, as an older adult. Check out the service with the Better Business Bureau. Ask the service how many of their clients are in your preferred age, racial, and/or religious group, whether or not background checks are done, and what geographical area is covered. (You may not be willing to travel to Kalamazoo for a date!) Before accepting a date, obtain as much information about the other person as possible. When you accept a date, tell a family member or friend and use your own car to meet for the first time in a public place. Accept dates from several people. That way, you will not be miserable waiting by the phone for only one person to call, and you will be less likely to feel that any one person is more important to you than is really the case. If you use the Internet, do not give out your real name or address.

Be honest about yourself, act pleasant, go slowly. Try to distinguish fact from fiction: What is real about the new relationship, what is an assumption, and what is simply an emotion? You may feel guilty about touching and being touched by someone new and about enjoying the feeling. This is natural. If you had died first, your former mate would have had the opportunity to love again. This can be a time for renewed energy and vigor. Listen to your own heart before the comments of your children and others.

Commitment

Beware: It is not unheard of for the first romantic approach to a widow to come from her boss or a married man. You have every right to set standards for a happy relationship or remarriage, and to get them. Don't give up short of your goals. If you give in to a live-in relationship out of convenience, you take yourself out of circulation for something better.

Get to know your suitor's background, his or her successes, financial situation, and past relationships. This information is more readily and reliably obtained if you are introduced by mutual friends rather than meeting at a singles bar. Be suspicious if someone can't wait to marry you or won't introduce you to his or her family.

Don't expect to remake the personality of a potential mate. You only have the power to change yourself. But have you learned what qualities your potential mate is seeking in a commitment? Do you know the qualities you want and need? For her book *Why Men Commit*, Susan Curtin Kelley reviewed 1000 questionnaires as well as interviews with married men of various ages to find out the priority order of the qualities that men seek in women. She discovered that men want (1) companionship, (2) love, and (3) sexual fulfillment, in that order.

A revealing study on commitment appeared in a 1999 issue of the American Psychological Association's *Journal of Personality and Social Psychology*. Susan Sprecher of Illinois State University tracked 101 unmarried couples for five years, periodically examining their feelings about relationships. By the end of the study, 59 percent of the couples had broken up. Of the remainder, 71 percent had married. She found that perceptions are the key to feelings, and that feelings affect behavior. There is a self-fulfilling prophecy: If you think your love is increasing, you are more likely to behave in ways to make it even better. Those people demonstrating optimism and cheer were the likeliest to be committed.

If a decision is made to marry, seek together the advice of an attorney about a prenuptial agreement so that inheritance issues can be settled before remarriage. The biggest areas of contention in second marriages are money-related and child-related. Older couples have comparatively more financial assets but less time to earn additional assets if some are lost. Men often want to merge the new family's finances but are willing to yield some control. Women often prefer separate accounts and want to be more financially involved than in their previous marriage.

Healthy Relationship Guidelines

I Love You, Let's Work It Out, by David Viscott, MD, prescribes the following guidelines for a healthy relationship:

- Each partner has the right to express what he or she feels or thinks.
- Each partner has the right to tell the truth.
- Each partner has the right to be trusted and believed.

- Each partner has the right to be listened to and to be understood.
- Each partner has the right to admit weakness without being ridiculed.
- Each partner has the right to express his or her needs and desires and to be taken seriously.
- Each partner has the right to be heard in the context of the moment without being reminded of the past.
- Each partner has the right to grow.
- Each partner has the right to seek help, friendship, and support.
- Each partner has the right to be forgiven.

The Singles Option

Sixty percent of second marriages end in divorce, says Mary Rowland in the August 1994 issue of *Working Woman*. Considering that grim statistic, the singles option may be very attractive to some people. This path does not mean that you must be completely without opposite (or same) sex socialization. In fact, most of life's socialization activities are open equally to couples and singles alike. Comparatively few are closed to one group or the other. Some would say that it is a mark of your inner resources, self-confidence, and self-knowledge to be able to both mingle enjoyably with others outside the home and then return to the peace and comfort of a private space in which you are the sole occupant. When newly single again, one might be well-advised to give the singles option a try for at least two years—a "Who am I really?" period—before making a commitment to another. You may actually conclude that the single life is really the best life for you.

Full Circle

You have come full circle. Now you are ready to look forward by looking back at the earlier chapters of this book and integrating those features not previously used.

Extend and enjoy your prime time, and feel GOOD as you age!

Selected Bibliography

Adams, Tom, and Kathryn Armstrong. *When Parents Age: What Children Can Do.* New York: Berkley, 1993.

Alberti, Robert E., and Michael L. Emmons. *Your Perfect Right: A Guide to Assertive Living.* San Luis Obispo, CA: Impact, 1990.

Anderson, Bob. *Stretching.* Bolinas, CA: Shelter, 1980.

Anderson, Patricia. *Affairs in Order.* New York: Macmillan, 1991.

Anderson-Ellis, Eugenia. *Aging Parents and You.* New York: MasterMedia, 1993.

Athearn, Louise Montague. *What Every Formerly Married Woman Should Know.* New York: David McKay, 1973.

Baron, Renee, and Elizabeth Wagele. *Are You My Type, Am I Yours?* HarperSanFrancisco, 1995.

Bateson, Mary Catherine. *Peripheral Visions: Learning Along the Way.* New York: HarperCollins, 1994.

Bearnson, Lisa, and Gayle Humpherys. *Joy of Scrapbooking.* Birmingham, AL: Oxmoor House/Leisure Arts, 1998.

Bennett, Allegra. *Renovating Woman: A Woman's Guide to Home Repair, Maintenance, and Real Men.* New York: Pocket, 1997.

Benson, Herbert, and Mary Stark. *Timeless Healing.* New York: Scribner, 1996.

Billig, Nathan. *Growing Older and Wiser.* New York: Lexington Books, 1993.

Blum, Laurie. *Free Money and Services for Seniors and Their Families.* New York: John Wiley, 1995.

Bortz, Walter. *Dare to Be 100!* New York: Simon & Schuster, 1996.

Borysenko, Joan. *Fire in the Soul.* New York: Warner, 1993.

Brilliant, Ashleigh. *Appreciate Me Now and Avoid the Rush.* Santa Barbara, CA: Woodbridge Press, 1981.

Brothers, Joyce. *Positive Plus: The Practical Plan for Liking Yourself Better.* New York: Putnam, 1994.

Burns, David. *The Feeling Good Handbook*. New York: Plume/Penguin, 1989.

Byock, Ira. *Dying Well*. New York: Riverhead, 1997.

Caine, Lynn. *Being a Widow*. New York: William Morrow, 1988.

Callanan, Maggie, and Patricia Kelley. *Final Gifts*. New York: Bantam, 1992.

"Can Your Loved Ones Avoid a Nursing Home?" *Consumer Reports*, October 1995, 656–662. Pt. 3 of a 3-part series, Nursing Homes: When a Loved One Needs Care.

Carter, Donna. *The Family Reunion Planner*. Old Tappan, NJ: Macmillan, 1997.

Cassel, Christine K., ed. *The Practical Guide to Aging: What Everyone Needs to Know*. New York: New York U.P., 1999.

Chapman, Joyce. *Journaling for Joy*. North Hollywood, CA: Newcastle, 1995.

Crose, Royda. *Why Women Live Longer Than Men*. San Francisco: Jossey-Bass, 1997.

Csikszentmihalyi, Mihaly. *Flow*. New York: Harper & Row, 1990.

DiGiulio, Robert. *Beyond Widowhood*. New York: Free Press, 1989.

Doka, Kenneth J., and John D. Morgan. *Death and Spirituality*. Amityville, NY: Baywood, 1993.

Dossey, Larry. *Beyond Illness*. Boulder, CO: New Science Library, 1984.

———. *Recovering the Soul*. New York: Bantam, 1989.

Emery, Marcia. *Dr. Marcia Emery's Intuition Workbook: An Expert's Guide to Unlocking the Wisdom of Your Subconscious Mind*. Englewood Cliffs, NJ: Prentice Hall, 1994.

Epstein, Gerald. *Healing Visualizations*. New York: Bantam, 1989.

Falk, Ursula A. *On Our Own*. Buffalo, NY: Prometheus Books, 1989.

Fisher, K. R. *Writer Grace: Spirituality for the Later Years*. New York: Paulist, 1985.

Freedman, Michael L. "Physical Activity Can Affect How We Age." *Seattle Times*, 31 December 1996, C2.

Frey, William H. *Crying: The Mystery of Tears*. Minneapolis, MN: Winston, 1985.

Fries, James F. *Living Well*. Reading, MA: Addison-Wesley, 1994.

Fumento, Michael. *The Fat of the Land: The Obesity Epidemic and How Overweight Americans Can Help Themselves*. New York: Viking, 1997.

Garfield, Charles G. (producer). *Peak Performance*. Indianapolis, IN: Kartes Video Communication, 1985.

Ginzberg, Eli. *Tomorrow's Hospital*. New Haven, CT: Yale University Press, 1996.

Goleman, Daniel. *Emotional Intelligence*. New York: Bantam, 1997.

Gray, John. *Men Are from Mars; Women Are from Venus*. New York: HarperCollins, 1992.

Greene, Bob, and D. G. Fulford. *To Our Children's Children.* New York: Doubleday, 1993.

Greene, Bob, and Oprah Winfrey. *Make the Connection:Ten Steps to a Better Body and a Better Life.* New York: Hyperion, 1996.

Grollman, Earl A., ed. *What Helped Me When My Loved One Died.* Boston: Beacon Press, 1981.

Haber, David. *Health Promotion and Aging.* New York: Springer, 1994.

Harder, Patty G. "How Can I Help You?: More from Bernie Siegel, M.D." *Holistic Health News* 5, no. 6 (June 1997): 1–3.

"Health Clubs." *Consumer Reports,* February 1999, 32–34.

Hedrick, Lucy H. *Five Days to an Organized Life.* New York: Dell, 1990.

Hendel, Joanetta. "Count on Grief." *Bereavement Magazine* 4, no. 1 (January 1990): 40–41.

Hill, T. Patrick, and David Shirley. *A Good Death.* Reading, MA: Addison-Wesley, 1992.

Hooyman, Nancy R., and H. Asuman Kiyak. *Social Gerontology.* Needham Heights, MA: Allyn & Bacon, 1988.

Hooyman, Nancy R., and Wendy Lustbader. *Taking Care of Aging Family Members.* New York: Free Press, 1986

Hughes, Marylou. *The Nursing Home Experience.* New York: Crossroad, 1992.

"In Search of the Right Home." *Consumer Reports,* August 1995, 518–528. Pt. 1 of a 3-part series, Nursing Homes: When a Loved One Needs Care.

James, Jennifer. *Twenty Steps to Wisdom.* New York: Newmarket, 1997.

Kabat-Zinn, Jon. *Full Catastrophe Living: Using the Wisdom of Your Body and Mind to Face Stress, Pain, and Illness.* New York: Delacorte, 1990.

Kalish, Nancy. *Lost and Found Lovers: Facts and Fantasies of Rekindled Romances.* New York: Morrow, 1997.

Kates, Ann. "The Widowed: When Can They Accept a New Relationship?" *Single Parent,* May 1985, 24+.

Keirsey, David, and Marilyn Bates. *Please Understand Me.* Del Mar, CA: Prometheus, 1984.

Kelley, Susan Curtin. *Why Men Commit.* Holbrook, MA: Bob Adams, Inc., 1991.

Kemper, Donald W. *Healthwise Handbook.* Boise, ID: Healthwise, 1995.

Klatz, Ronald, and Carol Kahn. "Can We Grow Young?" *Parade Magazine,* 20 April 1997, 20+.

Klatz, Ronald, and Robert Goldman. *Stopping the Clock.* New Canaan, CT: Keats, 1996.

Kübler-Ross, Elisabeth. *Death: The Final Stage of Growth.* New York: Simon & Schuster, 1975.

————. *On Death and Dying.* New York: Macmillan, 1969.

Lange, Margie. "The Challenge of Fall Prevention in Home Care: A Review of the Literature." *Home Healthcare Nurse* 14, no. 3 (1996): 198–206.

Levine, Stephen, and Ondrea Levine. *Who Dies?* New York: Anchor Books, 1982.

Lewis, C. S. *A Grief Observed.* New York: Bantam, 1976.

Lombardi, Vince. *Coaching for Teamwork.* Bellevue, WA: Reinforcement Press, 1996.

Lopata, Helena Z. *Widowhood in an American City.* Cambridge, MA: Schenkman, 1973.

Martel, Leon. *Mastering Change: The Key to Business Success.* New York: Simon & Schuster, 1986.

Moore, Thomas. *Care of the Soul.* New York: Harper Perennial, 1994.

Morgan, Ernest. *Dealing Creatively with Death: A Manual of Death Education and Simple Burial.* Bayside, NY: Zinn Communications, 1994.

Morse, Theresa. *Life Is for Living.* New York: Doubleday, 1973.

Moss, Richard. *The Black Butterfly.* Berkeley, CA: Celestial Arts, 1986.

Myss, Caroline. *Anatomy of the Spirit.* New York: Harmony Books, 1996.

Nuland, Sherwin B. *How We Die.* New York: Knopf, 1994.

Ory, Marcia G., and Gordon H. DeFriese. *Self-Care in Later Life.* New York: Springer, 1998.

Peck, M. Scott. *Denial of the Soul: Spiritual and Medical Perspectives of Euthanasia.* New York: Harmony, 1997.

Perry, J. Mitchell. *The Road to Optimism.* San Ramon, CA: Manfit, 1997.

Pogrebin, Letty Cottin. *Getting Over Getting Older.* New York: Little, Brown, 1996.

Pokorski, Doug. *Death Rehearsal.* Springfield, IL: Templegate, 1995.

Quinn, Jane Bryant. *Making the Most Out of Your Money.* rev. ed. New York: Simon & Schuster, 1997.

Rees, Shan, and Roderick S. Graham. *Assertion Training.* London: Routledge, 1991.

Rowe, John W., and Robert L. Kahn. *Successful Aging.* New York: Pantheon, 1998.

Ryan, Regina Sara, and John W. Travis. *Wellness.* Berkeley, CA: Ten Speed Press, 1991.

Ryback, David. *Look 10 Years Younger; Live 10 Years Longer.* Englewood Cliffs, NJ: Prentice Hall, 1995.

Schut, Michael, ed. *Food, Faith and Sustainability: Environmental, Spiritual, and Social Justice Implications of the Gift of Daily Bread.* Seattle: Earth Ministry, 1997.

Segell, Michael. "Reality Checks." *Sports Afield* 217, no. 4 (April 1997): 61.

Shealy, C. Norman. *Miracles Do Happen: A Physician's Experience with Alternative Medicine.* Rockport, MA: Element, 1996.

Siegel, Bernie. *Peace, Love & Healing.* New York: Harper & Row, 1989.

Silverstone, Barbara, and Helen Kandel Hyman. *Growing Older Together.* New York: Pantheon, 1993.

Slobody, Lawrence B., and David Oliphant. *The Golden Years.* Westport, CT: Bergin & Garvey, 1996.

Stanny, Barbara. *Prince Charming Isn't Coming: How Women Get Smart About Money.* New York: Viking, 1997.

Starr, Bernard D. *The Starr-Weiner Report on Sex and Sexuality in the Mature Years.* New York: Stein & Day, 1981.

Staudacher, Carol. *Men and Grief.* Oakland, CA: New Harbinger, 1981.

Tagliaferre, Lewis, and Gary L. Harbaugh. *Recovery from Loss.* Deerfield Beach, FL: Health Communications, 1990.

Thomas, William H. *Life Worth Living: How Someone You Love Can Still Enjoy Life in a Nursing Home—The Eden Alternative in Action.* Acton, MA: VanderWyk & Burnham, 1996.

Tilman, Norma Mott. *How to Find Almost Anyone, Anywhere.* Nashville, TN: Rutledge Hill Press, 1994.

Titus, Meredith. "Living Successfully with Chronic Illness." *The Menninger Letter: Your National Resource for Mental Health* 3, no. 16 (June 1995): 5.

Vickery, Donald M., and James F. Fries. *Take Care of Yourself.* Reading, MA: Addison-Wesley, 1996.

Viscott, David. *I Love You, Let's Work It Out.* New York: Simon & Schuster, 1987.

Vos Savant, Marilyn. "Ask Marilyn." *Parade Magazine*, 20 July 1997, 12.

Weil, Andrew. *Spontaneous Healing.* New York: Knopf, 1995.

Weiss, Robert J., and Genell J. Subak-Sharpe, eds. *The Columbia University School of Publc Health Complete Guide to Health and Well-Being After 50.* New York: Times Books, 1988.

Weenolsen, Patricia. *The Art of Dying.* New York: St. Martin's Press, 1996.

"Who Pays for Nursing Homes?" *Consumer Reports*, September 1995, 591–661. Pt. 2 of a 3-part series, Nursing Homes: When a Loved One Needs Care.

Wolfelt, Alan D. "Toward an understanding of complicated grief: A comprehensive overview." *The American Journal of Hospice and Palliative Care*, March/April 1991, 28–30.

Wylie, Betty Jane. *Beginnings: A Book for Widows*. rev. ed. New York: Ballantine, 1982.

Web Site Resources

OncoLink, run by the University of Pennsylvania, page 100
http://www.oncolink.upenn.edu/

National Depressive and Manic-Depressive Association, page 103
http://www.ndmda.org

National Institute of Mental Health, page 103
http://www.nimh.nih.gov

Depression Central, page 103
http://www.psycom.net/depression.central.html

Online Depression Screening Test, page 103
http://www.med.nyu.edu/Psych/screens/depres.html

American Council for Headache Education, page 106
http://www.achenet.org

National Heart, Lung, and Blood Institute, page 109
http://www.nhlbi.nih.gov

Obesity.com, page 110
http://www.obesity.com

PubMed: National Library of Medicine Database, page 118
http://www.ncbi.nlm.nih.gov/PubMed

Healthfinder: U.S. Department of Health and Human Services, page 118
http://www.healthfinder.gov

Agency for Health Care Policy and Research, page 118
http://www.ahcpr.gov

The National Organization for Rare Disorders, Inc., page 118
http://www.rarediseases.org

National Institute of Child Health and Human Development, page 118
http://www.nih.gov/nichd

CHAPTER SEVEN: Help Your Doctor Help You

The Senior Law Home Page, page 133
http://www.seniorlaw.com/index.htm

CHAPTER TEN: Make Your Home Work for You

Contractor legality resource, page 166
http://www.Improvenet.com

Online grocery delivery service, page 176
http://www.peapod.com

CHAPTER ELEVEN: Understand Your Financial and Legal Options

HCFA (Health Care Financing Administration) free publication "Medicare & You," page 198
http://www.medicare.gov

U.S. News & World Report, page 199
http://www.usnews.com

CHAPTER TWELVE: Is It Time to Move?

National Association of Realtors, page 210
http://www.realtor.com

Eden Alternative, page 223
http://www.Edenalt.com

National Association of Geriatric Care Managers, page 224
http://www.caremanager.org

AARP: rights of nursing home residents, page 224
http://www.aarp.org/getans/consumer/rights.html

CHAPTER FOURTEEN: Help Others Celebrate Your Individuality

PowerSolutions for Business, page 247
http://www.funeralsoftware.com

Index

do's and don'ts with patient, 289–291
emotional and spiritual needs, 255–257
hospice, 269–272
hunger and thirst, 285–286
institutional placement, 269, 283–284
pain control, 284–285
stages of, 286–287

E

ear care, 116
Eastern versus Western medicine, 36, 126
Eden alternative, in nursing homes, 223
education, 40–43
effective communication, 141–142
Eisenberg, Mickey S., 107
elder abuse, 146, 222
Elder Care Locator, 180
Elder Cottage Housing Opportunity
    (ECHO), 214
Elderhostel, 41, 44
e-mail, 149–150
Emanuel, Linda, 288
emergency calls, 150–151
Emery, Marcia, 67
Emmons, Michael, 142
emotional health
    family relationships, 48–49
    friendships, 48–49
    goals, 11–12
    needs of dying person, 255–257
    news broadcasts, effects of, 49–50
    socializing, 47–48
    See also health and well-being, mental
      health
end-of-life issues. *See* dying person
Enneagram, 325
estate taxes, 202–203
euthanasia, 262–263
exercise, 17–18
    aerobic, 19
    for arthritis, 21–22
    for balance, 23, 25
    function, 27
    range-of-motion, 21
    stretching, 23

walking, 20–21
eye care, 116

F

faith. *See* spiritual health
faith communities, 63–64
Falk, Ursula A., 47
falls, prevention of, 167–171
family
    decisions after a death, 299–301
    financial support, 193
    living with, 215
    –patient communication, 259
    relationships, 48–49
    restructuring, 311
    reunion, 236
fats, 76, 77–79, 85, 86
Fauza, Dario, 108
fiber intake, 81
Field, Tiffany, 30
files. *See* documents, personal
financial
    information file, 158–161
    management, 206–207
    planning, 187–189
fire prevention, 171
fitness clubs, 25–26
flexibility, 23, 25
flu, 109
Foege, William H., 95
food
    alcohol, 88
    chewing of, 83
    diary, 80
    dining habits, 83, 176–177
    environment and, 89
    fats, 77–79
    Guide Pyramid, 76–77
    nutrition, 79–80
    processed, 81
    servings, 81–83
    shopping, 85–86
    snacking, 86–87
    water, 88
    See also diets